Classical Sanskrit Tragedy

Classical Sanskrit Tragedy

The Concept of Suffering and Pathos in Medieval India

Bihani Sarkar

I.B.TAURIS

LONDON • NEW YORK • OXFORD • NEW DELHI • SYDNEY

I.B. TAURIS
Bloomsbury Publishing Plc
50 Bedford Square, London, WC1B 3DP, UK
1385 Broadway, New York, NY 10018, USA
29 Earlsfort Terrace, Dublin 2, Ireland

BLOOMSBURY, I.B. TAURIS and the I.B. Tauris logo are trademarks of Bloomsbury Publishing Plc

First published in Great Britain 2021
This paperback edition published in 2022

Copyright © Bihani Sarkar, 2021

Bihani Sarkar has asserted her right under the Copyright, Designs and Patents Act, 1988, to be identified as Author of this work.

For legal purposes the Acknowledgements on p. viii constitute an extension of this copyright page.

Cover design: Adriana Brioso
Cover image Heaven and Hell Gallery, Bas Relief, Angkor Wat Temple, Cambodia.
© AMS Images / Alamy Stock Photo

All rights reserved. No part of this publication may be reproduced or transmitted in any form or by any means, electronic or mechanical, including photocopying, recording, or any information storage or retrieval system, without prior permission in writing from the publishers.

Bloomsbury Publishing Plc does not have any control over, or responsibility for, any third-party websites referred to or in this book. All internet addresses given in this book were correct at the time of going to press. The author and publisher regret any inconvenience caused if addresses have changed or sites have ceased to exist, but can accept no responsibility for any such changes.

A catalogue record for this book is available from the British Library.

A catalog record for this book is available from the Library of Congress.

ISBN: HB: 978-1-7883-1111-3
PB: 978-0-7556-3924-3
ePDF: 978-0-7556-1786-9
eBook: 978-0-7556-1787-6

Typeset by Newgen KnowledgeWorks Pvt. Ltd., Chennai, India

To find out more about our authors and books visit www.bloomsbury.com and sign up for our newsletters.

To Anguish –
I leave you heaping flowers on your breast
Blue kissed with dew
White flecked with light
I let you go, O Anguish, to your rest.

Contents

Acknowledgements viii
Preamble: A Note on the Indian Medieval x

Introduction, Part I: The tragic middle 1
Introduction, Part II: Doubt, obstacle, deliberation, death, disaster: The trial in Indian aesthetics 25
1 Kālidāsa and his inheritance of grief 55
2 The map of melancholy: Lamentation and the philosophical pause 87
3 On losing and finding love: Conflict, obstacle and drama 109
4 The altered heart: Anguish, entreaty and lyric 139
Conclusion 165

Notes 169
Bibliography 193
Index 201

Acknowledgements

Many have been life-giving in the writing of this book as rainclouds in the monsoon bring life to the parched Indian plains. I am grateful in particular to Prof. Diwakar Acharya for reading passages from Nyāya, Mīmāṃsā and the *Abhinavabhāratī* and for clearing their occasional turbidity. The genesis of the thought underlying this book, the seed of which was implanted by the *De Profundis* and George Eliot's novels, is linked in part to those readings. To Dr Sarah Shaw, I am ever grateful for stimulating discussions on Buddhist narrative, tragic middles in Indian and English literature and for indicating relevant Pāli resources to me. Discussions on the *Raghuvaṃśa* would not have been possible without the generosity of the editors of the *Raghupañcikā*, Prof. Dominic Goodall, Prof. Harunaga Isaacson, Dr Csaba Dezső and Dr Csaba Kiss, who gave me their draft edition of the earliest version of the text as read by Vallabhadeva and allowed its use. I am sincerely grateful to Dr Csaba Dezső for his time and patience in reading through and commenting on one of the draft chapters. To Prof. Alexis Sanderson, who read with me the *Nandabhāryāvilāpa*; Prof. Harunaga Isaacson, who read and commented on draft editions and translations from the *Dīnākrandanastotra*, as well as shared a number of resources; Dr Andrew Ollett for his detailed reading of and meticulous commenting on the chapter on aesthetics; and Prof. James Benson who advised on resources and suggested alternative verse-interpretations: I express my heartfelt thanks. I am especially grateful to the anonymous peer-reviewer for his/her in-depth reading and astute comments, due to which the final form of the book took shape. Dr Elizabeth Tucker and Dr Antonia Ruppel provided indications to additional resources. Christ Church, Oxford, provided a refuge during the writing process. Dr Bergljot Chiarucci's detailed proof-reading of the text, including the Sanskrit, refined and improved the final manuscript.

The completion of the book was made possible by a grant from the Indian Institute Fund, Oriental Institute, University of Oxford.

This book coincides with my own tragic middle: my long and arduous struggle with mental health. Each of the tragic middles studied here, among which I first began with Rati's in the hard summer of 2014, affected and comforted me profoundly. They were and remain my friends, and in their voices I hear my own voice and experience. They know as I do the long darkness of the soul.

To my parents, siblings and kindred spirits, for their love and support in this difficult time: *namaḥ*.

A Note on Translations

The English translations of Sanskrit verses in the main body are literary, mainly in blank verse.

Preamble: A Note on the Indian Medieval

Whether there at all exists a medieval period for Indian history and what it may have been remain moot points. There is no time-span exactly contiguous to the European medieval, which stretches across the intervening centuries between the decline of Roman influence in Europe and the onset of the Renaissance. Nor do many of the major political and philosophical characteristics of the European Middle Period, such as the notion of constitutional rule (exemplified for example in the Magna Carta in England), feudalism and humanism (exemplified for example in Chaucer's *Parlement of Fowles*) apply – or *seem* to have applied – to the corresponding age in India.

Scholars, though, have generally accepted a very long 'middle period' comprising the twelve centuries between the demise of the great ancient empires in *c.*fifth century CE and the decline of Muslim rule with the advent of colonialism in the seventeenth century. In this vein: Stein 2010 holds the medieval to start at the end of Gupta rule during which 'different forms of monarchy, culture and economy had developed' that 'persisted until the decline of the Muslims'.[1] According to Stein on this basis the 'notion of an intermediate historical period has proven as legitimate and useful in India as in Europe'.[2] Kulke and Rothermund 1998 accept an Indian period on the same broad temporal lines but divide it into two phases: the early medieval, spanning the end of Gupta Imperialism to about the eighth century CE,[3] and the late medieval from 1000 CE century onwards when Islamic rule began (ibid., pp. 152–3). The early medieval age is marked in particular by the replacement of imperialism by regionalism. Until 500 CE, the history of India came to be dominated by northern (Gangetic) empires beginning with the Mauryas and ending with the Guptas. After the decline of the Guptas, the period of large northern empires ended with the rise of regional kingdoms, which vied for supremacy, leading thereby to the growth of central and southern Indian lineages and cultural complexes.[4] In particular, Kulke and Rothermund view the medieval to be inaugurated by the rule of King Harṣa of Kanauj (606–47 CE) (ibid.).

In this book, the understanding of the Indian medieval is based largely on Kulke and Rothermund, with a difference in opinion in one vital aspect. Arguably, the Indian 'middle period' can go back even further to the second century CE when Hellenized empires and cultures from Central Asia and Bactria ruled successively by the Scythian Śakas, their descendants the Kṣatrapas and the Yuezhi Kuṣānas ended their considerable influence on subcontinental terrain. In this view the medieval lies between the Kuṣāṇas and the decline of the Mughals (the 1600s). This would make the medieval period in India coterminous with late antiquity right till the early modern periods in Europe. In drawing most of my materials from both the age of the Gupta rulers *and* what Kulke and Rothermund call the early medieval period (*c.*seventh century to the eighth century CE), I have understood the Indian medieval to begin from the end of Scythian and Yuezhi rule, in other words with the end of Central Asian rule in India.

The advent of the Guptas marked the decline of these cosmopolitan political dynasties in the Gangetic basin and in central India, who were culturally linked via Bactria to Greece and Rome and who were kaleidoscopic in their religious preferences, tying together the worship of Iranian and Greek deities with Hinduism and Buddhism. Their end coincided with the death of a profoundly fertile period of cultural dialogue – visible for instance in sculpture from Gandhāra – and with the expression of a more parochial attitude in art and literature that emphasized the 'middle' culture of the kingdoms of Avantī and Vidarbha in present-day Madhya Pradesh and Maharashtra, respectively. Kālidāsa, reputed in tradition to have links to 'an enemy of the Śakas' (*śakārāti*), the Gupta King Vikramāditya, and to Ujjayinī, a major city in Avantī wrested back from the Śakas by Vikramāditya, is one of the key voices of this new post-Śaka, post-Central Asian era.

Introduction, Part I: The tragic middle

The legacy of looking

> *I now see that sorrow, being the supreme emotion of which man is capable, is at once the type and test of all great art. … Behind joy and laughter there may be a temperament, coarse, hard and callous. But behind sorrow there is always sorrow. Pain, unlike pleasure, wears no mask. Truth in art is not any correspondence between the essential idea and the accidental existence; it is not the resemblance of shape to shadow, or of the form mirrored in the crystal to the form itself: it is no echo coming from a hollow hill, any more than it is a silver well of water in the valley that shows the moon to the moon, and Narcissus to Narcissus. Truth in art is the unity of a thing with itself; the outward rendered expressive of the inward: the soul made incarnate … There are times when sorrow seems to me to be the only truth. Other things may be illusions of the eye or the appetite, made to blind the one and cloy the other, but out of sorrow have the worlds been built, and at the birth of a child or a star there is pain.* (*De Profundis*, pp. 109–10)

Thus wrote Oscar Wilde in the *De Profundis*, shortly after his imprisonment in Reading Gaol, understanding grief in his final years to be the very essence of life and art, their truth. Western culture has been dominated by the central place of calamity and grief in artistic expression ever since the Greeks. And yet if such be the 'supreme emotion of man' and the 'type and test of all great art' in the West, then classical Sanskrit poetry and drama (*kāvya*) can in this respect only disappoint the modern reader. It is said to be barren of confrontation with truth, for, if, as Wilde felt, 'sorrow seems to be the only truth', then most modern critics have looked for it in vain in *kāvya*: there is no final spectacle of death because death is inauspicious in Indian beliefs.

As a typical example of tragedy, a lay-auteur would usually think of *Hamlet* or *King Lear*. Were one to use Shakespearean tragedy as a measure for the preoccupation with the tragic in classical Sanskrit literature as a whole, one would inevitably be led to the conclusion, through the sheer paucity of that genre, that death, conflict and downfall – all the elements of tragedy – are inessential to *kāvya*. Apart from a few works that fit the European description – to wit a princely two (the *Vibudhānanda* and the *Ūrubhaṅga*) – there *are* no tragedies in the repertoire. Closest to Western tragedy is a dramatic type mentioned in Indian poetics called *utsṛṣṭikāṅka* or *aṅka*, a one act cathartic play predominated by the pitiful sentiment (*karuṇarasa*), ordinary men rather than gods, the lamentations of women, speeches that cause aversion (*nirveda*) to the world, and violence,[1] but it is hardly exemplified in the extant literature.

And so, *kāvya* is viewed as a spiritually impoverished frippery stepsister to tragedy, its serious and sad Western counterpart.

Literary critics of *kāvya* in the past two centuries – largely classically trained readers of Greek and Latin – have persistently remarked on the absence of tragic endings as a stand-out feature, generalizing the overall atmosphere of all *kāvya* to be that of an optimistic fairy tale: gentle, graceful, fantastic – in a word, unproblematic. Thus, for example, the Sanskritist T. Holme in his introduction to an edition of several early poetic translations including William Jones's *Sakontalá; or, the Fatal Ring* ('the most outstanding feature in the dramatic literature is the entire absence of tragedy');[2] or a hundred years later in similar vein M. Coulson, arguably one of the most insightful readers of Sanskrit poetry ('the atmosphere of the Sanskrit drama is of the fairy story').[3] Interestingly, the analogy is based on a misunderstanding about fairy tales, which are far more emotionally complicated[4] than either scholar chose to acknowledge.

Implicitly, tragedy for these scholars was typified by core elements of Greek tragedy (a tragic flaw, conflict) and premodern European and English inheritors. When they appraised *kāvya*, it appeared in stark opposition, and to be distinguished instead by the absence of these traits, especially by final harmony and union. This opposition represented a disjunction in aesthetics and views on the purpose of art: while Western tragedy gives expression to existential anxiety, Indian poetry to an implicit trust in a wider order. Thus the learned scholar of *kāvya* Edwin Gerow: 'Just as Western tragedy expresses a fear of disintegration, classical Indian drama [and by implication lyric] celebrates the ideal of union'.[5] For the author of the monumental *A Glossary of Indian Figures of Speech* (1971), conflict, the trigger to disintegration, did not form the chief concern of Sanskrit drama, unlike in Western tragedy.[6] Gerow viewed what he saw as an absence in Indian drama of moral conflict in the Greek sense 'self-induced in terms of a tragic flaw' in the hero, to lead to unchanging characters. For him, the characters were without hamartia, the tragic flaw which is the seed of personal tragedy. As a result, he saw Sanskrit characters more as universal types than as personalities adventitiously formed by changing external forces. This leads him to conclude that 'the exploration of failure in the Indian view is a self-defeating task', that, therefore, 'the tragic perspective is an inappropriate way of viewing Sanskrit drama' and, moreover, that 'tragedy is fundamentally antithetical to the Indian notion that the ultimate good of the individual is bound up to a wider social good.'[7]

Such views stem from prior assumptions of literary genre, and, moreover, those who strictly adhere to them consider *kāvya* to be essentially disinterested in complicated human experience. Largely unchallenged, this perspective has in fact led to an all-consuming attitude in modern readership that connoisseurs of the pleasures of Sanskrit poetry and drama avoid totally the grim abyss of sorrow that is the wellspring of serious art; that they rebuff the shrieks and screams of woe turned to rapturous elegies in Western culture, from Greek poetry to opera to the blues. Classical Sanskrit literature, unlike its predecessors, the great Indian epics, which are filled with blood, gore and broken hearts, is only the apogee of the happy – and by implication silly – fairytale, where love is triumphant and heroic characters untarnished. No grief is expected to mar the perfections of this world that should ever delight, ever soothe, ever pour the unctuous balm of the erotic on the tired soul, much as in the life story of the Buddha, in which his father had tried to keep away all signs of the painful realities of life from his halcyon youth.

And so, it becomes inevitable to ask, if sorrow is thought to constitute the gravest, the most philosophical expression of art (as Wilde held in the *De Profundis*), then would the (apparent) lack of it in *kāvya* mean that it is barren of matter truly essential for the understanding of the nature of existence?

In what follows, I argue against such a conclusion. The works of Kālidāsa place singular value on inherent failure and its consequences on psychology, and in the greater part of this book we will map out the progress of consciousness processing tragic occurrence in five of his compositions. How and with what words, actions, intentions and images are the range of tragic experience and the psychology of the anguished represented? How are they, like William James's mystical states that are characterized by a 'noetic quality': 'states of insight into depths of truth unplumbed by the discursive intellect … [they are] illuminations, revelations, full of significance and importance' that 'as a rule … carry with them a curious sense of authority for after-time'?[8] What kinds of philosophical consolation are offered in these representations? In fact can these passages of grieving and in some cases of derangement be read as philosophical confrontations?

First, in order to begin to truly appreciate the centrality of the tragic in Sanskrit *kāvya* through the lens of Kālidāsa's works, as the noetic, one would need to interrogate the identity of tragedy itself: what constitutes it? If there is almost nothing of Western tragedy in *kāvya*, then what is an Indian tragedy?

The closest idea to tragedy from the Indian perspective may seem to be the *rasa* of grief *karuṇarasa* a notion described in Indian aesthetics, but it too does not fully overlap with Western tragedy. Western tragedy is understood, by certain authors in terms of its design, necessarily nihilistic, but the *rasa* of grief is the affective experience of tragic design in poetry by the actor and/or by the spectator. In this sense the *rasa* of grief derives from tragic events in poetry as their psychological affect, rather than being strictly cognate with tragedy as a poetic mode; its understanding as affect is arguably more subtle and complex than conventional tragedy. We shall come to *karuṇarasa* later in this chapter. For the poet Kālidāsa, tragedy seems to be less about the event or action or poetic mode and more about its psychological perturbation and its alteration of the spirit (which in turn has or may have serious impact on the mode).

In the following chapters, we shall find that tragedy for Kālidāsa can have a broad inner spectrum, including frustration, crisis, failure, tension or conflict, confrontation/recognition, grief and pathos. These events and emotions can be imagined as centred implosions that cast a long and dark shadow over the remainder of the story, threatening to severely thwart narrative development. These experiences may not include death in the physical sense though they may include a painful – for some characters traumatic – absence, estrangement and what is referred to later in this book as 'alteritas' (a state of disengagement and otherness produced by shock). These may not terminate the plot, but they may appear prior to the end. In the Indian theory of narrative development, tragedy is registered in the idea of narrative plot behaving as the human heart matures, by having to confront internal failure or jeopardy in order for the final motive to be achieved.

My interpretations of these centred implosions in Kālidāsa's poems attempt to understand and explain the fundamental structure to the process of grief experienced by the characters – because in its minute attentiveness to first person subjectivity, Kālidāsa's perspective makes it impossible for us not to. I approach 'tragedy' as an internal rather than an external/formal phenomenon: as the poetic representation of the various stages of consciousness as it confronts and explains to itself loss or failure. This is a phenomenological landscape that Kālidāsa, it seems, understood well. There are certain recurrent patterns to this tragic process for the poet: a disturbance of temporality; an alienation and an impoverishment of the self; an alteration of the person; the persistent interpenetration of the past into the present, leading to the mourner living two lives as it were; a sense of circularity and entrapment; a frenzied urge to commit suicide; a sense of amputation through loss of a familiar past and a familiar body. In Kālidāsa, these subtle modalities of consciousness may be shown in a long monologue by the subject, or in a pause in the flow of events when the character may seem to the audience and to others in the narrative to go mad. Thus, in this book I use terms such as grief, melancholy, anguish and sorrow interchangeably with tragedy, for my concern is with the phenomenology of grief. Conflict and change, elements of tragedy that the legacy of looking have insisted are absent from *kāvya*, do indeed appear in Kālidāsa: certain characters undergo profound internal conflict and most in fact change as a consequence of failure in medias res. What makes Kālidāsa's tragic middles truly tragic is less that a death or absence has occurred and more that such events precipitate a detailed depiction of the subject's response to that event. In all cases the full kaleidoscopic experience by Kālidāsa's subjects of a tragic breakage in the middle of things leads to a psychological resolution of some kind, which in turn leads, or may, proleptically, lead (as in the case of the *Meghadūta*), to a structural resolution in the end.

There are deep resonances of this literary conception of tragedy as an inner process with a purpose in classical Indian religions. Since the body is subject to age, blindness, lameness, being maimed, evils, sorrows and ultimately death, the condition of being human is naturally tragic (*Chāndogyopaniṣad* VIII, iii–iv;[9] VIII, ix;[10] and VIII, xii[11]). The tragic condition is subject to endless continuity through rebirth. On the other hand, embodied experience makes and tests the soul, provided it is ready to understand and purify itself (ibid., V, x[12]), preparing it for a state free of the binding effects of temporality. Upaniṣadic thought sees this state to be one in which all dualities, including that between grief and not-grief, dissolve (*Bṛhadāraṇyakopaniṣad* II, iv;[13] and IV, iii[14]). It is a state in which the fundamental self is exempt from evil, age, death, sorrow, and hunger or thirst (*Chāndogyopaniṣad* VIII, vii[15]). As such the condition of sorrow leads to the two highest goals in the gnostic path, greater awareness and thereby freedom from suffering. It is preparatory and purificatory for the cessation of embodiment with which it is one and the same – this especially so in Buddhist traditions, in which *dukkha* (Pāli: suffering) is one of the three marks of existence.

When we permit ourselves to widen our conceptual map of the identity and nature of tragedy, we begin to think of it less as something structural (defined by an ending) and more as something experiential – as consciousness encountering and being readied by the world. The history of tragic identity shaped by the

Western genre has imposed upon us a formal view. Here suffering is determined by a 'trope', the death of the body in outward representation, while inward action, or the content of experience, while richly depicted, is shown to invariably lead to that trope, as a kind of artistic design. Hence European plays that end without the spectacle of death but contain tragic content are called 'tragicomedies' not tragedies, even though the inherent crisis might be profound. To put it another way, the European conception of 'tragedy' suggests that something is tragic not by virtue of how the character feels, however significant and altering, and how he or she may choose to learn from this feeling but by delimitation of the contextual structure that leaves them with no choice to respond but gives only one negative consequence: destruction.

The cry of the *Krauñca*

Within the history of poetic utterance in Sanskrit, tragic experience is first given importance as an experience in the author, and, second, this inward experience has a primary creative place in external eventuality. The composition of the *Rāmāyaṇa*, which Indian tradition regards as the first poem (*ādikāvya*) and whose author, Vālmīki, it regards as the first poet (*ādikavi*), has its origin in sorrow felt by the poet. Moreover, the very first verse of poetry composed by the first poet is not, as one would expect, a pleasantry but a curse – *śāpa*.

It is said in the first book of the *Rāmāyaṇa*, the *Bālakāṇḍa*, that Vālmīki witnessed the sundering of the lovemaking of two *krauñca* birds through the slaughter of the male bird by a hunter, and that he witnessed the consequent pain and mourning of its wife. Grief-stricken and enraged at the cruelty of their idyll irreparably broken, Vālmīki cursed the hunter. Later, reflecting on the finesse and even rhythms of the curse he had spontaneously uttered in passion, he called it *śloka*, which is a type of metre in Sanskrit, a verse of a poem and by extension poetry in general.

> Nearby, that holy man saw an inseparable pair of sweet-voiced *krauñcha* birds wandering about. But even as he watched, a Nisháda hunter, filled with malice and intent on mischief, struck down the male of the pair. Seeing him struck down and writhing on the ground, his body covered with blood, his mate uttered a piteous cry. And the pious seer, seeing the bird struck down in this fashion by the Nisháda, was filled with pity.

Then, in the intensity of this feeling of compassion, the brahman thought, 'This is wrong.' Hearing the *krauñcha* hen wailing, he uttered these words:

[I switch now to the Sanskrit original]

mā niṣāda pratiṣṭhāṃ tvam agamaḥ[16] *śāśvatīḥ samāḥ* |

yat krauñcamithunād ekam avadhīḥ kāmamohitam || *Rāmāyaṇa* I.2.14

'Never, for all time, O Hunter, may you find peace, since you slew one among the pair of *krauñcas* while they were entranced in lovemaking!' [translation in this instance mine[17]]

And even as he stood watching and spoke in this way, this thought arose in his heart, 'Stricken with grief for this bird, what is this I have uttered?'

But upon reflection, that wise and thoughtful man came to a conclusion. Then that bull among sages spoke these words to his disciple: 'Fixed in metrical quarters, each with a like number of syllables, and fit for the accompaniment of stringed and percussion instruments, the utterance that I produced in this access of *shoka*, grief, shall be called *shloka*, poetry, and nothing else.' But the delighted disciple had memorized that unsurpassed sutterance even as the sage was making it, so that his guru was pleased with him. (*Rāmāyāṇa* I.2.9–19, pp. 45–7, Goldman translation)

Vālmīki is commissioned by Brahmā to compose the great history of Rāma in this brand new form arisen as a spontaneous overflow from his grief:

Then the mighty four-faced lord Brahma himself, the maker of the worlds, came to see the bull among sages. … Once the holy lord was seated in a place of honor, he motioned the great seer Valmíki also to a seat. But even though the grandfather of the worlds himself sat there before him, Valmíki, his mind once more harking back to what had happened, lapsed again into profound thought: 'That wicked man, his mind possessed by malice, did a terrible thing in killing such a sweet-voiced *krauñcha* bird for no reason.' Grieving once more for the *krauñcha* hen, given over wholly to his grief and lost in his inner thought, he sang the verse again right there before the god.

With a smile, Brahma spoke to the bull among sages, 'This is a *shloka* that you have composed. You needn't be perplexed about this. Brahman, it was by my will alone that you produced this elegant speech. Greatest of seers, you must now compose the entire history of Rama … fashioned into *shlokas* to delight the heart. As long as the mountains and rivers shall endure upon the earth, so long will the story of the *Ramáyana* be told among men. …'

When the holy lord Brahma had spoken in this fashion, he vanished on the spot, and the sage Valmíki and his disciples were filled with wonder.

> Then all his disciples chanted that *shloka* again. Delighted and filled with wonder, they said over and over again: 'The *shoka*, grief, that the great seer sang out in four metrical quarters, all equal in syllables, has, by virtue of its being repeated after him, become *shloka*, poetry.' Then the contemplative Valmíki conceived this idea: 'Let me compose an entire poem, called the *Ramáyana*, in verses such as these.'
>
> And thus did the renowned sage with enormous insight compose this poem that adds to the glory of the glorious Rama, with hundreds of *shlokas* equal in syllables, their words noble in sound and meaning, delighting the heart. (*Rāmāyāṇa* I.2.22–41, pp. 47–51)

From the throes of Vālmīki's sorrow was born the first masterpiece and with it the first verse in the metre that would predominate Sanskrit composition from the religious to the belletristic. Poetic speech and poetic history, according to Indian tradition, were the children of tragedy, and the correlation is further evoked in the phonetic correspondence between *śloka* and *śoka*.[18] Thus the clinching statement of the legend: *śokaḥ ślokatvam āgataḥ* (*Rāmāyāṇa* I.2.39d), 'grief became poetry'. True poetry, primordial poetry, according to the Indians, arises from the tragic.

Although much of the *Bālakāṇḍa* of the *Rāmāyaṇa*, in which this episode is to be found, is considered by scholars in the field[19] to be apocryphal, there has emerged speculation in scholarship about its independent provenance. Vaudeville argued that this episode is 'an ancient tale or popular belief concerning the origin of lyrical poetry',[20] far older than the epic. Originally centring on two waterbirds symbolically representing a nobleman and his lady, the tale was about the female bird's curse upon the death of her mate by a hunter, which was representative of the first lyric. This symbolic ur-tale was modified so that Vālmīki was included as an observer and as the utterer of the curse, and then added to the *Bālakāṇḍa* to explain the composition of the *Rāmāyaṇa*, fittingly so, given the status of the latter as the first poem. The idea that 'grief became poetry' and its association with a legend about the killing of the *krauñca*, whose mate served as a metaphor for bereaved women and who was associated with mournful music, could have far deeper roots in the conception of Indic poetry, anteceding the *Rāmāyaṇa*.[21]

Though possibly apocryphal, by the fourth century the death scene had come to be seen by composers of classical Sanskrit literature as integral to the *Rāmāyaṇa*. The episode of the *krauñca*'s death was revisited by three luminaries of *kāvya* between the fourth and the twelfth centuries CE: Kālidāsa in *Raghuvaṃśa* 14.70, Bhavabhūti in *Uttararāmacarita* II.5 and Kṣemendra in *Rāmāyaṇamañjarī*

I.19.[22] For each of these authors, the imagery of the birth of poetry is invested with different quasi-mystical and mystical associations. What they are equally interested in is how Vālmīki's inward response to tragic occurrence generates an outward, creative effect.

For Kālidāsa, the female *krauñca*'s cries are evoked in Sītā's lamentation in the woods, after Rāma had banished her: when Vālmīki, gathering grass and firewood nearby, hears her wails, he responds with pity.[23] Kālidāsa introduces him, using the Rāmāyana's words, as 'he whose grief had become poetry' (*ślokatvam āpadyata yasya śokaḥ*, *Rāmāyaṇa* 1.2.39d) which, he adds, had 'arisen from the vision of the bird pierced by the hunter' (*niṣādaviddhāṇḍajadarśanotthaḥ*): an allusion to the *Rāmāyaṇa*, the latter compound qualifying 'grief' reminds of what is quintessential about Vālmīki for Kālidāsa, that the birth of poetry is the outcome of his inner anguish. This reminder is evoked at the moment most symbolic to Kālidāsa of the bereavement of the female *krauñca* bird – the abandonment by Rāma of Sītā. A parallel between the female *krauñca* and Sītā (and implicitly also the difference between Rāma and Vālmīki) is illuminated.

For Bhavabhūti (*c.*eighth century CE) too, tragedy is a process resulting in a creative effect, the curse, the first poem, and it is the exalted quality of this effect that is of interest to him. The moment of the curse becomes a philosophical epiphany: the manifestation in the poet of *śabdabrahman*, ultimate reality in the form of the sacred word.[24]

Kṣemendra (fl. *c.*eleventh century CE) revises the episode the most faithfully to the ur-text of the *Rāmāyaṇa*. However, he interprets the moment as the source of one of the key philosophical concepts regarding tragedy, *karuṇarasa*, the aesthetic experience – or distillation – of grief. He too repeats the *ādiśloka*, the first verse of poetry (though amending *mā* … *agamaḥ*, which must have seemed to him problematic, to *mālabdhāḥ*).[25] As it was for Bhavabhūti, for him too the first verse is a mystical revelation of something otherworldly: the luminous flash of the goddess of speech Sarasvatī in her conduit, the poet.[26]

In the tradition of the *Rāmāyaṇa*, all three poets interpret tragedy to involve a physical loss, a phase of inward emotional response to the loss leading to inner, spiritual change, and the external outcome of that change, which could even be ultimate reality or the goddess Sarasvatī.

But how does that change occur? Long before Kṣemendra, the psychological-aesthetic process underlying how 'grief became poetry' had become a rich topic of discussion among Ānandavardhana and Abhinavagupta, Kashmiri literary critics from the ninth and tenth centuries.[27] Intensely preoccupied in particular with the culminating statement of the *krauñca* death scene, *śokaḥ ślokatvam āgataḥ* as well as with the first poetic verse, which they repeat, these critics saw the first poet's empathy for the death of the innocent bird to be the genesis of the principle of aesthetic beauty: *rasa*.

In the tradition of the *Rāmāyaṇa*, Ānandavardhana believed that poetic expression is a transformation of real grief felt by the composer. This came to form a view in the history of Indian aesthetics that 'the literary artwork is an expression of the author's own emotion'.[28] On the other hand, his commentator Abhinavagupta felt that Vālmīki's curse was the origin of an aesthetic experience of grief, *karuṇarasa*, and thereby of *rasa*, which was in nature different from the actual grief experienced by the poet on seeing the killing of the bird. This aesthetic overflow of real emotion, the versified curse *mā niṣāda* – in other words the turning of emotion into art – was born out of a complex psychological processing of sorrow to poetry that Abhinavagupta explains in detail. Moved by the slaughter of the *krauñca*, the poet felt real pain; this pain stirred a memory of a past experience of pain latent in his consciousness; and this recognition is transformed into a process of mental relishing freed of the constraints of time and space and also of one's ego, a generalized form of awareness finding its shape in the words of the curse. Called *rasa*, this state of mental relishing 'differs from ordinary grief by its being experienced primarily as a melting of one's thoughts. Then, like the spilling over of a jar filled with liquid, like the pouring forth of one's emotion into a cry of lament, this [grief now transformed into the *rasa* of compassion] found its final form in a verse cast into fixed form of meter and into appropriate words'.[29]

And yet modern readers of Indian literature have largely forgotten this broken idyll even though its significance was profound to Indians in the tenth century, the origin even of the very thing distinguishing all poetic expression – *rasa*.

The *Rāmāyaṇa* presents the *krauñca* bird's death as a sacrifice out of which commences the genesis of *kāvya* and of poetic history (*itihāsa*). It imbues the profane nature of the hunting scene with a momentous sanctity to be found only in religious myths that tell of the beginning of time and corporeality. For the *krauñca*'s death is no ordinary event, and in its wake appears a tremendous creation. As such the death of innocence, however cruel and undeserved, is shown to propel a second rising. This secondary genesis serves to invert the ghastly spectacle of bereavement. Such was the underlying metaphor for Indian tragedy – tumultuous inward experience leading to transformative external event – for this is the way that later poets interpreted the original episode, as the conduit of a secondary genesis. Let me begin by paying obeisance to this primal sacrifice long forgotten and to the cry of the *krauñca* whose note reverberates in every lamentation and tragic utterance made subsequently in Indian poetry from Aśvaghoṣa to Kālidāsa.

The politics of looking

As we have seen, modern expectations of the tragic – certainly those of Holme, Coulson and Gerow – are to a large degree shaped by Western, specifically Greek and Shakespearean tragedy,[30] which ends unhappily, usually with a descent of the narrative from repleteness into a moral and circumstantial nadir. One purpose of such ineluctable disintegration, brought about by either a fatal flaw in the hero or even by pure chance, is emotional cleansing (catharsis).[31] Dante, evidently with tongue firmly in cheek, compared tragedy to the braying of a goat: 'tragedy in the beginning is good to look upon and quiet, in its end or exit is fetid and horrible; for this reason it gets its name from *tragos*, which is goat, and *oda* (meaning song) as though to say *goatish song*, that is, fetid in the manner of a goat; this is made plain by the example of Seneca in his tragedies' (quoted in Bhat 1974, p. 3).

This 'pleasant-to-unpleasant' direction is inverse to the movement of Sanskrit literary narrative which, underpinned by a theory of the purposeful (one might also say teleological) manifestation of action, progresses while overcoming various catastrophic hurdles towards a final positive outcome. The model of Western tragedy makes us – literary critics at large – look for suffering in the end and not inside the work. The politics of looking means that we bring those expectations of deathly or disastrous culminations into our evaluation of Indian literature, leading us to ignore its central point of crisis.

George Eliot and endings

Greek tragedy has not just constrained perceptions of 'Oriental' literatures. Even writers within European literary traditions felt stifled by the formal determinism of dramatic tragedy and comedy. Their questioning enabled the maturation of the novel, in which the understanding of both tragic and comic was more indeterminate, more like the older tragicomedy. In the wake of Goethe, early novelists in the nineteenth century critiqued an overemphasis on the dénoument in Western literature and privileged instead the slow development of things rather than their forced culmination. In 1809 George Henry Lewes, man of letters and close companion of George Eliot, writes thus on Goethe's leisurely expansive technique:

> A great writer, and one very dear to me, thinks that the long episodes which interrupt the progress of the story ... are artistic devices for impressing the reader with a sense of the slow movement of life; and, in truth, it is only in fiction that the dénoument usually lies close to the exposition.[32]

Indeed, George Eliot's own view lay close to Goethe's idea that 'the novel must go slowly forward' (see previous footnote): the author A. S. Byatt writes in her introduction to Eliot's *The Mill on the Floss*:

> George Eliot had the true novelist's distaste for the arbitrary artificiality of endings. Thus, to Blackwood in 1857: 'I will pay attention to your caution about the danger of huddling up in my stories. Conclusions are the weak point of most authors, but some of the fault lies in the very nature of a conclusion, which is at best a negation.' Or '... endings are inevitably the least satisfactory part of any work on which there is any merit of development.' Or, in a review, '... even Shakespeare flags under the artificial necessities of a dénouement'.[33]

Eliot, interested in what Goethe called *epische breite* (epic breadth), structured her narratives as development, in which internal conflict and moral crisis form critical stages of growth in medias res, in the middle of things. The modern novel in general might be seen to represent a move away from the artificial stranglehold of the end that characterizes its ancient predecessors in Greek and European tragedy and comedy. Among all forms, it is the novel with its 'slow movement of life and truth' that is closest in progress and process to the *epische breite* of Sanskrit literature. But the interest in narrative as growth/development can nevertheless be said to be a relatively new phenomenon in Western literature. It arises out of the modern interest in the reality of human experience – first outward in the Victorian period, then inward in the fin de siecle. This interest was particularly focused on the tension between individual human experience and wider external forces. Thus for instance, Eliot, rejecting 'that conspicuous far-echoing tragedy which sweeps the stage in regal robes and makes the duller chronicler sublime', favoured the 'unnoticed', 'hidden' reality common to men and the world:

> The pride and obstinacy of millers and other insignificant people, whom you pass unnoticingly on the road every day, have their tragedy too; but it is of that unwept, hidden sort, that goes on from generation to generation and leaves no

> record – such tragedy, perhaps, as lies in the conflict of young souls, hungry for joy, under a lot made suddenly hard to them, under the dreariness of a home where the morning brings no promise with it, and where the unexpectant discontent of worn and disappointed parents weighs on the children like a damp, thick air, in which all the functions of life are depressed; or such tragedy as lies in the slow sudden death that follows on a bruised passion, though it may be a death that finds only a parish funeral. (*The Mill on the Floss*, p. 207)

While this might be a product of a view of literature being what Wilde called 'the outward expressive of the inward', of the importance of the everyday for the individual, the *epische breite* of Sanskrit narrative poetry and drama is a product of a particular view of the flow of action itself, of, in other words, not of the individual but of the formal structure underlying the literary universe.

This view of formal structure draws a parallel with natural growth and maturation and with the 'struggle for life'. As in nature, individuals and their actions develop as they confront inevitable difficulties. The moral agents of the story must fight against the omnipresence of Death. To succeed against Death and to multiply – to attain *phalaprāpti* 'the acquisition of the narrative fruit' – forms indeed the innate natural intention of all beings inhabiting this aesthetic universe (more on this in part 2 of the introduction).

Interestingly, Eliot herself acknowledged at one point that the principles of natural causation underlie the novel, writing that 'nothing will be seen to be irrelevant to my design, which is to show the gradual action of ordinary causes rather than the exceptional'.[34] Natural development, or even a primeval 'green world' in the words of Northrop Frye, might then be said to underlie, to some extent, the idea of the episodic narrative in general throughout time and culture.

Paradoxically, generated by this natural universe of 'ordinary laws' that shapes Sanskrit literature is the utterance of human free will in the form of lamentation (*vilāpa*). Through lamentation, the laws of universal determinism in its two forms of fate and karmic retribution are severely rebuked by the characters. The inevitable progress governing the development of the plot with its multitude of obstacles, including separation in the middle of things, is not accepted with abject quietism by characters. Complaint is a central mode of expressing discontent with 'the way things are' in early *kāvya*, particularly in Kālidāsa and in his forebear Aśvaghoṣa. But it is also the mode of ripening the core of characters who are confronted with the deep mystery of a larger aegis and of instituting moral change wrought by this profound philosophical confrontation. The conception of purposeful action in *kāvya* thereby both formally constrains and accommodates individualism because it provides the conditions for philosophical deliberation (*avamarśa*/*vimarśa*).

William James and the 'second birth'

This, the rumination expressed in the Sanskrit lament, is what William James may have called 'the second birth' of the individual: a religious state of conversion marking the progress of the individual from a feeling of abject meaninglessness to a reaching out toward God. In one place in *The Varieties of Religious Experience* (1902) James is critical of the melancholic attitude exhibited in lamentation, here religious, zestily describing it as 'kicking and screaming after the fashion of a sacrificed pig', later complaining that Schopenhauer and Nietzsche 'remind one, half the time, of the sick shriekings of two dying rats'.[35] Excoriating though he may be about lamenting in the initial part of his book, in a later chapter aptly called 'The Sick Soul', James sees the tribulations of the soul as forming the doorway to philosophical contemplation:

> [Depression] … is a well-marked case of anhedonia, of passive loss of appetite for all life's values; and second, it shows how the altered and estranged aspect which the world assumed in consequence of this stimulated Tolstoy's intellect to a gnawing, carking questioning and effort for philosophic relief. … When we come to study the phenomenon of conversion or religious regeneration, we shall see that a not infrequent consequence of the change operated in the subject is a transfiguration of the face of nature in his eyes. A new heaven seems to shine upon a new earth. In melancholiacs there is usually a similar change, only it is in the reverse direction. The world now looks remote, strange, sinister, uncanny. Its color is gone, its breath is cold, there is no speculation in the eyes it glares with. 'It is as if I lived in another century,' says one asylum patient. – 'I see everything through a cloud,' says another, 'things are not as they were, and I am changed.' – 'I see,' says a third, 'I touch, but the things do not come near me, a thick veil alters the hue and look of everything.' – 'Persons move like shadows, and sounds seem to come from a distant world.' – 'There is no longer any past for me; people appear so strange; it is as if I could not see any reality, as if I were in a theatre; as if people were actors, and everything were scenery; I can no longer find myself; I walk, but why? Everything floats before my eyes, but leaves no impression.' – 'I weep false tears, I have unreal hands: the things I see are not real things.' – Such are expressions that naturally rise to the lips of melancholy subjects describing their changed state.… If the natural world is so double-faced and unhomelike,

> what world, what thing is real? An urgent wondering and questioning is set up, a poring theoretic activity, and in the desperate effort to get into right relations with the matter, the sufferer is often led to what becomes for him a satisfying religious solution.' (*The Varieties of Religious Experience*, pp. 149–52)

It is in the writer Tolstoy's personal journey from grief to God that James finds the key story of the transmutation of the sick soul. Tolstoy experienced severe depression at the age of fifty, which led him to contemplate suicide. However, at the end Tolstoy found that his 'heart kept languishing with another pining emotion. ... a thirst for God,' that 'this feeling of dread was mitigated by the hope of finding the assistance of some one [i.e. God]'.[36] James finds this process, 'intellectual as well as emotional', accommodates an understanding, even an acceptance, of 'natural evil':

> The only thing that need interest us now is the phenomenon of his absolute disenchantment with ordinary life, and the fact that the whole range of habitual values, may, to a man as powerful and full of faculty as he was, come to appear so ghastly a mockery. When disillusionment has gone as far as this, there is seldom a *restitutio ad integrum*. One has tasted of the fruit of the tree, and the happiness of Eden never comes again. **The happiness that comes, when any does come, – and often enough it fails to return in an acute form, though its form is sometimes very acute, – is not the simple ignorance of ill, but something vastly more complex, including natural evil as one of its elements, but finding natural evil no such stumbling-block and terror because it now sees it swallowed up in supernatural good. The process is one of redemption, not of mere reversion to natural health, and the sufferer, when saved, is saved by what seems to him a second birth, a deeper kind of conscious being than he could enjoy before** [my emphasis]. (*The Varieties of Religious Experience*, pp. 156–7)

'One has tasted of the fruit of the tree, and the happiness of Eden never comes again.' This then would be absolute loss, the nadir of European tragedy. But, for some, happiness does come, as it did for Tolstoy: the loss of innocence by tasting of knowledge can be – for those able to make it – a step to a second birth. The second birth then tells of spiritual revival through awareness of some new thing and the remodelling of one's existential framework.

In the development of characters in *kāvya*, the second birth is in one respect a gnostic moment, a renewal through epiphanic self-knowledge. Showing a second birth through a 'supernatural good' that includes the 'natural evil' innate to existence forms the very function of the position of a disruption in Sanskrit poetry from the classical period. Kālidāsa's *Śakuntalā*, in particular, is a striking embodiment of James's idea of the 'second birth': the happiness that eventually comes is 'not the simple ignorance of ill, but something vastly more complex, including natural evil … swallowed up in supernatural good'; it is the result of grief that does not bring 'mere reversion to natural health', for all primary idylls are irretrievably broken for Śakuntalā and Duṣyanta. The second birth is for her and her husband an arrival at a 'deeper kind of conscious being' (this even more so for Duṣyanta).

James sees the second birth as redemption. In Kālidāsa's *kāvya*, the loss and separation that we encounter in the middle of things show not just Death but also a second rising through Death, another creation. A sacrifice – James's tasting of the apple of the tree of Knowledge – is enacted in the centre of the Sanskrit narrative in order for renewal to be activated. Kāma dies in the *Kumārasambhava*, Indumatī in the *Raghuvaṃśa*, Śakuntalā is forgotten by Duṣyanta, the *yakṣa* is separated from his wife in the *Meghadūta*. (Indeed the *Meghadūta* though not embedded in a story clarifies the contextual plot from within.) To characters largely blameless, as their punishments are disproportionately heavy to their transgressions, are delivered the inexplicable blows of profound severance. What are they then if not sacrifices in the image of the murdered *krauñca*? And yet from their period of mourning – their deep deliberation over Self, World and Beyond, found in verse after verse of the richest laments in the hearts of the narratives – comes a new beginning. Wholeness is achieved. The wounds in the universe of the narrative are healed. Time is renewed. We must read these tragic middles as philosophical poetry, indeed as philosophy itself, born from the breaking forth of Death, either of the body or of the heart. Its archetypal form is the female *krauñca*'s crying when her mate died. And this vision of Death in the universe of *kāvya* is the necessary preamble to a new state of things, a new order of being.

Northrop Frye and unfinished comedy

The second birth in *kāvya* sits very closely to Northrop Frye's idea of the metaphoric sacrifice and rebirth in Greek comedy and in its later European inheritors. In 'The Argument of Comedy' Frye argues that while the purpose of Greek tragedy is catharsis – 'tragedy … is expected to raise but not ultimately to accept the emotions of pity and terror'[37] – it contains an implicit but pre-empted step toward an acceptance of evil, of things that strike terror. This is because premodern Western literature imaginatively stages a primeval prototype: an ancient sacrificial ritual of a divine man out of which the world is reborn:[38]

> Many things are involved in the tragic catharsis, but one of them is a mental or imaginative form of the sacrificial ritual out of which tragedy arose. This is the ritual of the struggle, death, and rebirth of a God-Man, which is linked to the yearly triumph of spring over winter. The tragic hero is not really killed, and the audience no longer eats his body and drinks his blood, but the corresponding thing in art still takes place. The audience enters into communion with the body of the hero, becoming thereby a single body itself. Comedy grows out of the same ritual, for in the ritual the tragic story has a comic sequel. Divine men do not die: they die and rise again. The ritual pattern behind the catharsis of comedy is the resurrection that follows the death, the epiphany or manifestation of the risen hero. … Aristophanes … [whom Frye talks about previously] is not only closer to the ritual pattern but contemporary with Plato; and his comedy … is Platonic and dialectic: it seeks not the entelechy of the soul but the Form of the Good, and finds it in the resurrection of the soul from the world of the cave to the sunlight. The audience gains a vision of that resurrection whether the conclusion is joyful or ironic, just as in tragedy it gains a vision of a heroic death whether the hero is morally innocent or guilty.[39]

This leads Frye to argue that Western tragedy is in fact 'uncompleted comedy' and that grief is latent in comedy:

> Two things follow from this: first, that tragedy is really implicit or uncompleted comedy; second, that comedy contains a potential tragedy within itself. With regard to the latter, Aristophanes is full of traces of the original death of the hero which preceded his resurrection in the ritual. Even in the New Comedy [the tradition following the Athenian dramatist Menander who is later than Aristophanes] the dramatist usually tries to bring his action as close to a tragic overthrow of the hero as he can get it, and reverses this movement as suddenly as possible. … Thus the resolution of New Comedy seems to be a realistic foreshortening of a death-and-resurrection pattern, in which the struggle and rebirth of a divine hero has shrunk into a marriage, the freeing of a slave, and the triumph of a young man over an older one. ('The Argument of Comedy', p. 8)

Western comedy then, metaphorically recalling an old pre-Christian rite of the sacrifice of a man and his rebirth, contains a death and then a resurrection of life after death, spring after winter. This revival is curtailed in tragedy. Frye sees this ancient pattern even in Restoration comedy: 'its theme is once again the triumph of life over the wasteland, the death and revival of the year impersonated by figures still human, and once divine as well' ('The Argument of Comedy', p. 9).

The memory of a 'green world' in which winter signals the death of the sap of spring remains buried within the enactment of death in both Western tragedy and comedy: 'The green world charges the comedies with a symbolism in which the comic resolution contains a suggestion of the old ritual pattern of the victory of summer over winter' (p. 10).

Kālidāsa and 'the second birth'

The symbolism of the internal deaths and separations in Kālidāsa is tied up more with the idea of a trial that we shall come to in the next chapter, than with an archaic ritual (though one might be tempted to find a possible prototype in the sacrifice of Puruṣa in the *Puruṣasūkta* close to Frye's divine man sacrifice). Nevertheless, while a ritual prototype for the inner death staged in Kālidāsa's Sanskrit *kāvya*s remains a moot point, Frye's pattern of dying and ascent to a Platonic 'Form of the Good' *is* indeed the implicit design in *mahākāvya* and drama by Kālidāsa, as it is in the *mahākāvya* of his predecessor Aśvaghoṣa and even in a close successor to Kālidāsa, Bhavabhūti. The awareness of loss – the revelation of Absence – forms the very womb of their works especially in Kālidāsa, for the underlying idea of growth/development – the 'form of the good' described in classical Sanskrit aesthetic philosophy – incorporates a vision of etiolated winter when characters face Death before the successful fruiting in verdant summer. Unlike Western tragedy, which has a pessimistic (one can even say anxious) view of crisis because it leads only to destruction, Sanskrit narrative sees crisis optimistically, for it leads toward an end-gain (*prāpti*), which is wholly contingent upon calamity. This is why the conception of grief here is teleological, for there is a fundamental intention, an end point, to it: *phala* 'fruit'. In the *Śakuntalā*, Duṣyanta's memory and his love die only to be regained along with the gaining of his child. In the *Meghadūta*, the loss of the *yakṣa*'s lover is soon to be replaced, we learn in verse 107, with reunion in four months' time.[40] In the *Kumārasambhava* the death of Kāma is replaced with a divine marriage and the birth of Kumāra. In the *Raghuvaṃśa* the tragic deaths of Indumatī, Aja and Daśaratha are replaced by the most celebrated exemplar of the Raghu lineage, Rāma. The 'death and resurrection' pattern is integral to Kālidāsa's vision. It reminds us of the primary bereavement in the *Rāmāyaṇa*, the death of the *krauñca*, out of whose sacrifice the birth of poetic form became possible.

For James, the second birth had been gnostic/spiritual. For Frye the rebirth is social, represented when everyone gathers on stage in the final scene. In

Kālidāsa, it is both these and more. The renewal staged after death is gnostic – a spiritual awakening, two elements of which are a manifestation of free will and the inclusion of 'natural evil'; it is collective – the harmonization of the social fabric; and finally it is natural – occurring in the deep underlying scheme of the kernel of human endeavour growing fruitful only through the struggle for life.

Pathos in Indian aesthetics

According to Indian aesthetics, the representation of grief can result in an aesthetic experience called *karuṇarasa*, the tragic *rasa* (*rasa* being the principle, according to Indians, that makes poetry poetry). Arising from a curse, travail, calamity, the destruction of a loved one or of wealth, a death or captivity, the tragic *rasa*, according to the tradition of Bharata, manifests when things are hopeless.[41] Bharata's aesthetics contrasts this state of hopelessness inherent to the tragic *rasa* with the sense of hopefulness in love-in-separation, *vipralambhaśṛṅgāra*, one of two types of *śṛṅgārarasa*, the erotic *rasa* (the other *śṛṅgāra* is love-in-union). Bharata says that the need for this contrast arises because love-in-separation is represented with exactly the same range of transitory emotional reactions (*saṃcāribhāvas*) as the tragic: despair, fatigue, disquiet, resentment, exhaustion, anxiety, madness and so on.[42] Where the tradition says they separate is at optimism. Love-in-separation is said to arise from a mixture of anxiety and eagerness (thus it is *autsukyacintāsamuttha*). It is a state of tension. On account of being hopeful, even if such hope continually deflates to despair, *vipralambhaśṛṅgāra* is not considered tragic by the tradition.

On the other hand, by calling one kind truly tragic and the other not so, Bharata draws too harsh a line between them.[43] As he had noticed, hopeful *śṛṅgārarasa* and hopeless tragedy are portrayed in *kāvya* with exactly the same repertoire of imagery and language: the 'transitory emotions' that are typically thought to belong to a work of *karuṇarasa* belong, too, to the depiction of love-in-separation, the most ubiquitous mode of representing sorrow in *kāvya*. Hence, though traditional aesthetics would disagree, when it comes to *karuṇarasa* and *vipralamabhaśṛṅgārarasa*, we are dealing not with two different *rasa*s but with two modes of exactly the same thing, namely tragedy. In their representation, both kinds of tragic experiences, one hopeful and one desperate, closely overlap, and indeed, as shall be shown in this book, are cognate. Given that they are modes of one thing, one can say that the idea of tragedy in the Indian case moves a step beyond the Western understanding. Where Western tragedy would regard pathos only as utter hopelessness, the Indian view presents an alternative, subtler, but no less important type – pathos rooted in ambiguity wherein the inner death wish grapples with and is reined in by hope. Such is the kind present in, for example, the *Meghadūta*. This kind of tragedy aligns with what George Eliot called 'the unwept, hidden sort' because it is a type of 'everyday grief' that arises from, and constantly confronts, uncertainty (will he? won't he? will she? won't she? will I? won't I?). Fundamentally it is philosophical in nature, rooted in doubt (*sandeha*), because given that it is not easily resolved, such grief shapes the self as it searches for answers. Though without an inevitable prospect of doom, it has its own gravitas and conflict, born from a severe oscillation between hope and despair.

Looking elsewhere

Given such a particular, layered understanding of the place of grief, it is doubtless that in order to do full justice to sorrow in Sanskrit literary writing, one needs to look beyond the Western understanding of tragedy. One must reconsider familiar Sanskrit plays more sensitively than previously done and in doing so one will come to find that some are actually tragic in their core, even though on the surface sorrow is eventually obviated. Rather than focusing on what is narrowly tragic, as the Greek understanding sets us up to do, it is necessary to re-orient our perception of works, including plays seen to be formally comic, and thereby arrive at a fresh conceptualizing of tragedy.

It is for these reasons that this book assesses the articulation of grief, not through the lens of the tragic ending as understood by the Greeks but through the lens of the tragic middle. The tragic middle is represented most fully in early writers of *kāvya*, in Aśvaghoṣa, Kālidāsa and Bhavabhūti, but, among them, only in Kālidāsa do we find it systematically in the full body of his oeuvre. The tragic is embedded within the phases of growth in his characters, in both dramatic and 'audible' (*śravya*) narratives. Inner conflict and moral transformation, the effects in character of an adventitious universe rather than a designed one, which Gerow had felt to be absent from Kālidāsa and Indian narrative as a whole, manifest with powerful clarity – one can even say as epiphanies – within the tragic middle. Among Kālidāsa's dramatic corpus, it is the familiar and beloved *Śakuntalā* that most clearly represents maturation through embedded crisis, and the second birth after crisis has been processed. In the 'audible' type of poetry the tragic middle is sounded to us through the lamenting voices of

Aja and Rati in his *mahākāvyas* (narrative poetry in cantos), the *Raghuvaṃśa* and the *Kumārasambhava*, and in his independent lyric, the *Meghadūta*, all elegies in which the theme of Death – or Absence – forms the glue as it were of the subject. Expressions of grief in the form of laments are emotional trials in full view, when characters confront and attempt to come to terms with a cruel universe. It is the place when the narrative pauses to deliberate on forces beyond human agency. As such, these moments are fundamentally contemplative and thereby formative. The purpose of grief in *kāvya*, as made clear in the placement and content of Kālidāsa's laments, is to create a philosophical pause – to foster our ruminative capacity about such causal forces as Fate and Accident – unlike in Western drama in which its main purpose is to produce cathartic activity.

Within the wider view of literature, in terms of where we look to find tragedy – in terms of where we stand in the history of the politics of looking – this means holding our gaze, far longer and more carefully than we have, on the middle, what the Indians called the *vimarśa* and the *avamarśa* – rather than the end of a work.

A précis of plots

All the works are well-known and well-loved, hence many readers would, doubtless, be familiar with the storylines, particularly, of the *Śakuntalā* and the *Kumārasambhava*, two of the most famous works of Sanskrit literature. Nevertheless it is useful to remind ourselves where exactly and why the tragic middle appears, and how it is resolved in the full sequence of events, especially since Kālidāsa's plots are intricate and meticulously crafted. For this reason I provide below their outlines.

The *Meghadūta*, comparatively the simplest structurally among all the works, is the love-lyric of a *yakṣa*. Banished from his wife by his master Kubera because of an infraction, he is condemned to a year-long exile in the Rāmagiri mountains. Here, weak with longing for his beloved, he composes a message to her and recites it to a cloud. The message tells a story of a journey through northern India and the plight of the *yakṣa*'s wife, including the path the cloud should take to the city of Alakā where the *yakṣī* dwells, how he should find her, and what he should say to her.

The *Abhijñānaśakuntalā*, or simply the '*Śakuntalā*', is about the love of a nymph's daughter, Śakuntalā, for King Duṣyanta. Out on a hunt, Duṣyanta meets Śakuntalā in the hermitage of Kaṇva where she has grown up and both fall in love. Remaining there to protect the sage's hermitage, he marries her. When he has to leave to return to his palace, he promises to send for her, leaving with her his signet ring as proof of their marriage. One day the sage Durvāsas visits Kaṇva's hermitage. Śakuntalā, now pregnant, lost in reverie of her beloved, neglects to welcome the sage, who growing angry curses her that the object of her affection would forget her. Her friends learning of this calamity beg him to soften, and on their pleas he amends his curse: on seeing a token of remembrance, would the king remember what he had forgotten. When Kaṇva learns of the secret marriage, he arranges for Śakuntalā to go to the palace, sending with her a coterie. On the way, Śakuntalā loses the signet ring while bathing in a river. In the palace, Duṣyanta, now in the grip of Durvāsas's curse, fails to recognize his pregnant wife, the absence of the ring preventing him from regaining his knowledge. In the courtroom, in front of all, he spurns her. Śakuntalā's mother, the nymph Menakā, takes her daughter away to heaven. Soon, the ring is found in the stomach of a fish, and Duṣyanta, remembering all, enters into a severe depression over what he had done. Menakā's friend Sānumati, seeing Duṣyanta's depression, goes back to the world of the nymphs to convey the news that he is remorseful. Six years pass. Duṣyanta, returning from an expedition to protect the gods from demons, stops at the hermitage of sage Mārīca and Aditi, where Śakuntalā has been raising her son, Sarvadamana. He sees a young and beautiful boy playing with a lion cub. He learns that this is his own son and gradually is reunited with Śakuntalā. Mārīca explains to him about the curse.

The *Vikramorvaśīya* is about the love affair between the nymph Urvaśī and King Purūravas. On her way back home with her friends after visiting Kailāśa, Urvaśī and her friend Citralekhā are accosted and captured by demons. Purūravas hears the nymphs' cries and rescues them. Urvaśī and the king fall in love. Back in heaven, while performing a play directed by Bharata, Urvaśī, lost in contemplation of Purūravas, confuses her lines. Bharata, infuriated, curses her to descend to earth. Indra takes pity and modifies the curse so that she would remain on earth until she bore the king a child. The curse allows Urvaśī to be reunited with Purūravas. Purūravas's wife, the queen, blesses their union, and all seems to be well. Purūravas while sporting with Urvaśī in the Gandhamādana is momentarily distracted by a Vidyādhara's daughter, angering Urvaśī. She runs away into the grove of Skanda, forbidden to women, and there she is turned into a vine. The curse is only to be broken by the recovery of a magical jewel.

A period of estrangement follows. Purūravas, distraught and mad with grief, runs through the grove talking to plants and animals. Finally he recovers the magic jewel, and Urvaśī is regained. They return to the palace. Meanwhile a vulture swallows the jewel which the king had intended for his crown. An arrow brings the bird down, and the jewel is recovered. The arrow is inscribed with the name of Urvaśī and Purūravas's son Āyus. Satyavatī, an ascetic lady to whom Urvaśī gave up the baby on his birth and who had brought up the child, reunites the king and Urvaśī with Āyus. Urvaśī recollects her curse. But Nārada intercedes at this point with a message from Indra: he had lifted the curse as Purūravas would be needed to fight against the demons on behalf of the gods. Urvaśī remains united with her husband.

The *Kumārasambhava* is about Śiva and Pārvatī's union. Pārvatī is the daughter of the mountain king Himālaya and Menā. She is the reincarnation of Śiva's first wife Satī, who had committed suicide after her father Dakṣa had humiliated Śiva. Thereafter Śiva, disconsolate in his bereavement, becomes an ascetic. The sage Nārada informs Himālaya that his daughter is destined to marry Śiva. Śiva one day arrives with his entourage at the Himālaya to meditate. Hearing of his arrival, the mountain god sends his daughter to attend to his spiritual needs. Meanwhile a demon Tāraka, empowered by a boon from Brahmā, usurps heaven and subjugates the gods. Brahmā prophesies that a son of Śiva would be able to defeat the demon and that the only suitable bride for Śiva was Himālaya's daughter. In order to rouse Śiva from his asceticism, Indra hatches a plan. He bids Kāma, along with his friend Spring and his consort Rati, to make Śiva fall in love with Pārvatī. Kāma infiltrates the grove but, as he is about to cast his arrow on Śiva, is burnt by the god in anger noticing him about to take action. Pārvatī is disconsolate, and Rati laments. Pārvatī decides to win Śiva herself and begins to practice fierce austerities undaunted by difficulty. In time Śiva is won over. He comes to her disguised as a young stroppy *brāhmaṇa* youth and begins to denounce Pārvatī's choice of groom. When she is riled up and answers back defending Śiva eloquently, he reveals himself to her and declares himself to be her slave. He asks permission from the Himālaya for Pārvatī's hand in marriage. His entrance into the capital city is accompanied by fanfare and excitement among the residents, especially the womenfolk. Śiva and Pārvatī's post-nuptial lovemaking is described in glorious detail. They dwell in the Gandhamādana mountain for twenty-five years making love.

The *Raghuvaṃśa* is a collection of interdependent tales about the kings in the line of Raghu, in which Rāma was born. It begins with the tale of pious Dilīpa and his protection of the sacred cow Nandinī, who granted him the boon of a son; then tells the tale of the generous conqueror Raghu and his protection of the sacred horse of the horse sacrifice from Indra and of his munificence towards the *brāhmaṇa* Kautsa; then of Aja, Dilīpa's son, and his marriage to and subsequent loss of Indumatī, the princess of Vidarbha; then of the hunt-loving Daśaratha, Rāma's father, and the curse that would doom him to death out of grief for his son; then of Rāma, the most celebrated descendant of Raghu and his loss of Sītā; then of Kuśa and the resumption of lost Rāghava power to Ayodhyā, and the marriage of Kuśa to a Nāga princess; and finally of the last king, Agnivarṇa, lover of sensual pleasures. Among these, the tale of Aja and Indumatī contains the tragic core. Indumatī selects Aja in a *svayaṃvara*, a ceremony where a high-born woman chooses her groom. One day while the couple are roaming in a park, a fatal flower garland falls from Nārada's musical instrument, as he is flying above them and lands on Indumatī breasts. She dies suddenly. Later we learn this is because of a curse she had received in her previous life as a nymph for tempting a sage. The king sinks into a deep depression for eight years, only enduring his grief for the sake of his son. When Daśaratha is crowned king, Aja commits ritual suicide.

Introduction, Part II: Doubt, obstacle, deliberation, death, disaster: the trial in Indian aesthetics

Introducing the Trial

The importance invested in the representation of disruption *in medias res* in Kālidāsa's works may be contextually framed, and formally explained, by the theory of narrative development in classical Indian aesthetics. Indian aesthetics views narrative development to follow a line of progression, in which failure is embedded in the middle and plays a critical role in the subsequent unfolding of the story, regarded as the endeavour of a hero and a heroine toward a final goal. One idea, in particular, is connected to embedded crisis – *avamarśa* or *vimarśa*, a trial characterized by an obstacle, conflict, death, a period of rumination or disaster, making the goal of the narrative unreachable. This is the aesthetic category that overlaps with the tragic middle in the works of Kālidāsa studied in the subsequent chapters. However, Kālidāsa expands the scope of crisis from a mere obstacle to a deep and nuanced representation of its experience by an afflicted character. In his works, the Trial, being *duḥkhātmaka*, 'characterized by suffering', is *truly* a tragic middle. However, the historical understanding of the Trial seems to have been entangled in various debates, which require clarification because they contribute a variety of perspectives, increasing the conceptual scope of tragedy as it is conventionally understood.

Below, I shall recapitulate the main elements of the narrative structure, of which the Trial is a middle component, as first outlined in Bharata's *Nāṭyaśāstra*. I will then introduce the problems surrounding the *vimarśa*/*avamarśa*. I shall use as my chief source for the latter Abhinavagupta's *Abhinavabhāratī* (*c.*tenth century CE), one of the oldest and most descriptive commentaries to the *Nāṭyaśāstra*.[1] While my comments on the narrative model are largely based on the views of several others,[2] I offer as new the discussions of Abhinavagupta on the *vimarśa*. Abhinavagupta's comments are unique in that they narrate a history of the interpretation of the *vimarśa* by various schools. How authentic his history of such debates is is uncertain, for none of the works he cites are available to us. Nevertheless, its value cannot be underestimated, for, among all works of literary criticism, his discussion offers the most penetrating and detailed analysis of the *vimarśa*.

An overview of the theory of narrative structure

Bharata's *Nāṭyaśāstra* (*c.*300 CE[3]), *Teachings on Drama*, the basis of the aesthetic tradition,[4] envisages a detailed theory of narrative art comprising three sets of 'five categories'. Described in the order of their appearance in that work (*Nāṭyaśāstra* 19.1–106) they are: (i) stages of action (*avasthā*s), (ii) means of securing the goal of action (*arthaprakṛti*s) and (iii) junctures (*sandhi*s). The five *avasthā*s elaborate a theory of narrative eventuality, as exemplified by purposeful deeds in the world and by rituals conducted for a specific reward. This sequential eventuality, 'regarded as inevitable even in real life' (Warder 1972, I, p. 60), is demonstrated through the effort of the main character towards the goal when it unfolds properly, and as such a connection to reality is seen to be implicit in artistic design. The five *prakṛti*s, or narrative means, are the particular instruments that bring about the final aim of the action. The five *sandhi*s provide the structural contexts in which the means, and through them the stages of narrative action, can unfold.

This theory of narrative development is adumbrated with few and minor changes, in spite of the passage of time, in a number of other treatises, such as the *Abhinavabhāratī*, Dhanaṃjaya's *Daśarūpa* 1.11–68[5] (*c.*tenth century CE), Dhanika's commentary thereon called the *Avaloka* and Viśvanātha's *Sāhityadarpaṇa*.

While the terminology in the *Nāṭyaśāstra* and in its aforementioned inheritors refers to drama, it is clear that among the three sets, the idea of the *sandhi*s applied also to the structure of epic poetry in cantos, *mahākāvya*. Thus Daṇḍin (*c.*seventh century CE) in an influential passage on the characteristics of *mahākāvya*: 'it [a *mahākāvya*] is … endowed with cantos, not too long, consisting in pleasing metres, in which there are well-depicted *sandhis*' ([*mahākāvyam*] *sargair anativistīrṇaiḥ śravyavṛttaiḥ susaṃdhibhiḥ … upetam*, *Kāvyādarśa* 1.18). Or Bhāmaha, a contemporary: 'A *mahākāvya* is … joined with the five *sandhis* (*mahākāvyam … pañcabhiḥ sandhibhir yuktam*, *Kāvyālaṃkāra*

1.20cd). Or Kouhala (*c.*eighth century CE) speaking of his epic poem in Prakrit the *Līlāvaī*: 'the matter of [this] tale, which is in a beautiful sequence of *sandhis*' (*susaṃdhibaṃdhaṃ kahāvatthuṃ* | *Līlāvaī* 42d[6]). Or Viśvanātha, a fifteenth-century literary theorist: 'A *mahākāvya* is a sequence of cantos. Therein ... there are all the dramatic *sandhis*' (*sargabandho mahākāvyaṃ tatra ... sarve nāṭakasandhayaḥ* | *Sāhityadarpaṇa* 6.315–17cd). Citrabhānu analyses Bhāravī's *mahākāvya Kirātārjunīya* according to the *sandhis*,[7] and a more recent effort is Tubb's (1979), who analyses the *Kumārasambhava*, also a *mahākāvya*, likewise according to the traditional narrative categories. Great efforts were taken by poets, it seems, to design their compositions through the *sandhis*, and it would not be unusual to assume that Kālidāsa too composed his works according to this aesthetic design though of course it is evident that he was highly original and used the style as it suited his expression. This is evident in the way the *sandhi* called *vimarśa* in his hands becomes a tragic moment.

It is not clear though how the *prakṛtis* and the *avasthās* were used in the composition of *mahākāvyas*. Given that the *sandhis* would be normally associated with the *avasthās* and the *prakṛtis* in the time of these writers – Abhinavagupta felt that the *sandhis* generated the *avasthās* (and in this vein Kane 1983, see ahead in 'Controversies about the *vimarśa*', and Tubb 1979, pp. 123–33) – it is possible that even those too may have been associated with *mahākāvya*. Such critics as Abhinavagupta and those of his school who saw a concomitance of the *prakṛtis* and the *avasthās* in mention of the *sandhis* may have explained the inherence of these in *mahākāvyas* in the following way. The *prakṛtis*, which are the constitutive matter of the story, chief of which is the Seed, the *bīja*, the starting point of the enterprise, activate the states of the goal-oriented action (*avasthās*). The constitutive matter is contextualized by periods of time called the *sandhis*. In other words, the *avasthās* 'answer a question – where to? and the *prakṛtis* furnish an answer to a question – how to?' (Byrski 1974, p. 117). The *sandhis* would in that case answer 'when?' The three are made possible only through their codependence and simultaneity. As such, the *pañcakatraya* may have been seen as a general theory of narrative causality for both visual (*dṛśya*) and audible (*śravya*) poetry.

The avasthās

In the prototypical vision in the *Nāṭyaśāstra*, it is made clear at the very beginning that the entire purpose of the main plot (*ādhikārikam itivṛttam*) is the Acquisition of Fruit (*phalaprāpti*) toward which is directed all the creative elements involved in the literary process.[8] The secondary plot (*prāsaṅgikam itivṛttam*) lays out the winning of the goals of the secondary characters. For example, Rāma's winning of Sītā is understood to be the *ādhikārikam itivṛttam* of the *Rāmāyaṇa*, while the stories of Vibhīṣaṇa and Sugrīva or the death of Rāvaṇa the *prāsaṅgikam itivṛttam*.[9] The Acquisition of Fruit, along with four other conditions preceding it, derives from five states of action that underlie any undertaking in the everyday world, including rituals performed for reward: 'In accordance with the operation of causation in something that has to be achieved and in a ritual with an aim, actors understand five conditions [to exist in a story] – the Initiation (*prārambha*), the Effort (*prayatna*), the Possibility of Success (*prāpteś ca sambhavaḥ*), the Certain Attainment of Fruit (*niyatā ca phalaprāptiḥ*) and the fifth, the Addition of Fruit (*phalayogaḥ*)' (*saṃsādhye phalayāge tu vyāpāraḥ kāraṇasya yaḥ / tasyānupūrvyā vijñeyā pañcāvasthā prayoktṛbhiḥ / prārambhaś ca prayatnaś ca tathā prāpteś ca sambhavaḥ / niyatā ca phalaprāptiḥ phalayogaś ca pañcamaḥ* || *Nāṭyaśāstra* 19.7–8). This statement explicates the teleological nature of narrative action: action is undertaken by the lead character for a specific effect, a *phala* (literary fruit), as it is in many examples in real life or in religious acts that fulfil certain needs (such as rainfall in times of drought). When arising altogether in sequence, they become the causes of the Fruit: 'Different in their natures (*svabhāvabhinnānām*), when they arise one after another (*āsām parasparasamāgamāt*), their unfolding (*vinyāsa*) as a single sequence (*ekabhāvena*) is said to be the cause of the Fruit (*phalahetu*)' (*āsāṃ svabhāvabhinnānāṃ parasparasamāgamāt / vinyāsa ekabhāvena phalahetuḥ prakīrtitaḥ // Nāṭyaśāstra* 19.15). And they are to be shown until the end of the full enterprise: 'The [stages] starting with the Initiation of that (*tadārambhādi*) which is the principal plot (*itivṛttam ādhikārikam*) mentioned at the very beginning (*samākhyātam pratyag eva*) must be shown (*kartavyam*) so that their ending in the Fruit (*phalāntaṃ*) may occur (*yathā bhavet*)' (*itivṛttaṃ samākhyātaṃ pratyag evādhikārikam / tadārambhādi kartavyaṃ phalāntaṃ ca yathā bhavet // Nāṭyaśāstra* 19.16). As such, the endeavour of the hero must involve all five stages of action, even though the degree to which the other sets of five are used is left at the discretion of the composer.[10]

The goal-oriented conditions underlying narrative development are then sequentially described in general terms so as to indicate their applicability in all purposeful endeavours. First: the Initiation (*prārambha*) in which an eagerness (*autsukya*) for the final goal is expressed by either the chief agent or by the secondary agents of the action, even in the form of wistful yearning. This eagerness for a wish is the propelling force of the principal action.[11] For example, Dhanika says that the first act of the seventh-century play *Ratnāvalī* by Harṣa, in which the wily minister Yaugandharāyaṇa hatches a plan to unite the heroine Sāgarikā with the hero King Udayana, is the Initiation of the effort (*Avaloka* 1.20ab).

This is followed by Effort (*prayatna*) during which the chief agents make an endeavour to acquire their goal, driven by eagerness for it, even though its attainment remains unclear.[12] In the *Ratnāvalī*, Dhanika says that Sāgarikā's efforts to portray her love for Udayana in a painting demonstrate Effort by the agent toward the Fruit (*Avaloka* 1.20cd).

Then the Possibility of Success (*prāptisambhava*), during which phase of action, the Fruit of the endeavour is thrown into jeopardy so that it appears both possible and impossible at once. This phase of action involves encountering obstacles and consequent doubts. These obstacles may be caused either by the actions of the main agents or by something external.[13] At *Daśarūpa* 1.21ab (*upāyāpāyaśaṅkābhyāṃ prāptyāśā prāptisambhavaḥ*), it is even said explicitly that there is a grappling with *śaṅkā*, profound anxiety about obstacles, during this state. Dhanika's commentary to this part explains that 'The Acquisition of the Fruit, that is the hope for the Fruit, is fully (*ekānta*) unsettled because of the presence of both a means of its attainment and a doubt concerning non-attainment' (*upāyasyāpāyaśaṅkāyāś ca bhāvād anirdhāritaikāntā phalaprāptiḥ prāptyāśā*, *Avalokā* 1.21ab)'.[14] Dhanika exemplifies this with the episode in the *Ratnāvalī* in which Sāgarikā meets Udayana in disguise but which also contains the fear of the chief queen, Udayana's wife, Vāsavadattā intruding into their surreptitious rendezvous. The agents begin to see that the desired wish, though striven for, is not a fait accompli. This is a phase of maturation, during which the characters must process the fear of failure. Only after this critical confrontation with tension is there Certain Attainment of the Fruit (*niyatā phalaprāpti*), an auspicious state in which the prospect of attainment of the fruit becomes visible again, after hindrances have been overcome. Now that jeopardy has gone, the fruit is fully settled.[15] On the other hand, as we shall see later, the interpretation of *niyatā* as 'certain' was historically not without controversy. Finally, the action culminates in the Addition of Fruit (*phalayoga*) in which the chief agents of the action win the fruit, and both the principal and subsidiary courses of the narrative end, with the ending of the action.[16,17]

Byrski 1974 compares the *avasthās* of narrative action with the theory of action in Vedic sacrifice. In the ritual model of action there are four stages, beginning with desire (the propellant for action) and ending with resolution, which seek as the *phala* to ultimately reunite the dismembered body of the god Prajāpati, to whom the ritual is addressed. The penultimate stage comprises counteracting dangers that obstruct this process in the form of demons. Only when the threat of danger has been overcome and the demons dispelled, can the action culminate in its final purpose – the reconstitution of the god. These stages coincide closely with and seem to form the prototype for the *avasthā*s of action guiding narrative-manifestation.[18]

Thus, like narrative development, ritual development includes a tragic middle as it were in which hindrances must be confronted in order for it to move forward.

Moreover, the teleological, goal-oriented form of the model parallels the Mīmāṃsā theory of language. The Mīmāṣakas explained how total, single sense is generated by a complexly ordered text composed of various semantic components through unity of purpose. It is this total, single meaning towards which sense-comprehension strives. Since words by themselves carry a universal meaning (a cow would convey the property 'cowness' rather than a particular cow), the particular meaning of a sentence is only made possible by an ultimate purpose to which all individual words forming the sentence are subordinated. Individual words in mutual juxtaposition delimit their universal senses through a set of expectations generated by the verbal component – what? how? by what means? It is in fulfilment of the need created by the verb that the component words of a sentence carry a particular meaning. To fulfil other expectations generated by the verbal component, the reader would have to look at the surrounding sentences for more information: in this way an interdependent single sense is generated through discrete linguistic parts. The process ends only when the ultimate, single purpose of the text is arrived at, towards which all component parts are hierarchically arranged.[19] The way the *avasthā*s unfold parallels the idea of unified textual sense-comprehension, which moves towards a final ultimate total sense: the flow of narrative is coterminous with the sense process; it is generated by the action (*kriyā*) of an agent, just as the sense process is activated by the capacity of the verbal element in a sentence; to the fulfilment of the final need of the agent of action, all individual narrative components, even subplots within the main plot, are subordinated. The action of the agent ends only when the final, single goal is achieved. Unity of purpose, here the purpose of the agent, is thereby made into the defining criterion of narrative.

The prakṛtis

Next, the artistic means whereby the narrative is constructed (*prakṛtis/arthap rakṛtis*) and the manner whereby the main effort is achieved.[20] There are five methods outlined in the foundational model in the *Nāṭyaśāstra*.

They are explained as follows.

The Seed (*bīja*): The cause of the goal according to Dhanaṃjaya and Viśvanātha, the objective of which alone must be taken into regard by the composer.[21] Sown or implanted in the beginning of the endeavour at the *prārambha*, it expands multitudinously, ending in the Fruit (*phala*).[22]

The Drop (*bindu*): Statements or memories or incidents which, when there is a cutting-off of the principal needs[23] of the enterprise, is the cause of their resumption till the end of the composition.[24] The analogy used at *Abhinavabhāratī* 19.23 is a drop of oil pervading as a continuum in water. Like the *bīja* it can recur at different points in the story, bringing the focus back to the aim of the chief character and the *ādhikārikam itivṛttam*. A further example of a *bindu* is the episode of the fisherman finding the fish with the ring that restores memory in the *Śakuntalā*: it is a drop that is the cause of the narrative purpose – the recognition of *Śakuntalā* – resuming. This is also where the second birth in the *Śakuntalā* takes place.

The Flag (*patākā*): An episode forming a part of the secondary story, but to be envisaged like the main plot. It is undertaken for the sake of some other character but will also help the main endeavour of the hero, which it promotes like a banner. Abhinavagupta cites the tales of Vibhīṣaṇa and Sugrīva as examples.[25]

The Interlude (*prakarī*): a shorter, isolated episode that unlike the *patākā* only helps the Fruit of the hero.[26]

And the Purpose (*kārya*): The purpose is the chief undertaking of the hero, the goal of the plot.[27] It overlaps with the objective of the main plot, in its potential state with the *bīja* and in its fully realized state, occurring at the end of the plot, with the *phala*. In its first manifestation as the *bīja*, it is revealed in the beginning, either through statements or actions made by the chief characters or by secondary characters revealing what is earnestly desired. It may recur at different points of the story. While Abhinavagupta sees it to mean the principal story itself, which leads to the Fruit, Dhanaṃjaya reduces the scope of the term to mean the three aims of man which form the overall narrative effect, either alone or in combination.[28] The three aims of man being the purpose of narrative seem nevertheless to be a later restriction of the sense. Viśvanātha sees the *kārya* to be the motivating factor, the 'wished for target' *apekṣitaṃ sādhyam*, behind the attainment of the goal rather than the goal itself.[29] He exemplifies this with the death of Rāvaṇa in the Rāma story.[30] As such, the *kārya* can be thought of as a sense of constant purpose or desire in the chief character, perhaps equivalent to the eagerness (*autsukya*) manifesting in the beginning of the action in the first *avasthā*.

The Flag and the Interlude are optional instruments. Only the Seed, Drop and the Purpose are considered to be necessary to accomplish the hero's aims, and to thereby serve in achieving the successive stages of action that the plot must demonstrate, in Abhinavabhāratī 19.27, the *Daśarūpa* and the *Avaloka*. In the last two the Flag and the Interlude are simply named in the context of the *prakṛtis* but not explained. They are discussed separately as types of secondary plots (*prāsaṅgikam itivṛttam*).[31] Clearly then the story in germ form, its restorative episode, and its main objective were seen as fundamental even as the other aspects became minor given their optionality.

The instruments can best be thought of as the primary manipulators of the growth of narrative action, components that galvanize the development of the story and its overall shape. (Thus Byrski 1974, p. 133: 'the five *arthaprakṛtis* constitute flesh.') Their strategic addition activates a desired condition of action. Among these the *bīja*, the Seed, is the most important instrument to the Fruit as further discussions of other aspects of narrative representation in the *Nāṭyaśāstra* and elsewhere return to it time and again.[32] In fact *Daśarūpa* 1.27ab identifies the Seed with the motivator, the *kārya*, by calling it the very cause – the driving force – of the primary objective of the plot: 'The cause of this [*kārya*] is the *bīja*, [at first] implied minutely, [then] expanding variously' (*svalpoddiṣṭas tu tad dhetur bījam vistāry anekhadā*). Similarly Dhanika, who calls the Seed 'the special cause' (*hetuviśeṣa*) of the unfolding action (*Avaloka* 1.27ab). Just as the *bīja* is the initial manifestation of the *kārya*, the *bīja* and the *phala*, Seed and Fruit, too are closely related, the former being a minute prior state of the latter, the matured outcome of the potentiality of the Seed. In this vein, Abhinavagupta indicates that the *bīja* is equivalent with the *phala* ('Furthermore, the Fruit is called the Seed because the means [of procuring it] that are to arise are inevitable', *phalam api bhaviṣyadupāyāvinābhāvād bījam ity ucyate, Abhinavabhāratī* 19.22[33]). In Kālidāsa we often find the Fruit of the story prefigured in his titles – *The Recognition of Śaktuntalā, The Birth of Kumāra, The Lineage of the Raghus*. In this respect, his titles also indicate the Seed of his stories. The narrative *phala* and the *bīja* seem to be in some sense cognate, the beginning being a prefiguration of the end, and such also is the understanding of Kālidāsa.

The sandhis

Finally: the Junctures (*sandhis*) of the story, which in turn may readily corelate to other developmental models in the real world.[34] Here, the place of obstacles, thus far only suggested in the flow of action toward its purpose and in the constituent instruments bringing about the flow, is seen to progressively increase as the Seed of the story develops into a proliferating, complex entity.

According to the vision of the *Nāṭyaśāstra*, the Seed matures through five stages of development, which, as later clarified by Dhanaṃjaya, connect the various secondary goals with the main goal of the story line when there is a single sequence of events.[35]

First, the invisible germination, the Mouth or the Source (*mukha*): This, corresponding with the beginning of action and the opening of a narrative, is the place in which the Seed is implanted, and it provides a subtle indication of the various *rasa*s and desires of the characters. The body of the story follows this germinal source.[36]

Then, the intermittently glimpsed Reflection, the phase of narrative action 'in front of the Source' (*pratimukha*): in this stage of maturation, the Seed of the main character's enterprise has newly germinated in the Source, but in its delicacy seems to be invisible to the audience even when it is glimpsed, like a sprout obscured by dust, according to Abhinavagupta. Dhanika cites the second act of the *Ratnāvalī* as an example in which the budding love between King Udayana and Sāgarikā, sown in the first act, is sometimes visible to the side characters and is partly inferred by Udayana's chief queen, Vāsavadattā, from the picture drawn by Sāgarikā (*Avalokā* 1.30).[37]

Next, the search and gestation through uncertainty, the Embryo (*garbha*): In this juncture, the Seed of the enterprise is concretely manifested, as the efforts of the agents take effect, but there is also a deep uncertainty about the final outcome, as the chief characters' endeavours confront greater hindrances. This leads to a reinvigorated desire for the goal in the main characters, which propels a continued search for the enterprise.[38] Dhanika exemplifies this phase of mixed conditions and emotions with the third act of the *Ratnāvalī*, in which Vāsavadattā becomes an obstacle to the love of her husband, Udayana, and her new rival Sāgarikā, while the secret meeting of the king with Sāgarikā disguised as Vāsavadattā is also shown, indicating the possibility of their union. Reinforcing the mixed hopes of this juncture, the union is followed by an interruption and then by a search to remove the obstacle (*Avaloka* 1.36).

Then the deliberative pause, the Trial (*vimarśa/avamarśa*): In this juncture, the Seed of the characters' desire that has sprouted in the Embryo and is nearing its final desired outcome encounters greater obstacles caused by temptation, anger or a destructive predilection, among various possible causes. Depending on the tradition of literary criticism one was taught, as inferable from Abhinavagupta (see later), this phase was thought to be characterized by doubt, a fatal obstacle, a disaster or by reflective awareness in the hero. The goal is apparently unattainable due to various hindering causes, and the endeavours of the hero and the subsidiary characters could technically conclude. The story would then be an enterprise representing failure, or the triumph of calamity. On the other hand, certain literary critics, as we shall see later in the controversies surrounding the Trial, believed that such doubting led to reinvigoration, indeed a rebirth of striving for the goal, which in turn activated the fourth *avasthā*, in which the prospect of the Fruit becomes a fait accompli.[39] Dhanaṃjaya and Dhanika state that the purpose of the Seed is brought back into focus by means of the confrontation with crisis in the *vimarśa*. Dhanika exemplifies this with two incidents of crises, one from the *Ratnāvalī* and one from Nārāyaṇabhaṭṭa's play the *Veṇisaṃhāra*. In the former, he cites the ending of the fourth act in which there is shown the crisis of the fire breaking out, leading to the rescue of the endangered Sāgarikā, the softening of Vāsavadattā toward her and the ultimate union of Sāgarikā and Udayana, the goal of the endeavour. In the final act of the *Veṇīsaṃhāra*, Dhanika sees the shocking entrance of Bhīma soaked in Duryodhana's blood as such a moment of the Seed being restored: Bhīma, horrific in red, is unrecognizable at first to Draupadī and Yudhiṣṭhira (and also it is unexpected to the audience) but when his identity is cleared the victory over the Kurus is understood by all and Draupadī in happiness ties up her hair – the goal of the play as indicated in the title (*Avaloka* 1.46). While he does not clarify that the hero or some other character is undergoing a period of deliberation, Dhanika sees the *avamarśa* as a critical 'flare up' that necessarily pushes the goal of the initiating project toward its conclusion. In the later *Sāhityadarpaṇa*, the inherence of fatal obstruction persists in the conception of the Trial, which is there said to be the juncture in which the linear movement of action is stalled by impediments such as a curse, and Act IV till the middle of Act VII of the *Śakuntalā* are taken to exemplify disruption.[40] Byrski (1974, p. 112) sees Bhavabhūti's play the *Uttararāmacarita* to be the longest representation of a Trial, beginning with the report of the people to Rāma about their mistrust of Sītā and ending in the last act. As I argue subsequently, it is this phase of apparent but necessary failure shown with varying degrees of intensity by Sanskrit composers that is portrayed in Kālidāsa's works as a shocking, unexpected eruption of the tragic in the form of grief or of a shattering loss of the mind, as Purūravas's mental dissonance in the *Vikramorvaśīya*. *Vimarśa* is characterized by both doubt and reflective awareness in Duṣyanta's depression following his amnesia in the *Śakuntalā*, and as such can be thought of as a phase of not just narrative obstacle but of knowledge acquisition and philosophical maturation. The successful culmination occurs after he turns this phase into one of growth, rather than of adverse decline.

And finally the uniting, the End (*nirvahaṇam*): Here there is a culmination (*samānayana*) of the goals of all the junctures, beginning with the Source together with the Seed, followed by their various emotions.[41] The story concludes with the conclusion of the action, and bears Fruit, the desire of the chief characters sown as the Seed in the beginning of the enterprise.

In drama, the major forms, the *nāṭaka* and the *prakaraṇa*, are expected to explore failure in their development, for they are said to show all five junctures (*Nāṭyaśāstra* 19.44), even as certain minor forms, in which the middle two junctures are absent, are not thus expected to.[42] While the *pratimukha*, the *garbha* and the *vimarsa*, that is to say, the middle phases of development, are omitted in those narratives, the *mukha* and *nirvahana* are always required.[43] Abhinavagupta says that when narrative agents acting with deliberation strive to achieve an extensive and manifold goal then all five junctures must be shown.[44] On the other hand, while the *sandhis* and the *prakṛtis* were subject to artistic licence, what remained important was that narrative development unfolded in the way goal-oriented ritual and worldly action unfolded, in which inherent impediment plays a critical role in maturing towards the outcome.

Abhinavagupta and controversies over the avamarśa/vimarśa

When one sees each in relation to the other, as the *Nāṭyaśāstra* intends, the three models seem to descend from the more abstract to the more particular – the *avasthās* embody a theory of causation in general, the *prakṛtis*, the finite tools of artistic representation that condition the flow of action, and the *sandhis*, the temporality of literary representation, or even its 'growth', its progression through transition points. On the other hand, the relationship between the *avasthās*, the *prakṛtis* and the *sandhis* is far from clear. While the *Nāṭyaśāstra* presents them as mutually codependent and coterminous, it does not make the causal and locative relationships explicit. Which causes which and when does one thing start and end?

There were differences in historical opinion regarding these relations. Udbhaṭa believed that there was no fixed relationship between the stages of action and the junctures.[45] Abhinavagupta, Viśvanātha and the Jaina literary scholars Rāmacandra and Guṇacandra believed that the *avasthā*s directly overlap consecutively with the *sandhi*s,[46] while a second group, represented by Dhanaṃjaya, felt there was a rigid one-to-one correspondence between each of the *avasthā*s, the *prakṛti*s and the *sandhi*s: for example, the Seed of the enterprise activates the state of action called *prārambha* which then corresponds to the structural frame of the *mukha* while the *bindu* activates the *prayatna*, the phase of effort by the hero, and corresponds with the *pratimukha*.[47] In terms of causation Abhinavagupta felt the plot itself together with all the aspects involved in its construction, – the five *sandhis*, their inner divisions and their instruments the *prakṛtis*, to generate the *avasthā*s (*Dhvanyālokalocana* 3.14 in Tubb 1979, p. 138; Kane 1983, p. 44) – the *sandhis* form the starting point for the five stages of action, generated into being by the narrative instruments: primarily the hero's use of the *bīja*, the *bindu* and the *kārya* and, supplementarily, by the sub-characters' use of the *patākā* and the *prakarī*. In fact according to Abhinavagupta the *prakṛtis* associated with the hero are nothing but his own aspects – the *bīja* is his activity, the *bindu* his planning, the *kārya* his completion of the enterprise (Tubb 1979, pp. 140–1). Following Abhinavagupta's reasoning, Kane 1983 argued that when the *avasthā*s are understood to be activated by the *sandhi*s, their teleology is made less rigid ('the *sandhi*s also do not permit the *avasthā*s to become overly linear') as the middle three *sandhis* may postpone or thwart positive progression.[48] She argued that 'an *avastha* does not span the same extent as its corresponding *sandhi* but rather begins somewhere in the course of a *sandhi* and potentially extends into the following joint' (Kane 1983, p. 62). Warder 1972 on the other hand, noted their lack of correspondence, arguing that while the *avasthā*s are real-world phenomena, the *sandhi*s are artistic, making the literary literary ('We may conclude that a straightforward narration (without a "plot") is to be transformed into a work of art by the introduction of the conjunctions [*sandhi*s]').[49]

The *Nāṭyaśāstra*, by its statement that the *avasthā*s must pervade the entire narrative sequence while the depiction of certain *sandhi*s remain optional, makes the optimistic culmination of the teleological model of action binding upon the narrative. On the other hand, the *sandhi*s envisage a progressive increase of uncertainty in the expansion of the Seed: in *Nāṭyaśāstra* 19.40ab, the Seed 'seems to be lost as soon as soon as it is glimpsed' (*dṛṣṭanaṣṭam iva*) in the *pratimukha* in 19.41, the delicate sprout of the enterprise confronts both 'success and failure and a continued search' (*prāptir aprāptir eva vā punaś cānveṣaṇam*) in the *garbha*, and in 19.42 there is an obstacle-ridden, conflict-centred ruminative awareness – or a philosophical pause – 'caused by greed, or born in anger or an addiction' (*vilobhanakṛto ... krodhavyasanjo vāpi*) in the fourth juncture. This increasing prospect of failure nowhere seems to be registered in the *avasthā* model, a straightforward progression, even though later interpreters added the possibility of obstacles and their removal as a prior stage on which *niyatā phalaprāpti*, the Certain Attainment of the Fruit, is contingent.

Let us for the sake of the following argument accept Abhinavagupta and see each phase of action (*avasthā*) to be activated by the instruments (*prakṛti*) operational within a juncture (*sandhi*), Following this mode of perception, the correspondence of the first *avasthā* with the first *sandhi* and the Seed and that of the last *avasthā* with the final *sandhi* and the Fruit appears clear enough: the Seed is implanted in the Source, activating the Initiation, the onset of action; the Fruit is ripe in the End which activates the Addition of Fruit. On the other hand the relationship between the fourth stage of action, *niyatā phalaprāpti*, and the fourth juncture, *vimarśa*, is problematic and cannot be satisfactorily explained. The Certain Attainment of the Fruit is a positive state, which prevails when obstacles have been overcome. How then can it arise in a juncture in which fatal obstacles, caused by a variety of emotional outbursts such as anger or greed, or by the power of fate, are in active proliferation, and doubts about success arise constantly? There thus is a clear and marked opposition between the two.

Historically, the disjunction between the fourth action-state and the fourth juncture has not gone unnoticed, and attempts have been made to explain it. Abhinavagupta, arguing against an attacker who asks how there can be doubt after the Possibility of Success, feels that the obstacle led to a renewed zeal for triumph in the hero, which then led to *the niyatā phalaprāpti* (*Abhinavabhāratī* 19.42, see ahead for text and translation). This would mean that the state of the Certain Attainment of the Fruit started not at the beginning of the fourth juncture but somewhere in the middle or even towards the end, a view adopted by Kane (1983). Dhanaṃjaya and Dhanika too opined similarly, as we have seen, in viewing the obstacle of the *vimarśa* to instigate a second birth, as it were, in the form of a realignment of the *bīja* with the main movement of the story. Rather than hindering, the obstacle pushed the action of the chief character forward toward the goal, serving only to increase his/her eagerness (*autsukya*) for achieving the purpose. The traditional explanation in the light of these thinkers would be that the state of optimistic action in full view of success arises – can only arise – from the presence of jeopardy.

One of the most interesting interpretations has been by Byrski (1974, pp. 108–9) who reread *niyatā phalaprāpti* following a tradition of hermeneutics noted by Abhinavagupta in which *niyatā* meant *sandigdhā*, the [Fruit] 'cast into doubt', or 'held back'.[50] This reinterpretation of *niyatā* as 'held back' attempted to offer a resolution in the form of a smooth alignment with the Trial.

Byrski based his interpretation on a comment Abhinavagupta makes in his discussion of Bharata's verse on the *avasthā* of the Certain Attainment of the Fruit, which suggests that some in his time read *abhāvena* ('by absence') instead of *bhāvena* in Bharata's original text. The latter is as follows:

niyatāṃ tu phalaprāptiṃ yadā bhāvena paśyati /
niyatāṃ tāṃ phalaprāptiṃ saguṇāṃ paricakṣate // Nāṭyaśāstra 19.12

Abhinavagupta reveals in the following way how a certain camp of thinkers read this obtuse verse:

ye tv akārapraśleṣād abhāvena niyatāṃ sandehamayīm iti vyācakṣate te niyatā phalaprāptiḥ saṃdigdhā cet katham etad viruddhaṃ saṃgacchatām iti praṣṭavyāḥ | Abhinavabhāratī 19.12

But they, who, through inserting '*a*', understand [the attainment of fruit] to be restrained by an absence [of the fruit], [and] explain [the attainment of fruit] as 'doubtful', they should be asked how, if the Certain Attainment of Fruit *is* doubtful, does the contradiction fit together!

This group of interpreters read *yadābhāvena paśyati* in *Nāṭyaśāstra* 19.12ab as *yadā+ abhāvena, paśyati*, supplying an '*a*' before *bhāvena* and seemed to have understood the twice-repeated *niyatā* in 19.12a and 19.12c in two different ways: as 'restrained' in the first line and as 'certain' in the second. They thus seemed to have interpreted Bharata's original text as something like: 'when (*yadā*) [the hero] sees that the attainment of fruit is held back (*niyatā phalaprāpti*) by an absence (*abhāvena*) [of the fruit], they call that meritorious [state] to be 'the Certain Attainment of the Fruit' (*niyatāṃ … phalaprāptim*)'. It seems tempting to think that this camp – let us call them the *abhāva*-camp – may have thus interpreted the first *niyatā* as 'restrained' or 'held back' in order to smoothen the obviously disjunctive relationship with the crisis-centred Trial. On the other hand, they also seem to have seen this as a state of action in which the attainment of fruit is simultaneously assured, on which basis Abhinavagupta accuses them – and justly so – of logical contradiction: how can the certainty of success be possible when the fruit of the hero's enterprise seems to have failed?[51]

The implied controversy over the stage of action called *niyatā phalaprāpti* is paralleled by problems Abhinavupta points out with the *Nāṭyaśāstra*'s verse on the Trial, leading to, it seems, a variety of ways of interpreting the text so that its inconsistencies could be smoothed over.[52] Such fertility in interpretation may have been prompted by the mysteriously opaque language of the *Nāṭyaśāstra* verse on the fourth juncture:

garbhanirbhinnabījārtho vilobhanakṛto 'thavā /

krodhavyasanajo vāpi sa vimarśa iti smṛtaḥ // Nāṭyaśāstra 19.42

Among the traditional interpreters of Bharata here consulted, namely, Abhinavagupta, Dhanaṃjaya, Dhanika and Viśvanātha, only Abhinavagupta's comments acknowledge problems, offer a resolution to the unclear relationship with the fourth *avasthā* and provide multiple viewpoints. The passage is tricky given that some sentences appear vague – there may well be textual corruption in those cases – but I offer here a preliminary first analysis based on Ramakrishna Kavi's edition of the *Nāṭyaśāstra* with Abhinavagupta's commentary. The main problem Abhinavagupta identifies is that the literary tradition suspected corruption with the word *vimarśa*, which led to all manner of creative hermeneutical strategies to clarify the obscurity of the root text. According to him, some groups read *vimarśa* but others read *avamarśa*, leading to two schismatic hermeneutic traditions for the Trial: one that characterized *vimarśa* as an epistemological category involving doubts in the knowledge process that lead into clarification, another that characterized *avamarśa* as a fatal obstacle that annuls the enterprise.[53] The second school, interpreting *avamarśa* as an obstacle, was led to further squeeze the available text, according to Abhinavagupta, to ensure a smooth fit with their point of view, interpreting *bīja* (Seed) in the original verse to mean, through a secondary extrapolation, the Fruit (of the endeavour) arising from the Seed. Moreover, apart from the philosophical *vimarśa* schools and the tragedy-oriented *avamarśa* schools, Abhinavagupta discusses four more groups of interpretation. One of these uses clever interpretational tricks again to make sense of the original text. None of their interpretations seem to have been satisfactory to Abhinavagupta, suggesting that the Trial was the proverbial hot potato in classical Indian aesthetics. Let me present this interesting and lengthy text in discrete sections before summarizing what I feel are the main arguments of the six schools implied in the analysis:

[1] kecid vimarśa iti paṭhanty anye 'vamarśa iti | tatra sandehātmako vimarśaḥ | nanu pūrvaḥ sambhavanāpratyayaḥ tataḥ saṃśaya iti nedam ucitam | saṃśayanirṇayāntarālavartinaṃ hi tarkaṃ tārkikāḥ prāhuḥ

| kiṃ ca vimarśasandhir niyataphalaprāptyavasthayā vyāptaḥ tac ca niyatatvaṃ sandehaś ceti kim etat | atrāhuḥ – tarkānantaram api hetvantaravaśād bādhacchalarūpatāparākaraṇe saṃśayo bhavet kiṃ na bhavati | ihāpi ca nimittabalāt kutaś cit saṃbhāvitam api phalaṃ yadā balavatā pratyūhyate kāraṇāni ca balavanti bhavanti tadā janakavighātakayos tulyabalatvāt kathaṃ na sandehaḥ ||[54] *tulyabalavirodhakavidhīyamānavaidhuryavyādhūnanasandhīyamā nasphāraphalāv alokanāyāṃ ca puruṣakāraḥ sutarām uddhurakandharībhavatīti tarkānantaram atra saṃśayaḥ tato nirṇaya ity etad evocitataram | tathā hi – puruṣakāraśālina eva*

ślāghyante adbhutam adbhutaṃ prāṇasandehād apy anekātmā samuttārito yatra

saṃbhāvanāvinābhavati yata evānyaprayatnato vidhuraprayatnato ya upanipātaḥ

tata eva puruṣakārodyataḥ pumān api vijigīṣāgarbhatvena prodyamaṃ bhajatīti

tadāśayena niyatā phalaprāptir ucyate | śreyāṃsi bahuvighānīti paśyan tad atra

mayā vighnāpasāraṇaṃ kartavyam iti sābhimānaḥ svam udyogasūtraṃ

sahasraguṇīkurute tathā hi sāgarikābandhane'pi

mahāmātyaprayuktamaindajrālikavṛttaṃ sunipuṇam upanibaddhaṃ tāvat |

Certain people read '*vimarśa*', others '*avamarśa*'. Among those two [readings], *vimarśa* is characterized by doubt [following the Nyāya school in which *vimarśa* means doubt[55]]. [An objector to the Naiyāyikas may say] 'Surely, it is not right that there should first be a notion of the possibility [of attaining the fruit] followed by doubt, since [you the Nyāya] logicians say that the phase of reasoning (*tarka*) is between the phases of 'doubt' (*vimarśa*) and conclusion (*nirṇaya*)? Moreover, the Trial is pervaded by the condition [of action] called the Certain Attainment of the Fruit, and so to have the Certain Attainment of the Fruit and doubt [at the same time] is simply ludicrous!' To this [objection] [the Naiyāyikas] say: Even after the [the phase] of reasoning, there may be doubt due to some other argument, in the [process of the defender] repudiating [attacks] having the form of counter-arguments and quibbling – why should this be impossible? And even in this scenario, even though the fruit is made possible somehow by the strength of a [positive] cause, if it is hindered by something powerful, and, [furthermore], if the [other] causes [for a negative ending] are [also] powerful, then how should there not be doubt [about success], since the cause [of the fruit] and the obstacle [to the fruit] are equally forceful? Human effort becomes extremely eager[56] to see the fruit when its fullness is being joined [to the plot] through the shaking-off of an absence [of success] while such an absence is being created by an obstruction of equal power [to the cause of the fruit]. Thus, here there is doubt after reasoning [and] after this comes the settlement – this [sequence] is even better! For, only those amply possessing human effort are respected: where the possibility [of success] is inevitable (*saṃbhāvanā+avinābhavati*), [the fruit] having many lives (*anekātmā*), is rescued in miraculous ways even when its life is in doubt. Since the hero is besieged at this point either through [his own] effort or through the effort of an adversity[57], he for this very reason once again experiences an ascent (*prodyama*) because of his containing a desire to conquer even annihilation – on this basis it is said [that the equivalent *avasthā* to the Trial is] the Certain Attainment of the Fruit (*niyatā phalaprāpti*). 'I must remove the obstacle keeping in mind that many obstacles are [only conducive to] well-being!' Thus becoming confident, [a hero] makes the single thread of his effort a thousand-threaded! For example, even in the capture of Sāgarikā, the magical stratagems used by the Chief Minister were included with great style in respect of this (*tāvat*).

[2] anye tv avamarśo vighna iti vidanti | sa ca vyākhyāne bījaśabdena tadbījaphalam arthaśabdena nivṛttir ucyate | tena garbhanirbhinnapradarśitamukhaṃ yad bījaphalaṃ tasya yo 'rtho

nivṛttiḥ punas tatraiva saṃpādanaṃ niṣpratyūhaprāṇatayā phalaprasūtiḥ, sa

iti tacchabdena yatrety ākṣiptam | sā ca nivṛttiḥ krodhena ca nimittena lobhena vā vyasanena śāpādinā vā | apiśabdād vighnanimittāntarāṇāṃ

pratipadam aśakyanirdeśānāṃ saṅgrahaḥ | sa ca devyā vāsavadattayā

sāgarikāyāḥ kārānikṣepāt prabhṛti yeyaṃ turīye 'ṅke rājña uktiḥ –

kaṇṭhāśleṣaṃ samāsādya tasyāḥ prabhraṣṭayānayā |

tulyāvasthā sakhīveyaṃ tanur āśvāsyate mama ||

atra vighne vāsavadattākrodho nimittam | lobhas tu nimittaṃ yathā tāpasavatsarāje tvatsaṃprāptivilobhitena sacivaiḥ prāṇā mayā dhāritāḥ (6–3) iti | tadapare na sahante – na hy atra vāsavadattāprāptilobhaḥ prakṛte phale vighnakārīti idaṃ tadodāharaṇaṃ – tatraiva pariṇītāyām api padmāvatyāṃ

vāsavadattām alabhamānasya rājño maraṇādhyavasāyo mumūrṣoḥ tadalābhe[58] *mantriṇāṃ sutarāṃ rājyaprāptidīrghalobho nimittam iti |*

śāpavyasanaṃ tv amarṣanimittam iti abhijñānaśākuntale darśitam |

evam anyad utprekṣyam | tathā hi – sapatnyā vidyāprabhāvo nimittam avamarśe kvacid daivaṃ kvacit samayaḥ – yathā vikramorvaśyāṃ

putravadanāvalokanād urvaśyāḥ svargagamanādhyavasāye |

However, others [non-Naiyāyikas] understand *avamarśa,* [which means] the Obstacle. In their interpretation, by the word Seed this [*avamarśa*] is said to be the Fruit [arising from] the Seed of the [story] (*tadbījaphala*), and by the word 'purpose', 'cessation' (*nivṛtti*). That which is the purpose of the Fruit [arising from] the Seed that has sprouted from the Embryo, – that has been made to show its face – because of that Obstacle (*tena*), is [understood as its] cessation. Moreover, at that very juncture there is a bestowing, that is a growth, of the Fruit, because of the unimpeded nature of its life. By the word 'that' (*tat*), 'in which' (*yatra*) is implied [in *garbhanirbhinnabījārtha*]. And that cessation [of the Fruit] is because of a cause in the form of anger, greed, addiction, a curse, etc. By the word 'also' (*api*) there is an understanding that it is impossible to identify each and every cause to an Obstacle. Such is this utterance of the king which is in the fourth act [of the *Svapnavāsavadattā*] after Queen Vāsavadattā had cast Sāgarikā into prison:

'[Because] I have experienced her embrace [around] my neck, this, my body, is consoled when she has fallen away, like her friend [my beloved] who shares an equal state.'

The cause for the obstacle here is Vāsavadattā's anger. But greed is the cause as for example in the *Tāpasavatsarāja*:

'The ministers make me, who am greedy to attain you, endure life (verses 3–6).' etc. Others do not accept this, for here the greed for acquiring Vāsavadattā does not cause an obstacle to the real Fruit [of the story]. Regarding this, an example is such: in that very work, even when Padmāvatī had been married, the resolve for death in the king desiring freedom [from life] because he had not acquired Vāsavadattā [and] in not winning her the intense deep-seated covetousness in the ministers for winning the kingdom is the cause [for the obstacle to the Fruit].

However, it is shown in the *Abhijñānaśakuntalā* that a destructive predilection is the cause of the obstacle. In the same way, another [example] may be imagined. Such as, [in some works,] for a co-wife, the power of knowledge is a cause for an obstacle, in some places, Fate, in some places, Time, as in the *Vikramorvaśīya* in Urvaśī's intention to return to heaven after [Purūravas] sees his son's face.

[3] anye tv āvṛttavimarśaśabdaṃ[59] *kalpayanta itthaṃ vyācakṣate – garbhānnirbhinnaṃ*[60] *bījārthaphalaṃ yasmin vimarśādikāraṇatvād vimarśarūpe kathāvayave sa vimarśo nāmeti | atra vyākhyāne mukhyam asya sandher yad rūpaṃ vighnakāraṇasaṃpātātmakatvaṃ nāma tad aspṛṣṭam eva syāt |*

Others, however, imagining the word *vimarśa* to be repeated [in Bharata's root text as 'having *vimarśa*' and then 'that *vimarśa*'] explain thus – that [section] in the part of the story having the form of doubt(?)[61] since it causes doubt, etc. [greed, addiction and anger] is called the Trial, in which the Fruit that is the goal of the Seed has sprouted forth from the Embryo. In this analysis, the principle character of this Juncture, characterized, indeed, by a confluence of reasons that make it remote, will [remain] totally unclear.

[4] anye tu lābhayogyatvaṃ nāśāvasthā anveṣaṇāvasthā ca yathāruci garbhe nibandhanīyā tatra yadā lābhātmikā prāptyavasthā pratimukhenaiva nibadhyate tadānye dve garbhe sandhau yadāpy avamarśe nāśāvasthāṃ tadā garbhe 'nveṣaṇam eva garbhe yadā nāśānveṣaṇe tadā cāvamarśe vicāro nibandhanīyaḥ | kathaṃ mayā prāptaprāyam ap yapahāritaṃ kim atra viguṇopāyānuṣṭhānaṃ mayā kṛtaṃ uta prāptiyogyam evaitan na bhavatīti yadāhodbhaṭaḥ yāsāv anveṣaṇabhūmir avamṛṣṭir avamarśa iti tac cedaṃ vyākhyānaṃ lakṣyaviruddhaṃ yuktyā ca pūrvoditaprārambhādyavasthāpañcaka gatakramaniyamasamarthanaprastāv-oktayā viruddham ity āstām |

On the other hand, others [believe] that the joining of attainment, a state of destruction and a state of searching must be inserted, according to taste, in the Embryo. Among these, when the state of attainment, characterized by a gain, is inserted in the Reflection itself, then the other two [states] are [to be shown] in the Embryo. Also, when there is a state of destruction in the Trial, then only the searching is [to be shown] in the Embryo; when both destruction and searching are in the Embryo then a deliberation must be inserted in the Trial (*avamarśa*). 'How have I removed [the Fruit] even when it is nearly obtained? Is it the case here that I have resorted to a deficient instrument [to my aim]? Or is this not suitable for success?' Such [are examples of deliberations in the hero]. As Udbhaṭa has said: That in which there is a deliberation, which is the ground for searching, is the Trial: this analysis contradicts the logic that was stated in the introduction [of Bhrata's text] establishing the fixity of the order inherent in the five *avasthā*s beginning with the Initiation described in the beginning – therefore, let it be!

[5] *aham anena viphalāyāṃ kriyāyāṃ vilobhya pravartita iti yatra kartā vimṛśati sa vilobhanakṛta iti krodhavyasanādes tu vyāpadyamāne phalavyāpattiviṣayo yaḥ kartur vicāraḥ sa krodhavyasanaje vimarśa ity evaṃ vimarśanasvabhāva eva vimarśaḥ kāryavinipātas tūttaranirvahaṇasandhinibadhyamānādbhutarasaparip oṣakatvena nibadhyate iti śrīśaṅkukaḥ | tanmate vicārasya sarvasandhyanuyāyitvāt pṛthagvimarśaśabdenābhidhānaṃ syāt |*

'In longing for this fruitless action, because of this [reason], I act' – where the agent deliberates thus, that [part of the narrative] is caused by greed. Such deliberation in the agent, whose content is the destruction of the Fruit when [the Fruit] is endangered through anger, a dangerous addiction, etc., that originating in anger or an addiction is *vimarśa* (deliberation): thus in this way, the Trial is nothing but something characterized by over-thinking (*vimarśana*). However, the ruining of the objective is inserted [into the composition] as a nourisher for a marvellous *rasa* embedded in the poem in the concluding *nirvahaṇa* juncture – thus according to Śaṅkuka. In his view, because deliberation attends all the *sandhi*s, there should be a designation [for it] as a different type of Trial.

[6] *vyāpattiviṣayo vicāra iti kecit | punar apy asya saraṇir eva*[62] *sā ca na vyākhyānena krameṇa darśitā | vilobhanakṛtodāharaṇaṃ tu na vyāpatīvimarśa iti sarvaṃ tvasamañjasaṃ yathāruci parikalpitamityalamanena* | Some hold that [*vimarśa* is] deliberation concerning disaster. Moreover, this is their only explanatory route, and it is not demonstrated step-by-step in their explanations. On the other hand, the example of [*vimarśa*] caused by greed is not *vimarśa* (deliberation) connected to disaster. Thus, all [their arguments] are unsuitable, devised according to their likes – therefore enough!

[1] Abhinavagupta implies that the school that read *vimarśa* were followers of the Indian epistemological tradition of Nyāya, for he calls them the Tārkikas (logicians). The Naiyāyika school Abhinavagupta discusses interpreted the fourth juncture in terms of their epistemological category *vimarśa*, a phase of reflective awareness involving doubts. Nyāya posits sixteen categories of knowledge among which logical doubt (*sandeha*) called *vimarśa* forms the third category of the knowledge process. *Tarka* 'reasoning' is the eighth category while *nirṇaya*, 'settlement', is the ninth. Objectors to this school seemed to have attacked it on the technical grounds that, if the fourth juncture was the stage of 'deliberation characterized by doubt' (*sandehātmakavimarśa*), and if it lay before the phases of 'reasoning' and 'settlement', in which there are definite moves away from doubt and toward a conclusive knowledge, then it would not be possible to invert the knowledge process and to follow success in attaining the Fruit with a phase of doubts about it. They also objected to the view that doubt could coexist with the state of action in which the fruit is certain, which they seem to have correlated with the *nirṇaya* phase of conclusive knowledge. To this Abhinavagupta replies, echoing the Nyāya point of view, that it is possible to have doubts even after reasoning if one is still being attacked by opponents, and similarly, the Fruit, too, may still be in jeopardy if the nexus of causes that hinder it are as powerful as the causes that propel it. In such a situation, the eagerness of the chief character grows even more intense and his efforts to procure the fruit are

ingeniously diversified, like a single strand becoming a thousand-stranded rope. Thus according to him to have *vimarśa* and *nirṇaya* consecutively follow *tarka* is an even better sequence of knowledge because it increases the will for victory. Abhinavagupta too sees the Trial in terms of Nyāya epistemology, as a form of ruminative, conflict-centred awareness in the chief characters that leads ultimately to resolution.

[2] Another group, non-Naiyāyikas, read *avamarśa*, possibly reading *so vamarśa*, and interpreted this as an obstacle to the Fruit rendering it to cease. Interpreting 'purpose' (*artha*) in the main verse of the *Nāṭyaśāstra* as 'cessation' (*nivṛtti*), Seed (*bīja*) in this particular instance as the fully realized goal of the story, the Fruit (*phala*), and correlating 'that' (*saḥ*) to an 'in which' (*yatra*) embedded in the compound *garbhanirbhinnabījārthaḥ*, they seemed to have interpreted the verse as follows: '[the juncture], in which the purpose [i.e. the cessation] of the Seed [i.e. the Fruit] has manifested from the Embryo, which is caused by greed or born in anger or a dangerous predilection, is known as the obstacle (*so 'vamarśa smṛtaḥ*)'. They saw this juncture to form the context in which the Fruit ceases to exist because of various hindering forces too numerous to enumerate. Some of these obstacles are exemplified: it might be a hero wishing to commit suicide, a destructive preoccupation, Fate, a jealous first wife, and such who might cause the narrative goal to cease. However, they also saw this to be the place where, just as the Fruit ceases to exist, it comes into being again in a miraculous rebirth as it were, because, in their view, its life is simply imperishable. This idea of the Trial as the place for the growth of the Seed of the plot into its Fruit possibly came about in order to maintain a smooth fit with the fourth *avasthā* of the Certain Attainment of the Fruit. Hence, for interpreters of this tradition, the Trial is a place for a paradox: the endeavour of the chief characters dies, or seems to die, but it simultaneously lives again and attains its prospect of success. This seems to be similar to the idea of narrative obstacle being a calamitous 'flare-up' that serves only to forcefully push the narrative forward to the concluding Fruit that Dhanika has in mind when he discusses the example of the fire in *Ratnāvalī*. In either way they chose to read the contested word, either as a stage of knowledge or as a destructive obstruction, both the Nyāya and this non-Nyāya tradition saw the process of doubt and cessation to be optimistic in effect, even though it is pessimistic in experience for the characters, and to cause a reinvigoration for a second ascendance.

[3] The third group performed an interpretative tour de force. They repeated the words *sa vimarśa* twice using a hermeneutical device often resorted to by philosophers called *tantra*, and they understood thereby two different meanings (through another hermeneutic tool called *yogavibhāga*).[63] The first time the words were read as a single compound *savimarśa* 'having a Trial', the second time as two words, '*sa vimarśa*', 'that Trial', leading to an interpretation of the root text that is something like: 'That [part of the story] containing a Trial (*savimarśa*) in which the Fruit which is the goal of the Seed has sprouted out from the Embryo, caused either by greed or born in anger or a dangerous predilection' is called the Trial (*sa vimarśa iti smṛtaḥ*)'. Abhinavagupta is deeply critical of this school, as he felt that they left unclear the core nature of the narrative Trial – whether it is an obstacle or doubt – looking at it only as a component of the story.

[4] Another group saw depictions of a gain, a death and a search to be portrayed according to the will of the composer in the Embryo, which made the nature of the Trial variable. If a search was shown in the Embryo, then death formed the nature of the Trial. If on the other hand both a search and a death were shown in the Embryo then a period of deliberation formed the Trial. This period of deliberation is characterized by questions by the hero about how and why he failed in his enterprise, and anticipates his efforts to reprocure the Fruit. Such a view of the Trial not as obstacle as such but as a mental state of deliberation – instantiated by the philosophical pause in the form of laments in the *Kumārasambhava* and the *Raghuvaṃśa* – seems to have been indebted to the earlier philosopher Udbhaṭa, who characterizes the Trial as 'pondering' (*avamṛṣṭi*) in the *nāyaka*, a form of critical revaluation that leads to a search for the Fruit. However Abhinavagupta is critical of Udbhaṭa since according to him Udbhaṭa's idea contradicted the underlying teleological sequence of action. In the *avasthā* model Abhinavagupta accepted as arising from the junctures, there is a straightforward movement to the goal – but in Udbhaṭa's view, the phase of deliberation is characterized by thoughts of failure and self-doubt (such is implied by the range of examples given), without the following step of the revival of confidence of the hero that ensures a smooth transition to the next *sandhi*. This contradicts Abhinavagupta's stance that the Trial only increases optimism and flows into the next phase of the Fruit secured, which is thereby made dependent on the previous.

[5] A middle way between the Nyāya-inflected understanding of *vimarśa* as doubt and the non-Nyāya understanding of *avamarśa* as a serious impediment is espoused by Abhinavagupta's philosophical predecessor, Śaṅkuka. In his view the Trial is the complete annihilation of the narrative purpose, an obstacle in this sense, but it is also inherently purposeful, like the Naiyāyika-influenced *vimarśa*, in nourishing and activating a positive outcome through the resolution of doubt: the final emotional quality of the poem, its *rasa*. The *rasa* in the conclusion is made more astonishing because of the destruction of the Fruit in the *vimarśa*, which also hereby facilitates its production.

[6] Finally Abhinavagupta ends his exposition by saying that another camp understood the *vimarśa* to be a disaster. Abhinavagupta's analysis of the section on *vimarśa* in the *Nāṭyaśāstra* is complex: he seems less interested with decoding Bharata's words and more with an in-depth engagement with the opinions of his predecessors and contemporaries. This is not unusual in his commentary on the *Nāṭyaśāstra*.[64] All these six groups, apart from the 'logical' school of the Tārkikas, are rejected – scathingly – by Abhinavagupta. His main aim in interpretation is to ensure that the process in the *vimarśa* coincides with the fourth *avasthā* in which the Fruit is at hand – this creates problems for him, since it is impossible to ensure a smooth fit, and as such he rejects those who see the *vimarśa* as a final and destructive obstacle, or comprised entirely of thoughts of destructive self-doubt, without a step up into either optimism in the hero or in the creation of the final *rasa*.

On the other hand, Abhinavagupta seems to me to be too harsh – these various threads in the tangled skein of the interpretation of the inner Trial that he identifies can be applied to each of the tragic middles in Kālidāsa's works. Doubt, the annihilative obstacle whereby the narrative fruit is completely thwarted, death, pessimistic even philosophical deliberation, positive impediment and calamity: all perspectives may be glimpsed in the Kālidāsean Trial. Taken together they exemplify how the Trial was understood both phenomenologically, as a form of inner experience of rupture, and mechanistically, as an effective part in an arrangement of components. As such they add considerable richness to our understanding of tragedy as an interaction between awareness and an objective destruction external to awareness. In all these schools the outcome of a fraught narrative middle, comprising an interaction of both these elements, was always envisaged as a maturing trial: though difficult it was necessary for and responsive to human effort, and led in fact to the achievement of the characters' ultimate goal.

The historical priority of the junctures

On the basis of several reasons: that the *sandhis*, and not the other sets, were said to have been used to construct drama in Kālidāsa's time (see the next chapter for mention of the junctures in the *Kumarasambhava*), that the *avasthās* and *prakṛtis* do not find mention with regard to *mahākāvya* in literary critics writing about *mahākāvyas*, and because of the increase of impediments in the *sandhi* model which does not appear in the other two sets of five, I would like to suggest that among the three, it is in fact the model of the junctures that is the original and the oldest.

Viśākhadatta (*c.*seventh/eighth century CE) in his play the *Mūdrārākṣasa* talks about the great efforts taken by a composer to design a play according to the *sandhis*, which are akin to the stratagems of a wily politician.

> *kāryopakṣepam ādau tanum api racayaṃs tasya vistāram icchan*
> *bījānāṃ garbhitānāṃ phalam atigahanaṃ gūḍham udbhedayaṃś ca* |
> *kurvan buddhyā vimarśaṃ prasṛtam api punaḥ saṃharan kāryajātaṃ*
> *karttā vā nāṭakānām imam anubhavati kleṣam asmadvidho vā* || *Mūdrārākṣasa* 4.3

> 'At first there is a hinting of the purpose [of the narrative in the *mukha* (Source)] however slender. [Then] in contriving an arrangement for [it] while desiring an expansion of [the narrative purpose] [in the *pratimukha* (Reflection]; in [then] causing the secret, deeply embedded fruit of the seeds that are in the *garbha* (Embryo) to sprout; in [then] fostering with intelligence a *vimarśa* (Trial) though the [purpose] has come forth; and in again wrapping up the entire purpose [in the *nirvahaṇa* (End)]– such is the hardship both a maker of plays and one such as I [a politician] experience!'

Nowhere though is it said that the composer takes into regard the *avasthās* and the *prakṛtis*.

The *avasthās* may have been retrospectively applied to the *sandhi* structure in response to a question about the apparent arbitrary nature of the *sandhis*. Such an imagined inquisitor may have asked of the *sandhis* – why or on what basis is poetry modelled thus? To such an objection, the answer provided by the *avasthās*, and the *prakṛtis* which support the hero's and sub-characters' actions, would be that because action in the world progresses in stages in a goal-oriented way, thus too the representation of action in literary narrative which follows the action of the world and, in particular, purposeful, always successful ritual action. The effect of the theorizing role of the *avasthā*s, taken from the model of ritual action, and their complementary *prakṛti*s which sustain and enable them, was to reduce – or hide from view – the place of tension and obstacle in the original *sandhi*-based model of narrative flow. These obstructions may have been perceived as inauspicious by some, and by subordinating them to the driving power of the auspicious ritual action model, the *avasthā*s emphasize the inevitability of the 'happy ending'. The *avasthā*s make it appear that it is they that are in fact the ultimate structure behind narrative – not the *sandhi*s, thereby suppressing the place of progressive uncertainty. By Bharata's time, this later association of the teleological action model, itself perhaps influenced by the Mīmāṃsā theory of goal-oriented meaning-generation, and all the instruments that bring it about had become fixed – but the awkward mismatch between them and the *sandhi*s, registered in that between *niyatā phalaprāpti* and *vimarśa*, remained a reminder of their forced association.

Character, survival and a universe of hazard

The *sandhi* model in its idea of the attainment of Fruit appears in one respect to also parallel the Mīmāṃsaka theory of the generation of a single sense from complex linguistic arrangements mutually interwoven. On the other hand, where the teleology of language, and in turn the teleology of the *avasthā*s, envisage a smooth, inevitable progress toward the final, ultimate goal, the telelogy of the *sandhi*s envisages significant obstacles so that the development of the component parts of the narrative process is clouded and impeded by constant, external uncertainty. In their lack of smoothness and assumption that it is inevitability that is artificial and obstacle that is inevitable, the *sandhi*s parallel a model of naturalistic and even psychological development: natural forms and human character mature, strengthen and survive only after facing up to the dangers of the world. To explain further using the example of botanic growth: a plant life cycle also goes through five phases from seed, to sprout, to seedling, to the first efflorescence to final fruit. The *mukha* is similar to the seed stage, the *pratimukha* to the sprout, the *garbha* to the seedling, when the sprout lives off the seed pouch, the *garbha* as it were, for food, the *vimarśa*, the efflorescence when the plant is close to maturity but may also perish, and the *nirvahaṇa*, the appearance of pods or fruits, with which the reproductive cycle starts again. This idea is evoked by some of the terminology of the *sandhis*: *bīja* (seed), *udbheda* (sprout) and the *phala* (fruit). One could also use the example of psychological development. In this sense the idea of narrative development is in close, mimetic synergy with growth models in the real world, where danger, perceived to be part of a process of sequential maturation, is a trial rather than an end.

The inevitable slings and arrows of obstruction envisaged as the *vimarśa* may even be correlated to what William James had called 'natural evil' (see Introduction, Part I, for a discussion of James's ideas) and the final fruit to a form of happiness that grows out of an encounter with it. 'Natural evil' – the danger inherent in the universe – may be seen to characterize the fraught middle. It is natural because it is a part of the environment that human endeavour within *kāvya*, and particularly within Kālidāsa's literary narrative, must confront. This – the tragic middle in the life of the story – is the point at which Western tragedy would conclude. In its vision of form, danger stymies. In the struggle for survival, human experience fails catastrophically. Our story – or rather the efforts of the principal agent of action – would perish. However in the Indian idea of narrative the enterprise faces two possible outcomes in the tragic middle: death or survival. Unlike in the Greek model, the first outcome is unimportant to the Indian theory of narrative because it wishes to explore imaginatively its alternative less available in the real world: a move from natural evil to a happiness that survives evil, a success, a second birth. It is not in this respect a mimetic representation of the world, because its movement, culminating in success, diverges from that of the world where failure of purpose can be a reality for many. At the same time it *is* mimesis in the sense that the model of plot is interested in the fulfillment of innate, natural capacity, expressed in the wish articulated in the agents of the enterprise at the beginning of the story to fulfil the goal. The vision of survival presented in *kāvya* parallels, in one sense, the Platonic 'form of the good', which seeks to move beyond the cave to the sunlight. Human experience presented here seeks transcendentalism in a similar way to that expressed by Plato: 'The true order of going … is to use the beauties of earth as steps along which one mounts upwards for the sake of that other Beauty … until … he arrives at the notion of absolute Beauty, and at last knows what the essence of Beauty is' (*Symposium* in *Varieties of Religious Experience*, p. 56).

The scholar Gerow, as pointed out above, had felt that the universe in *kāvya* was not adventitious, which meant that characters, and thereby the story, did not change according to changing external circumstances. Environment and character were unrelated. On the other hand, the model of the story as represented in Indian aesthetics shows us quite a different picture. From the point of view of the *sandhi*s, it assumes an entirely adventitious universe in which chances of survival for the enterprise are equally tipped between death and success during its development in the *vimarśa* as the protagonist confronts a whimsical environment. Character and environment in this vision are deeply intertwined, for the former responds – and indeed must respond – to the latter. This is how tragedy is provided the opportunity to unfold in the middle. The main enterprise has to withstand dangers arising without explanation from the point of view of the agents of the enterprise. Situations of disintegration that Kālidāsa envisaged in the fourth Juncture are expressions of the inexplicable fluctuations of a dangerous world. Moreover, in his works, the *vimarśa*, represented as the severe, inward self-doubt of a character, is also inner conflict. Inner conflict is shown in Duṣyanta both during his amnesia and in his period of remorse, in Aja at the death of Indumatī and also in Rati at the death of Kāma. In this way the theory assumes that the universe, externally and internally within the psyche, is indeed profoundly hazardous in the middle of the journey.

On the other hand, where the idea of the *sandhi*s departs in one fundamental aspect from being based on a strictly adventitious model of chance is in its notion of a literary character's innate instinct for success. This latent desire for success hardwired into the DNA as it were of narrative agents is its 'secret weapon' in battling an external universe of chance, chaos and doom and a concomitant inner world of conflict. It is *this* natural design – this hopeful gene so to speak, or in Kālidāsa's words from the *Meghadūta* this 'bind of hope' *āśābandha* – that gives characters courage to doggedly continue in spite of obstacles. In this way the aesthetic vision of the narrative in Indian literature is both like and unlike the Greek model of tragedy. It is like the Greek model in as much as it is aware that the potential for tragedy lies in external circumstances being out of one's control and in characters having to respond to things happening to them as best as they can. As such it does in fact show change in characters permanently affected by their external environment (we shall argue this further in our treatment of Śakuntalā and Duṣyanta), for this is the only way that the successive junctures in the journey of the story are attained and the final fruiting secured. It is unlike the Greek model in as much as it views the character to possess the tenacity to live. The characters of a story in *kāvya* possess an internal animus to survive chaos even if the changes wrought by tragic circumstances are profound and perhaps even unforgettable, though they may be for some forgivable. Characters in this respect have the ability to remain independent of the environment and not at its mercy because of their natural will for life.

If we imagine, as naive poets, a growing tree behind the model of the *sandhis*, we may further be led to imagine etched in the subtlest, the most imperceptible shades in the background when we hear or see Kālidāsa, an inner Eden. It is not, though, an Eden in the Christian sense, a place of eternal summer and unending felicity, over which the grace of higher power always shines benevolently and allays the fear of strange shadows. It is, as in the *Śakuntalā*, an Eden marked and buffeted by the struggle for survival, whose inhabitants, distant from a transcendent Overseer, must face consequences and in facing them make their own way in the world.

The Trial in the works of Kālidāsa

The fourth juncture represented by the *Raghuvaṃśa*, the *Kumārasambhava*, the *Śakuntalā*, the *Vikramorvaśīya* and the *Meghadūta* can be both a *vimarśa*, in the sense of doubt (conflicting awareness, the correct resolution of which leads toward knowledge) and an *avamarśa* in the sense of a fatal obstacle. In the *Raghuvaṃśa vimarśa*, registered in Aja's lament, is indeed characterized by doubt: Aja after the death of Indumatī doubts his continued existence and wants, and indeed actively finds, death (Chapter 2, pp. 87–108). In the *Kumārasambhava*, *avamarśa* is both doubt and an obstacle to the main endeavour, involving also the state of death: Kāma's murder leads Rati to doubt her life and makes Pārvatī and Śiva's union apparently impossible (Chapter 2, pp. 87–108). Thus too in the *Śakuntalā*, in which the curse of amnesia leads to Duṣyanta's doubts about Śakuntalā, and thence to the impossibility of their union; its lifting leads to another type of pessimistic rumination in the hero: Duṣyanta's self-doubt and depression (Chapter 3, pp. 109–31). In the *Vikramorvaśīya*, the *avamarśa* is characterized by an obstacle: the catastrophe of Urvaśī turning into a vine leads to the union with Purūravas becoming impossible. This in turn leads to another obstacle, Purūravas's own mental estrangement (Chapter 3, pp. 131–8). The *Meghadūta* can be thought of as the *avamarśa* made independent – it arises at the moment in which the obstacle of Kubera's curse delays the union of the *yakṣa* with the *yakṣiṇī* (Chapter 4, pp. 139–63). Characterized by the *yakṣa*'s deliberations of intense longing for union with his *yakṣiṇī*, it can also be seen in terms of Naiyāyika *vimarśa*, which increases eagerness in the hero for fruit. In all these treatments though, Kālidāsa is uniquely interested in how, through delaying the goal, *vimarśa* and *avamarśa* can construct a rich and nuanced phenomenology of grief, in which the experience of the subject to whom the calamity has occurred forms the chief artistic focus. He also shows that in securing the Fruit in the end, it is possible for characters to rise above adversity.

In the two *mahākāvyas* discussed here, the importance of free will in the *vimarśa* is registered in the *vilāpas* sung by the lamenters. Aja's and Rati's mourning is a rebuke to Fate, the architect of tragedy. Moreover, these *vilāpas* portray the full range of experience undergone by the grieving subject, painting for us a map of melancholy, in which the stages of lamentation, from a feeling of being in a vortex, a sense of the world becoming alien, individual personality estranged from itself, to a desire for suicide are meticulously plotted. The *Meghadūta* too is a *vilāpa* registering an experience of estrangement but of a different sort in which optimism, daydreaming and projection onto nature become the characteristics. In the *Śakuntalā* losing and finding knowledge, and the after-effects of this process, is a persistent theme of the *vimarśa*. In the *Vikramorvaśīya*, the *vimarśa* is a search for Urvaśī in which the grieving subject loses his mind. The human psyche and how it confronts calamity are at the centre of all these tragic middles. Kālidāsa's presentations posit an implicit connection between awareness and crisis. The nouns *vimarśa* and *avamarśa* derive from the verbal root *mṛś* (*mṛśati*), which means 'to touch' with the prefix *vi* in the case of the former and *ava* in the case of the latter. When connected with either of these prefixes, *mṛś* 'to touch' has the sense of a mental exploration, or deliberation. The idea in the five works treated here is that this process of *vi-/ava-marśa*, touching upon critical issues in one's mind or thinking through things, is triggered by some severe obstruction to the end-goal.

In the following chapters we shall, having first surveyed depictions of tragedy and tragic agency prior to Kālidāsa (Chapter 1, pp. 55–86), enter and explore with care the tragic middles of five of Kālidāsa's extant repertoire of six compositions (seven including the possibly apocryphal *Ṛtusaṃhāra*): the *Raghuvaṃśa*, the *Vikramorvaśīya*, the *Meghadūta*, the *Abhijñānaśakuntalā* and the *Kumārasambhava*.

1

Kālidāsa and his inheritance of grief

Why Kālidāsa?

Among all Sanskrit authors it is Kālidāsa (*c.*350–450 CE[1]) who, though fêted as the greatest voice of Sanskrit literature, has most acquired an unjust reputation for fairy tales that lull us to beatific complacency with dream-like worlds and unchanging characters. Coulson when speaking of the Sanskrit drama as a fairy tale (see Introduction, p. 2) was speaking in particular of Kālidāsa's play *Śakuntalā*. Indeed, it is this work that has been accused of unrealism more than others, as for instance by Warder, who writes:

> Here lyricism is carried to an extreme which disregards story and plot and is interested only in highly emotional, preferably pathetic, situations, The hero, Duṣyanta, is shown as doing nothing, though capable of a certain amount of feeling and anxiety. Things happen to him through fate, a curse, or divine intervention. His character remains a blank and we cannot believe in the depth of his feelings. The heroine, Śakuntalā, is more real but still the helpless plaything of supernatural powers. She can be seen as a thoughtless girl whose love is tested and matured by a long and harsh separation. (Warder, 1972, III, p. 148)

Like Coulson Warder concludes 'the play does not deal with human experience. It is a fairy story' (ibid., p. 149).

And yet nothing could be further from the truth.

Among all Sanskrit authors, it is Kālidāsa who is most interested in presenting embedded tension as a fully tragic middle. The previous chapter raised the idea of there being an inner pattern to the majority of Kālidāsa's narratives, and that this pattern was that of the *sandhis* as it has come down to us in Bharata's treatise. The confrontation with profound disturbance in the middle of a narrative and its resurrection thence coincide with the inner deaths, or experiences of absence, shown consistently in Kālidāsa's corpus, from which the 'second birth' of his narratives commence.

An imagined opponent might say at this point that to write a book about tragedy in classical Indian *kāvya* would require a representative sample whereby we can construct a wide history of the expression of grief diachronically plotted across various voices. At the commencement the net must be cast as widely as possible in order to do full justice to the topic. Starting at the very beginning, in the *Rāmāyaṇa*, the study must include the *Saundarananda*, one of the earliest examples of a *mahākāvya*, Loṣṭaka's hymn the *Dīnākrandanastotra* that tells of the link between sorrow and *nirveda*, the religious state in which aversion to the world is felt, Bhavabhūti's *Uttararāmacarita*, renowned for its *karuṇarasa*, and finally the only known tragedy of the Greek kind, the *Vibudhānanda*. The dramatist Bhāsa is often said to be the sole tragedian within the repertoire of *kāvya*,[2] his one-act play the *Ūrubhaṅga* often being held as a rare example of a Sanskrit play ending in death.[3] As far as Bhāsa is concerned, there is much ambiguity about the authenticity of his extant works. Against those who believe their ascription to Bhāsa to be genuine exists convincing scholarship arguing that the thirteen plays 're-discovered' by T. Ganapati Sastri in a single palm leaf codex in Malayalam script in 1912 were later compositions belonging to the theatrical repertoire of the Cākyārs of Kerala.[4] Given that the matter is still unsettled, I have for the time being felt it prudent to set aside Bhāsa until more convincing evidence emergences.

However, after *kāvyacarvaṇā* ('chewing on poetry') over a period of time, it became clear that the most persistent, eloquent and philosophical engagement with the internal tension of grief was shown in the early *kāvya* writer Kālidāsa in whose works disruption, loss and absence play a pivotal role in the overall grander vision of his narratives. Substantial *vilāpa*s spanning an entire canto appear in both his *mahākāvya*s while separation forms the theme and context for his lyric *Meghadūta*, and at least two of his three plays the *Śakuntalā* and the *Vikromarvaśīya*. Attaining the Fruit is truly impossible in the middle of the *Kumārasambhava* and in the *Śakuntalā*, until by an unexpected flash of resolution in Pārvatī, until then a somewhat weak plaything of the gods, leads her to pursue her love on her own, and the recovery of the ring of recognition in a fish by sheer, almost comical, chance, are both narratives made happy in their culmination. However, until these quirks of chance – episodes which can be thought of as the Drop (*bindu*) restoring the story to fulfilment – things are utterly hopeless, the characteristic of tragedy according to Bharata (see Introduction, pp. 19–20).

In the two plays – where we lack a consolidation of grief in the form of an extended *vilāpa* – separation is shown to have enormous repercussions on both the physical lives and the minds of central characters. Kālidāsa is deeply interested in their exploration, which is why entire acts exploring the psychological effects of grief, where very little in terms of action occurs, are to be found. In fact in the *Śakuntalā*, Kālidāsa invents the device of the ring, the chief dramatic symbol in that play, in order to show an extended tragic middle through Duṣyanta's six-year long remorse. Given the absence of the ring or similar device in the story's source in the *Mahābhārata*, it is no surprise that the earlier telling lacks such a focused depiction of grief. A similar argument may be made in the *Raghuvaṃśa* – Kālidāsa invents the marriage of Indumatī and Aja (as noticed by Abhinavagupta in his *Locana* to the *Dhvanyāloka*),[5] absent in Vālmīki's *Rāmāyaṇa*, in order to show the tragic middle caused by her death and Aja's heart-wrenching lamentation and painful death.

Much has been written about the style, the times, the metres and the sources of Kālidāsa,[6] and yet no publications have discussed at length, apart from comments inter alia,[7] the centrality of pathos in the body of his work and its importance for our understanding of the notion of suffering in general in early India.

Kālidāsa explores grief in a unique manner, both as a loss of mind (one hesitates to call it madness) and as a form of philosophical rumination on fate and other causes of tragedy, and often the twain overlap. This amalgamation of mental disturbance with philosophical contemplation is a hallmark of his work, and something that is something that is rare among the other voices of *kāvya*.

At the centre of Kālidāsa's perception of mental disturbance lies the altered heart, *anyathāvṛtti cetaḥ*, described in verse 3 of the *Meghadūta* as a quality that marks even happy people gazing at clouds. Its peculiar expression – characterized by confusion, dolour, longing, trance, mystical foresight, reverie, childishness and slowness – acquires a musical fluidity in his technique. For, though these states of grief are nebulous – just like the cloud of the *Meghadūta* – Kālidāsa's language is at its clearest, sharpest and most rhythmic in their description. Nothing is superfluous, nothing left to be said. The contrariness of the inner world becomes Kālidāsa's supreme subject and in his hands it turns into song. One can say that grief and music become inextricably intertwined in Kālidāsa's works so that to imagine one without the other becomes nearly impossible. In this sense Kālidāsa is directly in the tradition of the *Rāmāyaṇa*'s *krauñca* bird, which represents the cognate nature of mourning and primal musical-poetic utterance.

Part of the reason behind his engagement with the imagery, sound and purpose of grief might be to do with the fact that the rise of inward-looking lyric poetry, first in the Pāli canon, as argued by Warder, had begun to truly mark Sanskrit narrative, dramatic and epic. Kālidāsa felt this influence strongly – so much so (again *apud* Warder) that the story at times feels entirely unnecessary (such is, perhaps, best exemplified by the *Meghadūta*).[8] In Kālidāsa this apparent – in the words of Warder – 'neglect of action' is an opportunity to exploit through language in a manner unprecedented thus far the infinitely rich capacity of inwardness to become music, and music that tells a story of an inner life.

It is also evident that this persistent concern with grief has not been pointed out thus far and that there is a pressing need to intelligently challenge the stereotype of Kālidāsa as the writer of happy tales. For these reasons, my remarks on the history of grief have been confined to Kālidāsa in this book, even as my eye perceives his wider context.

In order to see how Kālidāsa stands out among other *kāvya* writers in his interest in tragedy, a comparison of him with writers of the period and an examination of their interrelations and departures are presented in this chapter. Here we shall see Kālidāsa's inheritance of grief, on which his conception of the tragic stands, derived from the *Rāmāyaṇa* (I follow herein Vālmīki's telling), constructions of grief in Buddhist literature and the works of Aśvaghoṣa.

This legacy culminates in the later author Bhavabhūti (*c.*eighth century CE), whose work the *Uttararāmacarita*, renowned in tradition for its profound concern with sorrow, engages conceptually and formally – as has been remarked by Pollock 2007 – with Kālidāsa's *Śakuntalā*.

> 'Shakúntala' is a 'Mahabhárata' play, and 'Rama's Last Act' [*Uttararāmacarita*] seems designed as a 'Ramáyana' counterpart to, and competitor of, Kali•dasa's masterpiece. Like the two epics the two plays share a deep resemblance. In their core they are stories about love, rejection, recovery, and ultimately – because this is the very reason behind the rejection – political power and its perpetuation. The star-crossed love of Dushyánta and Shakúntala is mirrored in that of Rama and Sita. The women, both of whom are pregnant, are repudiated because of doubts about their fidelity and (implicitly) the paternity of the progeny they are carrying. This is followed by a soul-searing acknowlegement of guilt on the part of the husband, reunion with his wife, recognition of the legitimacy of the offspring with the aid of quasi-divine agents (Marícha in 'Shakúntala', the magical anthropomorphic weapons in 'Rama's Last Act') and reconciliation of husband and wife. Both works hereby aim to emend and aesthetically enhance their epic models. (Pollock 2007, pp. 34–5)

Aside from its being the epic and thematic antipode to Bhavabhūti's play, the interlocking, antiphonal design characteristic of the *Śakuntalā*, which I discuss in Chapter 3, pp. 111–12, also shapes the *Uttararāmacarita*.

> Thus in Act I, the opening verse ... the viewing of the picture gallery ... the benediction that Rama pronounces regarding the magical weapons ... the reference to Sita as 'dear companion in my sojourn in Dándaka wilderness'; the request that Ganga protect Sita; the artistic representation that precedes the separation ... all this has crystal clear resonances with what occurs in Act 7. ... The same sort of excavation could be done for the remaining acts: 2 and 6 correspond [and] ... Acts 3 and 5 correspond closely, too. (Pollock 2007, pp. 36–7)

In this way, the *Śakuntalā* shaped and informed the vision of sorrow in the later literature from the early medieval period.

In order to examine Kālidāsa's tragic middle in light of aesthetic notions of internal rupture, it is necessary to first explore the relationship between Kālidāsa and traditional aesthetics – did Kālidāsa know and study the conventions of *alaṃkāra*? Close study, taking into account the views held by traditional commentaries, is indeed rewarded by a recovery of links with traditional ideas of development.

Bharata and Kālidāsa

The *Nāṭyaśāstra*'s discussion of *sandhis*, in its terms and phases, reminds one most of all and almost immediately of the Kālidāsean narrative model, especially the *Śakuntalā* (pointed out as well by the medieval commentator of the Devanāgarī recension of the *Śakuntalā*, Rāghavabhaṭṭa[9]). In particular, the Trial (*vimarśa*) harmonizes almost perfectly with the courtroom trial scene (Act V) of *Śakuntalā* and with the subsequent events (thus too Warder 1972, III, p. 149). Among modern interpreters, Tubb 1979, on the basis of traditional commentators of the text, finds Kālidāsa's *Kumārasambhava* – spanning the original eight cantos – to be arranged according to Bharata's plot structure. While I disagree with his point regarding where the *vimarśa* starts (for Tubb 1979, pp. 181–2, it starts at the end of Rati's lament), his argument shows convincingly how theoretical ideas of plot intricately thought out, at times even internally synchronized, were integral to Kālidāsa's compositional habits.

From internal evidence, it is certain that Kālidāsa was familiar with the idea of *sandhis*. In the seventh canto of the *Kumārasambhava*, we hear of an origin myth, in miniature form, of the first play and with it we are given a clear indication of what makes this art form a theatrical performance. During their marriage celebration, the gods Śiva and Pārvatī, after achieving their long-delayed and difficult union, 'beheld for a while the "first performance" (*prayogam ādyam*) of the nymphs, which was ravishing through its charming "limbs" (*lalitāṅgahāram*), which was composed with the *rāgas* of music (*pratibaddharāgam*), the divisions of whose action were shown (*vyañjitavṛttibhedam*) according to the narrative junctures (*saṃdhiṣu*) containing *rasa* (*rasāntareṣu*)' (*tau saṃdhiṣu vyañjitavṛttibhedaṃ rasāntareṣu pratibaddharāgam | apaśyatām apsarasāṃ muhūrtaṃ prayogam ādyaṃ lalitāṅgahāram* || *Kumārasambhava* 7.91).[10]

Moreover, Kālidāsa knew of a Bharata associated with the practice of drama and understood his aesthetic tradition to be canonical,[11] just as he seems aware of a set of conventions guiding composition. This is confirmed by the *Vikramorvaśīya*. In Act III there is a scene, telescoping previous events in the speeches of two side characters, in which Bharata remarkably appears as himself. We learn from two gossiping students of Bharata, Gālava and Pelava, about a play called *Lakṣmīsvayaṃvara* (*Lakṣmī's Choice of Husband*) written by the goddess of learning, Sarasvatī. Its producer was their *upādhyāya* (teacher) and guru (preceptor), the esteemed sage (*muni*) Bharata. As implied internally in the episode, the play is about the choosing by Lakṣmī of Viṣṇu as her consort. According to the students, Lakṣmī's role was played by the heroine of the *Vikramorvaśīya* the nymph Urvaśī. When one of the students, Gālava, asks the other, Pelava, if the assembly of the gods had been duly honoured with the play, Pelava replies that he did not know if it had been performed properly. Urvaśī, privately in love with the human king Purūravas, a love forbidden to celestials, was completely intoxicated with various emotions during its performance and made a terrible blunder. In front of the entire assembly of gods – the ten *lokapālas*, all the celestials from the three worlds and Viṣṇu – who had come to see Bharata's play, when asked by the nymph Menakā, in the role of Vāruṇī, to whom among the gods her heart was devoted, she replied 'Purūravas' instead of 'Puruṣottama' (Viṣṇu). Bharata, his masterpiece publicly ruined by this love-lost-lass, was implacable. He cursed her to lose her divinity and descend to earth, since his instructions had not been duly observed. Later Indra, taking pity on Urvaśī, modified the curse. He said that she would be with Purūravas, who was his aid in battle, till the time he saw his son by her. And so the principal story line of Purūravas and Urvaśī's love and its central travail begin.

Bharata's appearance in Kālidāsa's homage is doubtless slightly comical. He is the prickly, overbearing director, who loses his temper when his actress 'botches up'. However this episode is critical in revealing Kālidāsa's attitude to him. Bharata's role as the prototypical producer, whose method guides – indeed schools – artistic expression even in heaven, whose productions are not as much entertainments as modes of worship, reveals the mythical, quasi-divine status he had already achieved by Kālidāsa's time. The curse he places on Urvaśī for failing to remember his rules – an ironic reference it seems to the negligent composer – is also the central turning point in establishing the objective of the play, the love of the nymph and the mortal, otherwise an impossibility. Bharata is truly essential for the play, both for and as its internal self-reflection as a work of art and for its overall development toward *phalaprāpti*.

Once in a while, Kālidāsa uses his compositions to reflect on 'art as art' and episodes of performance appear in his works, reflecting, a more detached, conscious awareness of the practice and theory of poetry. It is as if in these moments the perspective begins to combine that of the artist – being sensitively immersed in the universe of the artwork – with that of the philosopher – being detached and critically aware of what is happening in art and what constitutes its beauty. Thus too in the close of Act I and in the beginning of Act II of the *Mālavikāgnimitra*: two venerable *upādhyāya*s of the performing arts in the model of Bharata compete against each other with the help of their best students. The competition is in fact a pretext for the hero, King Agnimitra, and the heroine, Mālavikā, one of the students, to begin a flirtation without the censure of Agnimitra's chief queen. In order to establish which of the warring preceptors, Gaṇadāsa or Haradatta, is the superior, their students are asked to exhibit a song called the *chalita* comprising four parts and associated with Śarmiṣṭhā. The judge for this performance is Kauśikī, a learned ascetic lady with high influence at Agnimitra's court. All, including the king, his wife, the two teachers and the scholar Kauśikī, assemble in the royal theatre hall. Mālavikā enters and before an enraptured king delivers the song, conveying to him her feelings and delighting him with her charming figure. Kauśikī, in on the surreptitious love affair, names Gaṇadāsa, Mālavikā's teacher, the winner, even before seeing the other performance. In her observation of what makes Mālavikā's art a winner (citing Tawney's translation):

> All was blameless and in accordance with the rules of art: For the meaning was completely expressed by her limbs which were full of language, the movement of her feet was in perfect time, she exactly represented the sentiments; the acting was gentle being based upon the measure of the dance; in the successive development of the action, emotion kept banishing emotion from its place: it was a vivid picture of a series of passions. (*Mālavikāgnimitra* I.8, pp. 41–2)

As in Act III of the *Vikramorvaśīya*, here too, much rides on the performance being accurate to the teaching. But, it is also of paramount importance to note that much depends on love. It is doubtless that, according to Kālidāsa, the theory of performance underlay the practice and its foundation, but this was not a guarantee of the inherence of *rasa*, the standard by which beauty in art was apprehended, which depended on the genius of the composer, the interpreter of the composition and the force of emotion ('by which', as *Nāṭyaśāstra* 7.7 says, 'the body is fully engulfed, as wood by fire'). In Mālavikā's case what grants her performance that touch of genius, as clearly hinted at by Kālidāsa, is the power of her love for the king over and above the perfection of her technique, a power of emotion that even makes her stumble at one point in the height of her passion. Kauśikī, the scholar, is well aware of this, but careful to hide the fact from the queen, and points out the outward quality of technical brilliance as a cover-up. This is clear to any audience of the *Mālavikāgnimitra*. In this way episodes of performance in Kālidāsa subtly reveal how his craft was in conversation with the established ideas of structure and performance as epitomized by Bharata's thought-world.

The *Viśvantarajātaka* of Āryaśūra

Now to return to Kālidāsa's inheritance of grief: in the history of the poetry of grief, Kālidāsa's is not a lone voice nor the first. The trope of the lamenter, the detailed interest in the process of grief and the culmination of crisis and its stages in the middle of a work appear in the *Rāmāyaṇa* and in Pāli literature from before the second century BCE.

In *Rāmāyaṇa* III.59–62, Rāma laments pitifully on discovering Sītā's abduction. Unable to speak, his limbs shaking, unable to think clearly, he mourns to his brother Lakṣmaṇa, and then, like Kālidāsa's grief-maddened *yakṣa* and Purūravas, asks Sītā's whereabouts to a number of insentient beings: the River Godāvarī, the creatures on its banks and a mountain. The trope certainly provides an ancestral template for the mourning hero central to Kālidāsa's works – for example, like Aja, Rāma too 'stammers in his tears' (*bāṣpagadgadaḥ* 3.59.27c) – whose lament, even suggesting temporary madness, is in fact a sign of nobility rather than weakness.[12] On the other hand, the structural significance of the image of mental breakdown as an inner turning point towards an ascent in Kālidāsa's works is made more clearly visible with help from an example from Buddhist literature.

The *Vessantarajātaka*,[13] one of the most popular birth stories of the Buddha even to this day, with wide representation in art from the second century BCE,[14] existing in ritual and in literary versions in Burmese, Chinese, Khotanese, Sanskrit, Sogdian, Tibetan and Tocharian,[15] tells the tale of the selfless giving of King Vessantara of the Śibis, a Buddha-to-be. The largesse of this king culminates in the middle of the tale, in sections eight and nine, in the traumatic giving up of his two children to the *brāhmaṇa* Jūjaka. The work details the effects of this event on the emotional state of his wife Maddī, who is grief-stricken to the point of madness. As Cone and Gombrich 1977 (p. xx) note: 'opportunities for lamentation all cluster round the giving of the children; those opportunities are taken; and the episode becomes the story's centre of gravity, lengthy and heart-rending.' When the children are given away, the earth resounds in a roar, registering the enormity of Vessantara's generosity. At the time of the event, Maddī is in the forest foraging for food and does not know what has happened. However, she feels powerful presentiments of catastrophe: her spade falls from her hand, her basket trap slips from her shoulder and her right eye throbs. She feels shaken and confused. Gods disguising themselves as a lion, a tiger and a panther try and prevent her from returning home and discovering the awful loss, and in this way the forest becomes a succouring realm for distressed beings where grief, distress and despair can safely manifest untrammelled without condemnation from society. In Kālidāsa's *Śakuntalā* and in the *Vikramorvaśīya* too, the forest is a metaphor for quiet consolation and a realm of safety for characters tormented by misery from separation or states of madness. At night the animals finally let Maddī go and she arrives home. Unable to see her children where they usually ran out to greet her, she laments to her husband. She asks him why he is silent. She declares that her mind is in darkness. The birds do not sing, and her children must be dead. She goes through all possible reasons why they are not home. Perhaps her husband has sent the children on an errand? Perhaps they are asleep? Perhaps they are busy with games? The environment of the home reminds her of the children and emphasizes to her their absence: the fig and the breadfruit, the banyan and the portia, the gardens and the river where they played, the flowers, the little toy elephants and horses, all become symbols of absent love. She then runs out in derangement into the forest looking for her young, and, in a scene that is a literary prolepsis of the states of *alteritas* presented in the forms of the *Meghadūta*'s *yakṣa* and Purūravas in Act IV of the *Vikramorvaśīya*, she mourns to insentient beings:

> She grieved in the mountains, she grieved in the woods; She returned to the hermitage yet again, and in front of her husband wept. 'Sire, I do not see the children, or the means by which they have been killed. Even the crows are silent – surely my children are dead! Sire, I do not see the children, or the means by which they have been killed. Even the birds do not cry – surely my children are dead! Sire, I do not see the children, or the means by which they have been

killed even though I have searched at the roots of trees, in the mountains, and in the caves!' So Maddī, the renowned princess with the beautiful hips, stretched out her arms and cried out, and right there collapsed onto the ground. (Appleton and Shaw 2015, Vol. 2, p. 614)

The Pāli invests the tragic potential of the event with drama even before Maddī's discovery of her loss, in section 8 when the children are given away. While they are being taken away by the *brāhmaṇa*, they lament heart-rendingly to their father, bidding farewell to the dear trees, gardens and rivers, that Maddī will name later, where they once played, and the little girl beseeches the forest trees to protect them and to tell their path to their mother.[16]

The Buddhist literary prototype demonstrates a sustained interest in precisely mapping out the unfolding of grief, from the father's woe when he gives his children away, to the children's laments, to Maddī's premonitions, her questioning of her husband, her lament and then her mad rush out into the forest ending in her calm acceptance on finding out the truth that they are not dead but given up. This detailed map of grief appears in the middle of the narrative, which forms a critical juncture, a turning point for the tale. Appleton and Shaw comment at length on the palindrome structure of the story, whereby things given away, reaching their climax in the middle, are then returned at the end.[17]

Kālidāsa may not have known the Pāli text, though he may well have known some form of the story of Vessantara given its widespread popularity. Among literary versions, it is likely he was familiar with the Sanskrit poem composed by the poet Āryaśūra, who probably lived around the *c.*second century CE. Āryaśūra was translated into Chinese in 434 CE,[18] and the later poet Haribhaṭṭa, a follower of Āryaśūra,[19] is cited in a Chinese text of 445 CE,[20] so it is certain that he was both active and had grown famous well before that time, and he could have lived a few centuries before Haribhaṭṭa. It is possible that he preceded Kālidāsa, as many of the facets of Kālidāsa's construction of grief and the great care with which the figure of the mourner is shown within the middle resemble this version of the Buddhist narrative. Āryaśūra's Sanskrit *Jātakamālā* is a close rendition of the older Pāli, and in it the *Viśvantarajātaka*, the birth story of Viśvantara, the Sanskrit form of Vessantara, appears to have followed the Pāli version closely.[21] In the *Jātakamālā*, Āryaśūra describes the grief and lamentation of Maddī, called Madrī in Sanskrit, thus:

Then Madrī, her alarm roused by unwanted omens that foretold something undesirable, hurriedly gathered the roots and fruits. And despite being anxious to arrive [home], returned to the hermitage with much delay since her path had been blocked by beasts of prey. Not seeing her two children in their usual places of greeting and in the places of their play, she was overpowered by a fierce despair (*bhṛśataram arativaśam agāt*).

Then, agitated by anxiety from the unwanted omens[22] (*anīpsitāśaṅkitajātasaṃbhramā*), her eyes darting about in search of her offspring, seeing that her repeated calls had no welcoming from them, she lamented, overcome with grief (*vyalapac chucāturā*).

'That very wood which because it resounded in the past with the babble of my babes, resembled a community of friends to me, today by their absence becomes a place that grants no refuge, like a wilderness.

Have those younglings fallen asleep through fatigue from their play? Or are they lost in the deep forest? Or perhaps, angered by my late return, they might have hidden somewhere because of their childishness? Why do not even these birds wail? What if they are devastated having witnessed their deaths? Have they been stolen away by a torrential river of unabated temper by the billows of her waves?

Please[23] let these false suspicions prove groundless right now! Please may the prince and the children be well! Please may the consequence of these evil-portending omens manifest only in my body! Then, why does my heart, covered by the dark night of misery, false omens having inverted its joy, seem to be bursting? Why do my limbs seem to fall, the directions seem confused, this forest from which Luck has fallen seem to spin?'

Then having entered the hermitage, having dropped the fruits and roots in one corner, having approached her husband with due etiquette, she asked, 'Where are the two children'? Then the Bodhisattva, knowing that a mother's heart is frail in her love and because of the difficulty in communicating the unpleasant fact, could not say anything to her.

For, when someone deserving good news arrives, it is difficult for a compassionate person [to inflict] torment with the fire of unpleasant tidings. Then Madrī understanding that something bad had happened to her children since he was thus silent with grief and misery, her mind as if deranged (*kṣiptacitteva*), searched the hermitage everywhere and not seeing her children, said again, her voice stammering with tears, (*sabāṣpagadgadaṃ*): 'I do not see my children and you do not tell me [anything]. Miserable, I am indeed destroyed. For one does not talk about something evil.' Speaking thus, her heart overcome by the fire of grief, she fell like a vine whose roots were torn out.[24]

Āryaśūra's version compresses Madrī's grief into a dense, compacted section in which the altered nature of her mind and the sequence of her fears, from going through where her children could be, to pleading for good news or preferable alternatives, to final physical shutdown, are sequentially unravelled. Though it omits the final part where she runs out into the forest in madness, it preserves the lineaments of that state in Madrī feeling her body to fall, the directions to appear awry, the forest to spin and her heart to burst. As in the Pāli, Madrī is first plagued by omens (though in the Sanskrit the three mentioned in the original are not described), commencing from which the tragic builds up slowly, harrowingly, to the moment she steps into her empty home. The overall impression of the section is of tension, prolongation and slowing down, so that external action gives over to feeling and sensation, and we find many compounds registering with exactness distraught psychology (*arativaśam, anīpsitāśaṅkitajātasaṃbhramā, śucāturā, aratitamiśrayā, animittāpavṛttapraharṣam*). Even before the revelation of the lost children, these omens create a powerful frenzy, a terrible sense of the unheimlich, and this frenzy is what is developed and made to drive the narrative into the central confrontation with her silent, grieving husband, whose silence becomes the most expressive communicator of something unwanted. Madrī's deepest fear is that her children are dead. She first lists where her children might be, she then hopes that in fact she has interpreted the omens incorrectly and they might only mean something bad might happen to her body. The fear summoned up by these signs is what causes her *alteritas*, her physical and mental dislocation into feeling something wholly other and unwelcome. In fact, throughout Madrī's tale, we get the impression that the premonition – the ghost – of the unknown overpowers the actual event in creating an intense state of despair for the grieving subject.

There are particular aspects of the construction of grief in this tragic middle that we also find in Kālidāsa's presentations: the verb introducing Madrī's lament *vyalapat* (*Jātakamālā* 9.78b) derives from the same base *vi-lap* (to mourn) as Kālidāsa's preferred word for lament, *vilāpa*; omens or strong presentiments of the dreadful; shock and confusion in the mourner; the lamenter not finding loved ones where they are usually present; the transformation of symbols of love into symbols of dereliction; questions often concerning the causes of death; vortex (either captured in the feeling of spiralling, in images of spirals or in questions that lead to more questions); the description of grief as a thick black substance (*tamas, tamisrā, moha*) clouding or covering completely the mind; the sheer physicality of grief; the forest; and, above all, the alteration of consciousness. Striking too is that when Madrī questions her husband in the cottage, she 'stammers with her tears' (*sabāṣpagadgadaṃ*). When Aja laments in the *Raghuvaṃśa*, he too stammers through his tears and even the same phrase is used (*vilalāpa sa bāṣpagadgadaṃ*). Above all, Kālidāsa's descriptions of the tragic middle contain a high degree of precision and detail about the various stages and states, mental and physical, undergone in mourning – this exacting interest in the experience of grief tallies closely with the level of detailing found in the Buddhist narrative perspective.

There are some aspects of the Buddhist vision of the tragic middle that are especially reminiscent of the lament of Aja in the *Raghuvaṃśa*. The image of the mourner 'stuttering in tears' (*bāṣpagadgadaṃ*) has already been mentioned. Madrī when she falls into a swoon at the end of the section is compared to a vine (*latā*) torn up at its roots. The dislocated vine recalls a verse found in the oldest version of the *Raghuvaṃśa* (Vallabhadeva's) in which Aja compares the dying of his wife Indumatī to lightning (representing an action in an older birth) striking down a vine (Indumatī) from a tree (Aja).[25] The perfect of *ni-pat* (*nipapāta*, fell) used with *latā* in Āryaśūra's description is, moreover, evoked in the past participle of the causative of *pat* (*pātita*: caused to fall) used by Kālidāsa in that verse. Then, the part where Madrī runs through the meanings of the omens in her lament, wondering if her heart might burst, exclaiming about her body dissipating and the forest spinning recollects a similar expression in Aja's lament. Here (*Raghuvaṃśa* 8.64) Aja sums up the negating effects of his bereavement – 'Gone is contentment. Pleasure has lapsed. Song has ceased. The seasons are without festival. Gone the need for ornaments. Today my bed is empty'[26] – in the same way that Madrī describes the effects of her loss of children on her body and mind.

The remembrance and keeping alive of love through an array of mnemonic symbols is a key mode of the elegiac voice in this *jātaka*. The various trees and fruits and aspects of the house where the children played, which the lament of the mother summons up, are evoked in both the Pāli and the Sanskrit. This too appears in Kālidāsa. In the *Meghadūta*, the *Ajavilāpa* and the *Rativilāpa* signs of the absent lover, often a special tree, a special animal, a half-finished adornment, flowers, spring insects and birds summon up the ghost of the loved one, like a still life painting. The elegiac consciousness hones into and invests a miscellany of things with meaning as part of the grieving process. These then become totems (Indumatī's belt, *raśanā*, for example). Instead of mourning a person, lamenters often mourn such totems of the departed: this is an aspect of the mourning voice singled out in the lament of Maddī, in the songs of the *yakṣa*, and in the laments of Aja and Rati.

The *Saundarananda* of Aśvaghoṣa

The underlying structure in the Kālidāsean epic of a rupture in the middle, the result of which is a lament followed by a second birth, can in fact first be seen in Aśvaghoṣa's *mahākāvya Saundarananda*, in which the ascetic bliss of monkhood replaces the loss of love. However, bliss in monkhood or salvation, which forms the explicit point of the tale as Aśvaghoṣa informs us in the end (*ity eṣā vyupaśāntaye … mokṣārthagarbhā kṛtiḥ*), does not come about easily, and for a few cantos seems almost impossible for its hero. In other words the rupture in the middle is carefully and attentively represented. The story of the *Saundarananda* is about the ordination and ascent to salvation of Nanda, the Buddha's brother and his theological counterpoint (Nanda personifies the *bhogin* to the Buddha's *mukta*) who, at the beginning of the tale, and for much of it in the middle, is immersed in his love for his wife Sundarī. One day, while he was engrossed with his beloved, holding before her a mirror while she adorned herself (Canto IV), his brother paid him a visit, seeking alms. However so involved was the household in the preparation of various accoutrements for the couple's amusements that no one offered food to the Buddha, who left without being honoured. When news reached Nanda that his revered brother had been ignored, he followed the Buddha to make amends, but promised, on Sundarī's pleading, that he would return before her makeup dried.

But he never did. On following the Buddha to the hermitage, he is forced by his enlightened brother to renounce his householder's life, to forego his loving wife and take up the nobler path of the mendicant (Canto V). Full of reluctance, his face streaming in tears (V.53), Nanda is initiated into the Buddhist order of monks, but to Aśvaghoṣa, this is clearly a difficult and painful change, for both Nanda and his wife. In spite of the purpose of the work, to instruct in a way out of the world, and in spite of the religiously minded poet's appropriately monkish determination to see all women as sensual pleasures and a sheer waste of time, Aśvaghoṣa, for much of Cantos IV–X, manifests a deep, humane sensitivity to the bereavement of the lovers, and, remarkably, to Sundarī herself. In the middle of the narrative, in Canto VI, at the moment when Sundarī discovers that their marriage is irretrievably severed, and that she has been betrayed as it were for salvation, she utters her lament, the *Nandabhāryāvilāpa*.

Aśvaghoṣa in lieu of condemnation opens with extreme tenderness toward his subject: Sundarī is pictured at the beginning of Canto VI still waiting on top of the palace roof – where with her husband she had explored the delights of love – filling the window with her anxious, lovelorn face, her necklace of pearls hanging down, resembling, Aśvaghoṣa says (citing Covill's translation) 'one of the beautiful *apsarases* watching her lover fall from her celestial abode when he had used up his ascetically-derived credit' (*tapaḥkṣayād apsarasāṃ varaiva cyutaṃ vimānāt priyam īkṣamānā* 6.3 in Covill 2007, pp. 114–15). The top of the palace, the *harmyapṛṣṭha*, in which the couple had spent time away from the operations of the world, becomes a powerful symbol of love, while Nanda's departure to dharma, a descent – one might even say a plummet – from this paradisiacal idyll. This is a metaphor of lost love. From this descent from one world, Nanda will ascend again into another.

The opening words of the *nandabhāryāvilāpa* even reveal a veiled criticism of dharma: *tato hṛte bhartari gauraveṇa*, 'then when her husband was taken away (*hṛte*) by venerableness' (translation here mine). One might even be tempted to make the erroneous slip from *gauraveṇa* ('by venerableness') to *gautamena* ('by the Buddha'). Sundarī is described as *vipralabdhā* or 'deceived' in *Saundarananda* 6.9a. As the reason for her being duped she repeats the promise, now reneged, Nanda had made to her: 'He made me a promise that he would be back before my *viśeṣaka* dries. What reason could there possibly be for my dear husband to break his promise now, when his promises are so important to him?' (*Saundarananda* 6.13 in Covill 2007, pp. 118–19).

Her grief when she finds out that Nanda has taken up the mendicant's robes is intense. She throws away her ornaments, she tears the string of pearls that had formerly partaken of her lovemaking with her husband, she heaves, she swoons, she hurls her arms, she moans like a bird, she tosses about on her bed, she paces up and down, she scratches her face and her clothes (*Saundarananda* 6.25–34) and 'enters a state of darkness, howling loudly and collapsing as though sinking into the mire' (*Saundarananda* 6.32 in Covill 2007 p. 122). After the love play of Canto IV, where the emphasis had been on the refinement and beauty of the arts of love – the dazzling gems on the couch where the lovers lay, the jewellery heaped on the wife's body, the *tamāla* unguent used to make the *viśeṣaka* makeup pattern on her body, all enhancing an atmosphere of exquisite aesthetic pleasure – now appears its stark opposite. It is a visceral inversion from love-art to death-truth, in which the effect of truth is mourning, unadorned and rooted not in skilled words but in the inelegancies of the body wracked by uncontrollable grief.

Dharma is not unambiguous even for a Buddhist. Nanda's second birth in and through dharma from Canto VIIII onwards is marked by enormous anguish and reluctance. After Sundarī laments, we find that so does Nanda.

Canto VII, the *nandavilāpa* ('Nanda's Lament') finds Nanda disconsolate in the forest, lamenting the world, utterly transformed after his forced conversion. In vines, flowering trees and the birds, he finds only memories of his beloved (*Saundarananda* 7.5–10). We are reminded here once more of William James's observation – '*Such are expressions that naturally rise to the lips of melancholy subjects describing their changed state ... If the natural world is so double-faced and unhomelike, what world, what thing is real?*'[27]

Through Nanda, we are shown that love and dharma are in conflict: 'Today I comprehend that men who leave behind their weeping sweethearts to practice asceticism – and those who have done so in the past, and those who will do so in the future – they are doing something very difficult indeed, and so it was in the past and will be in the future. There is no bond in the world, whether of wood, fibre or iron, as solid as this bond – teasing words and a face with fluttering eyes!' (*Saundarananda* 7. 1314 in Covill 2007, p. 135).

While real bonds can be physically shattered, the bond of love, described as a *snehamayaḥ pāśaḥ* in *Saundarananda* 7.15d, bearing the opposite qualities to a *dāravaṃ*, *tāntavaṃ* or *āyasaṃ bandhanam* – unctuous, slippery, moist ('*sneha*', 'tenderness', can also mean oiliness) – can be broken either by supreme knowledge (*jñāna*) of the kind arisen in the Buddha, or by sheer cruelty (*raukṣya*). However Nanda lacks both: 'The former [material bonds] disappear when they are cut or broken, by one's own force or the strength of friends, but the snare of love cannot be undone without knowledge and cruelty. That knowledge which might make for peace I do not have, nor, being compassionate by nature, can I be cruel. I am naturally passionate, yet the Buddha is my guru; I am as if fixed to a turning wheel' (*Saundarananda* 7.15–16 in Covill 2007, pp. 136–7).

To be *shito 'ntare cakragater* (*Saundarananda* 7.16 in Covill 2007, p. 136) 'fixed inside the revolution of a wheel' is to be in conflict with a larger force. The *cakragati*, the wheel's motion, is an especially expressive image of tragedy. It conveys the determinism of fate against which human will is hapless and also the mental agony of returning to the same point, the inability, that is, to forget. It is a literal representation of the state of *sambhrama*, 'spinning around' or 'confusion', that is a key aspect of depictions of grief even in Āryaśūra. Once again, Nanda's promise to Sundarī is echoed, interlocking with his wife's lament in the previous canto: 'The words that the lass spoke to me, her eyes brimming with tears – Hurry back before my *visheshaka* dries! – those words lock up my mind even now' (*Saundarananda* 7.19 in Covill 2007, p. 137).

The compound *anāśyānaviśeṣakāyām*, 'while the *viśeṣaka* (*-viśeṣakāyām*) is not dry (*an-āśyāna-*), appears thrice, once when it is first made in the promise

Sundarī extracts from Nanda (*Saundarananda* 4.34), then it is revisited by Sundarī in mourning, finally it is recollected by Nanda in bereavement. It is a sound-link, weaving together, and thereby cohering thematically, the tragic middle. It is the symbol of the broken *pratijñā*, forming the background incantation as it were to the inner death of Sundarī and Nanda's relationship. An echo of this same shattered idyll appears in *Kumārasambhava* 4.19, in which Rati, mourning the dead Kāma, asks him to finish adorning her feet, an act of affection forestalled by his duty to the gods:

> *vibudhair asi yasya dāruṇair asamāpte parikarmaṇi smṛtaḥ /*
> *tam imaṃ kuru dakṣiṇetaraṃ caraṇaṃ nirmitarāgam ehi me //*
> *Kumārasambhava* 4.19 //

> Come back to me!
> On my left foot, daub the final paint-marks.
> While yet undone its ornamentation,
> The cruel gods recollected you just then.

Here in *asamāpte parikarmaṇi* ('while yet undone its ornamentation') we find a memory of *anāśyānaviśeṣakāyām*, and in the gods imposing their duty when the couple is together, an image of the Buddha interrupting Sundarī and Nanda's idyll. In both the heart is destroyed by dharma.

We are reminded also of love as a *snehamayapāśa* in Kālidāsa's *āśābandha*, the bind of hope described in the *Meghadūta* 11, and both Aśvaghoṣa and Kālidāsa are interested in the oxymoronic nature of Love: it is a firm bond (*pāśa/bandha*) even though its nature is viscose and fragile (*snehamaya/āśā*). Where Aśvaghoṣa seeks to break this bondage, and to show that love in religion is a more exalted experience than earthly love, Kālidāsa's stories seek to show its durability through delay and duress. But to a higher degree, both authors are interested in broken promises. For Aśvaghoṣa, Nanda cannot bear the thought of breaking his promise in the beginning. He decides to return to his wife, so acute is his grief, even after the most scathing opprobrium on women, including a catalogue of 'harlots' from history, from a pious monk in Canto VIII, and a denunciation of love-as-intoxication in Canto IX. It is only much later, in Canto X, when the Buddha reveals to him the greater pleasures in heaven, particularly the enticements of the celestial nymphs, that Nanda breaks his oath. On seeing the *apsaras*es Nanda's heart flies away – all too quickly – from Sundarī (*Saundarananda* 10.50), he begins to transform utterly, to see earthly love as lust and ensnarement as a good renunciate ought to, and thence he begins his second birth, which leads to liberation. The *Saundarananda* shows that Nanda's progress only begins after the death of his love for Sundarī through the tearing (*chedana*) of its noose (*pāśa*).

Apart from the death and lamentations in the tragic middle, the story of Nanda and his wife provides a parallel template to the story of Duṣyanta and Śakuntalā in its view of dharma – a higher duty – to be the destroyer of love and in its view of the tragedy experienced by women when their lovers desert them for a higher good. By and large in both narratives men's desertion is seen as necessary and justified for a wider social and religious purpose. It is only through the experiences of those deserted, Nanda's wife and Śakuntalā, that a critique of dharma is provided. For their wives, Nanda and Duṣyanta, though initially *dayitapratijña* (one who cherishes his promise) – echoing the words of Sundarī's lament – become *vitathapratijña* (one whose promise is false).

The *Rāmāyaṇa*

The roots of the wife injured by dharma go back to the tale of Sītā and Rāma, the primal tragedy of unfulfilled, hopeless love, the trauma of which returns time and again in Kālidāsa, who, in almost all his works, seeks to restore and heal the great throbbing wound in that tale and grant dignity to Sītā and her literary descendents. Behind Kālidāsa's *Śakuntalā* lies the tragic separation of the *Rāmāyaṇa*: Duṣyanta and Śakuntalā echo Rāma and Sītā, and Duṣyanta's repudiation of Śakuntalā is an echo of Rāma's repudiation of Sītā in the *Rāmāyaṇa*. In their symbolic association, Sītā and Śakuntalā are as contrapuntal notes to each other. Where Sītā is an emblem of the earth and of the belief in Indian kingship in the sacred marriage between earth and king, Śakuntalā is an emblem of heaven, Earth's other. Both are adopted after their mothers abandon them, Sītā by Janaka when he finds her in a furrow, Śakuntalā by Kaṇva when he finds her under a tree, watched over by *śakunta* birds. In Act V of the *Śakuntalā*, Kālidāsa makes the parallelism between Sītā and Śakuntalā more evident. Act V of the *Śakuntalā*, in which Śakuntalā's veracity is put to test in the eyes of the royal court, is an image of Sītā's final trial in the *Uttarakāṇḍa* where too she is publicly adjudged. After Śakuntalā is rebuffed by both her king and her entourage, as she is sent off with the court priest, she calls out to Mother Earth to rescue her: *bhaavadi vasuhe dehi me viaraṃ* ('Goddess Earth, give me an opening', *Śakuntalā* D, Act V, p. 253). This moment replays Sītā's final trial scene in the *Rāmāyaṇa*, when she cries out to her mother Goddess Earth to take her in order to prove her innocence. The words too recall Sītā's cry to Goddess Earth: *tathā me mādhavī devī vivaraṃ dātum arhati*

('So, may the Goddess Mādhavī give me an opening', *Śakuntalā* D, 7.88.10c). Apart from the general sense being the same, Śakuntalā's *viaram* is an exact rendering, in Prakrit, of *vivaram* (hole/opening) in Sītā's utterance. Sītā is rescued from this final ordeal by her mother after she cries out to her. In the *Śakuntalā*, the Earth does not rescue Śakuntalā, because she is not her mother, but we learn that after the trial, a similar *deus ex machina* takes place: Śakuntalā is whisked away to safety from the opprobrium of dharma by her mother, the nymph Menakā, who appears from the sky as miraculously as Goddess Earth appeared for Sītā from below. Whereas Sītā is never reunited with Rāmā, Kālidāsa, in portraying the king's remorse in Act VI, and in the subsequent union in Act VI – once he is judged by Sānumati, a heavenly nymph and friend of Śakuntalā, to be suitably regretful – shows a restoration of Śakuntalā's marriage and status. Through her acceptance and through Duṣyanta's severe emotional disturbance for much of the length of time he is separated from her, Kālidāsa writes a different ending to the story of Rāma and Sītā.

The tragedy of lost love in the *Rāmāyaṇa* also appears in the *Meghadūta*, in which it forms the musical shadow as it were, muffled and only occasionally heard, casting deeper colour and shade, when it is, on the song of the *yakṣa*. In verse 1, the *yakṣa* is said to be spending his banishment in the hermitages on Rāmagiri or Citrakūṭa (*rāmagiryāśrameṣu*). Kālidāsa's tenderness for the primal tragedy diffuses into his descriptions of those hermitages: 'in which there were friendly shade-giving trees (*snigdhacchāyātaruṣu*)'; 'in which there were waters sanctified by the baths of the daughter of Janaka (*janakatanayāsnānapuṇyodak eṣu*)'. The hushed, shaded woodland idyll in which he embeds his lonely *yakṣa* reverberates with deep symbolism. Citrakūṭa was the site of the happy union of Sītā and Rāma before the eventual doom of their love and as such it is a symbol for primal *sambhoga*, love-in-union, but it is also a prolepsis of *sambhoga*'s disintegration. Once again, in verse 97, the separation of Rāma and Sītā appears. Here, in the message that the *yakṣa* imagines the cloud will convey to his beloved, he compares her to Sītā (Maithilī) being revived by Rāma's message delivered by Hanumān 'the offspring of the wind':

ity ākhyāte pavanatanayaṃ maithilīvonmukhī sā
tvām utkaṇṭhocchvasitahṛdayā vīkṣya saṃbhāvya caiva |
śroṣyaty asmāt param avahahitā somya sīmantinīnāṃ
kāntodantaḥ suhṛdupanataḥ saṃgamāt kiṃcid ūnaḥ ||

When addressed thus she sees you with a face
Turned up in eagerness her heart
In longing trembling, just like Maithilī

> The offspring of the wind when she beheld,
> And recognizing you, she later will
> In rapt attention heed you gentle sir.
> For married women count their lover's news
> Brought by a friend to be but a little
> Less in happiness than actual reunion

The *yakṣa*'s separation from his wife replays for Kālidāsa the separation between Rāma and Sītā after she was taken captive by Rāvaṇa. Like Bhavabhūti known for his dexterity with grief and his preoccupation with the pathos of the *Rāmāyaṇa*, Kālidāsa too is marked indelibly by the understanding of the tragic in the epic.

Fate in the *Rāmāyaṇa*

The *Rāmāyaṇa* is filled with lamentation. So great is its weight of grief that it turns even powerful heroes to unrestrained mourners: epitomes of dharmic kingship, Daśaratha and even Rāma, meant to espouse appropriate self-restraint collapse time and again into laments that almost paralyse them. This is especially so in the second book, the *Ayodhyākāṇḍa*, in which the banishment of Rāma is portrayed, wherein Daśaratha is presented as a tragic – even weak – character, powerless against the machinations of those he considered nearest to him. For example, on hearing Kaikeyī's wish for Rāma's banishment, he 'cried in uncontrollable fury before he fell into a stupor, his heart crushed by grief' (*Rāmāyaṇa* II.10.32, p. 93). Elsewhere 'lost in lamentation', 'heaving burning sighs', 'begging [Kaikeyī] for mercy', 'his eyes reddened and dimmed by tears', he 'was taken faint, overcome with grief and dropped unconscious to the floor' (*Rāmāyaṇa* II.11.7–15, p. 97).

The engine for such tragedy is often characterized, even when there is clear indication of personal responsibility, as fate (*daiva*), the 'agent of ends' (*kṛtānta*). The *Rāmāyaṇa* unfolds in a sacrificially and karmically ordered universe. Fate represents the principle of chaos threatening that well-oiled predetermined order. Unlike the mechanized harmonious universe, fate is said to be its counterpoint 'running wild, like a careering elephant beyond control of the goad, in a frenzy of rut and might' (*Rāmāyaṇa* II.20.15, Pollock's translation, pp. 144–5). It can be controlled neither by the gods, nor by religious sacrifice, and in this independent capacity, precipitates the most tragic of episodes for Daśaratha: Rama's banishment. In this respect, the *Rāmāyaṇa*, just as it is concerned with the dharmic world it strives to protect, is pregnant with a meditation on fate, its antipode and the thing that sets it in disarray. This is seen, for instance, in Rāma's long rumination on fate in the *Ayodhyākāṇḍa*:

> It is nothing but destiny, Saumítri, that we must see at work in my exile and in the revocation of the kingship, which had been awarded to me. For, why should Kaikéyi be so determined to harm me were this intention of hers not fated and ordained by destiny? You know yourself, dear brother, that never in the past have I drawn any distinction between our mothers, nor did she ever differentiate between her son and me. I cannot credit anything but fate for those words of her, those hard and brutal words that meant the revocation of the consecration and my exile. ... What cannot be explained must surely be fate, which clearly no creature can resist; for how complete the reversal that has befallen her and me.
>
> What man has the power to contest his fate, Saumítri, when one cannot even perceive it except from its effect? Happiness and sadness, fear and anger, gain and loss, birth and death – all things such as these must surely be the effects of fate. ... People overmastered by fate say things they never wanted to – you know fate has such power. (*Rāmāyaṇa* II.19.13–22, Pollock's translation, pp. 141–3)

The curse in the *Rāmāyaṇa*

Not all suffering though is governed by fate, and often it appears to be only a scapegoat rather than a real entity propelling events. The *Rāmāyaṇa* shows that personal responsibility plays a powerful role in causing tragedy. When human error or misdeed occurs, it is not without repercussion but is often punished with a curse. A curse (*śāpa*) is a prophetic utterance drawing its power to generate tragedy from the anger of a sagacious or powerful individual, who is usually the curser. It has a correspondence with poetic speech, as shown in the death of the *krauñca* episode, and even incantation (*mantra*) for like those expressions of divine speech, *vāc*, it is a form of the powerful word that can affect and transmute reality.

Fate and the curse allow us to envisage two poles in the map of epic tragedy: while fate is seemingly causeless at one end, tragedy born from a curse is caused by individual will at the other. The first, fate, represents tragedy as inherent natural design, the whimsy of the governing gods (hence the *vṛddhi*-formation, *daiva*, 'of the gods'). The second, the curse, represents tragedy as human error, caused by some personal vice (such as, for instance, addiction).

Curses are present in the *Rāmāyaṇa* almost from the very beginning. In the *Bālakāṇḍa*, poetry is said to have originated as a curse uttered by the sage Vālmīki in grief. Again, the murder of the *krauñca* is echoed symbolically in Dasaratha's deathbed confession (*Rāmāyaṇa* II.57.10–58.46, pp. 330–41) of his accidental killing of a *brāhmaṇa* hermit boy. We learn while Daśaratha is dying that in his youth he killed a hermit boy in error while hunting, a fault that could have been avoided had he not been so addicted to the hunt. As a result of his crime he was cursed by the boy's distraught father to suffer the same fate of the loss of his own son. Within the narrative progress of the epic, this episode resurrects in memory the *krauñca*'s death. Both tragedies unfold during hunting. The innocent *krauñca* is a prefiguration of the murdered *brāhmaṇa* boy; the hunter, of Daśaratha. The boy's *karuṇāṃ giram*, 'piteous cry', on being shot by Daśaratha's arrow echoes exactly the lament of the female *krauñca* bird, also described as a *karuṇām giram*. The father's curse – 'Just as I now sorrow over my son's calamity, so you too, your majesty, shall end your days grieving for a son' (*putravyasanajaṃ duḥkhaṃ yad etan mama sāmpratam | evaṃ tvaṃ putraśokena rājan kālaṃ kariṣyasi ||* *Rāmāyaṇa* II.58.46, Pollock's translation, pp. 340–1) – structurally interlocks with Vālmīki's. Both for instance are divided into two sections: one, a reason for the punishment sign-posted by *yad*, used in the sense of 'since', and another, a wish for the accused to spend the rest of his days in mental agony. This sentence is meant to mirror the suffering of the victim of bereavement – and so the curse is envisaged as punishment truly fitting the crime.

When tragedy ensues in the second book, Daśaratha attributes his separation from Rāma to this curse. Just as the *krauñcavadha* curse is the *bīja* as it were of the first book out of which the tree of the *Rāmāyaṇa* sprouts, so in the second book the hermit's curse of Daśaratha is placed symbolically at the generative apex of a spiral of momentous events: the separation of wives from their husbands, parents from their children, a kingdom from its ruler. Like the dull thud of a drum that seems to continue through the unstoppable power of its own momentum, the *Ayodhyākāṇḍa* bristles with their laments.

Kālidāsa's vision of tragedy is shaped too by the epic model of the twin poles of tragic causation: *kṛtānta* at one and the *śāpa* at the other. What makes his poetic universe unalterably tragic is fate. A narrative aid to predetermined, innate tragedy is the centrality of the curse. Kālidāsa's vision of how a curse unfolds is very close to the epic vision. However, to fate and the curse as causes of tragedy, Kālidāsa adds two further culprits: the effects of action in a previous birth and God or the gods.

Fate (vidhi), curse (śāpa), retribution (karma), God (Īśvara): Tragic agency in Kālidāsa

Like the *Rāmāyaṇa*, Kālidāsa's understanding of the universe is that it is an essentially cruel place, where all things are prone to decline and where simply to survive is to be lucky. As the love of Chaucer's Troilus and Criseyde is subject to and finally doomed by the dominion of Lady Fortune turning her wheel, so human life in Kālidāsa, too, is subject to the turns of time.

The conception of fickle time in the tragic universe is revealed systematically in several verses in the *Raghuvaṃśa* (A, 8.85–94; V, 8.82–91), remarkable, in the corpus of Kālidāsa's works, for their illumination of a sustained, philosophical argument about existence. These verses articulate a consolation, which, however, remains unsatisfactory for King Aja, for whom it is meant. The context for these verses is a message sent by Aja's royal preceptor, Vasiṣṭha, explaining the futility of Aja's grief over his wife Indumatī's sudden and horrific death, as it was the result of a curse in a previous birth. The consolation includes the following telling remark that reveals how, for Kālidāsa, tragedy, as it is for the Buddhists, given the dominion of time over all, is implicit in transmigration:

maraṇaṃ prakṛtiḥ śarīriṇāṃ vikṛtir jīvitam ucyate budhaiḥ |
kṣaṇam apy avatiṣṭhate śvasan yadi jantur nanu lābhavān asau || *Raghuvaṃśa* A, 8.85

The natural state of all creatures is death
While embodied life is unnatural
Thus say the wise – so, should a creature breathe
Even for a moment then it's lucky!

The earliest commentator to the verse, Vallabhadeva, expands on the mutability of existence described in the verse thus: 'Scholars say that death is the nature of beings given that it is eternal and will invariably occur. However, life is an impermanent deviation. One may or may not be born in human form [even] after a thousand births. Thus should an embodied being remain alive even for a moment, then that is his/her good fortune. This is considered to be the mutability of a body. However [its] lord, the soul, [is not mutable] because of its eternal nature' (*prāṇināṃ mṛtiḥ svabhāvo nityatvād avaśyaṃbhāvitvāt paṇḍitaiḥ kathyate* | *jīvanaṃ tu vikāraḥ kādācitkatvāt* | *janmasahasrair hi mānuṣyakam āpyate na vā* | *ataḥ śarīrī kṣaṇam api yadi jīvan santiṣṭhate tat so 'sya lābhaḥ* | *etad vināśitvaṃ piṇḍasyābhimatam* | *na tv īśvarasyātmanaḥ nityatvāt* | *Raghuvaṃśa* V 8.88).

For the consoling sage, death is the natural, inevitable course: it is *prakṛti*, while life as a body is its opposite: uncertain. For him a powerful pain lies at the very heart of existence: the cyclical separation of the soul and the body, which at every death become like disjoined lovers. Their permanent union is thereby always pre-empted, always unfulfilled. Next to this truth of profound dislocation, any temporal, mundane suffering in the form of blows in life pales in comparison. Such is indicated in the verse at Raghuvaṃśa V 8.90 (= Raghuvaṃśa A 8.87,[28] I am citing Vallabhadeva's reading as it is clearer):

> *svaśarīraśarīriṇāv api smṛtasaṃyogaviparyayau yadā |*
> *virahaḥ kam ivānutāpayed vada bāhyair viṣayair vipaścitam || Raghuvaṃśa*
> V 8.90.

> When one recalls that the body and soul
> Shall also be sundered at the time of death,
> Whom should separation from attachments
> To organs of senses torment, do tell?

On the other hand, the sage explains, even if Aja were to die – which is the wish he feels and one that the sage desires to forestall – there would be no guarantee he would be united with his dead wife in the afterworld, for each person's karmic effects, the driving force of transmigration, differ, so that associations may not coincide again in the next life:

> *rudatā kuta eva sā punar bhavatā nānumṛtāpi labhyate |*
> *paralokajuṣāṃ svakarmabhir gatayo bhinnapathā hi dehinām ||*
> *Raghuvaṃśa* A 8.83

> Even if you followed her in death
> You would not win her back, then how on earth
> Can you reclaim her with your moans and groans!
> According to the worth of their actions
> The paths of farers in the afterlife differ.

In this way: 'For those who are born, calamity is permanent' (*vipad utpattimatām avasthitā*) (*Raghuvaṃśa* A 8.81d). Frustration and unfulfillment, then, are the cornerstones of what it is to exist as a body.

The same thought underlies the *Śakuntalā*. The rise and fall of fortune (*sampad*) and calamity (*vipad*) are like the alternate ascents of the sun and the moon. 'It is true', says a disciple of Kaśyapa in Act IV of the Kashmirian recension of the *Śakuntalā* on seeing the daybreak the morning after the sage curses Śakuntalā, 'the sun and the moon seem to demonstrate the mutability of fortune and calamity in this universe. For:

'On one side, the moon, lord of herbs goes to the peak of the setting mountain, on the other side, is the sun, preceded by the glow of dawn. By the simultaneous rise and fall of two effulgences is mankind governed in his particular[29] personal conditions' (*Śakuntalā* K IV.2: *yat satyaṃ sūryacandramasau jagato 'sya sampadvipattyor anityatāṃ darśayata iva* | *tathā ca* –

yāty ekato 'staśikharaṃ patir oṣadhīnām
āviṣkṛtārjunapuraḥsara ekato 'rkaḥ |
tejodvyayasya yugapad vyasanodayābhyām
loko niyamyata ivātmadaśāntareṣu ||)

The verse also registers the calamity that has just befallen Śakuntalā.

The disciple further goes onto allegorically describe how even love is subject to temporal mutability in what is a prolepsis of things to come for Śakuntalā. He says that when the moon disappears, the lotus that blooms only in moonlight, whose beauty is now concealed in the sunlight and which can only be remembered, cannot delight his eye as before. Surely the sorrows of womenfolk, when their dear ones are gone, are intolerable (*Śakuntalā* K IV.3). The lotus, or flowers whose beauties are no longer enjoyed, and the wives of travellers become two of the many symbols conveying the image of transient time in the *Śakuntalā* in which love is shown to be fickle.

The background to the view in the *Raghuvaṃśa* that life is essentially and unchangeably grounded in rupture, and that one must therefore carry on regardless of the turnings of life (this second point is one which Aja, though asked to accept, is unable to), lies in the ascetic traditions of ancient India. The mutability of the body – the incalculable deaths it suffers – is a conception that draws from the idea of *saṃsāra* common to the renunciatory traditions of Buddhism, Jainism and Upaniṣadic Brahmanism. According to this conception, the body is painfully wrenched from birth to birth in an unceasing manner. Life itself is painful because it is proof of endless deaths, of inhabiting 'the state of a ball' swerving violently from body, to heaven, to hell, to body again. Just how violent and how tragic the *vikṛti*, change, mentioned in the *Raghuvaṃśa* verse was felt to be can be gauged by a later verse from the ninth-century poet Loṣṭaka's lamentation on life, the *Dīnākrandanastotra* (*Hymn on the Lamentation of the Wretched*):

ghore kṣaṇaṃ vinipatan narake kṣaṇaṃ ca
puṇyaṃ padaṃ diviṣadāṃ sahasādhirohan |

mohena kandukadaśām iva nīyamānaḥ
svāmin sahe kim avadhīni gatāgatāni || *Dīnākrandanastotra* 4

Once plunging into fearful hell, and once
Soaring to the gods' auspicious regions –
Delusion seems to make me but a ball –
Lord how can I bear these cycles that are death!

The confessional tone of the lamentation is marked by an impassioned vividness, similar to that of Dante's *Inferno*. Life is either a desert or a well or a vortex, the latter two are images of spirals that also appear in other *vilāpa*s from Kālidāsa as metaphors of existential vertigo:

cuṇṭhījalair[30] *iva sukhaiḥ pariṇāmaduḥkhair*
āsvāditair api manāg aviluptatṛṣṇaḥ |
śrānto'smi hā bhavamarau suciraṃ caritvā
tac chāyayā caraṇayoḥ śiva māṃ bhajethāḥ || 1

Ah tired am I from wandering long
In *saṃsāra*'s desert, my thirst unquenched
By pleasures that I've tasted that just turn
Finally to sorrow like ditchwater
Therefore O Śiva grant me grace
With the shadow of your feet.

durvārasaṃsṛtirujā bhṛśakāṃdiśīkas
tvām oṣadhīpatibhṛtaṃ sukṛtair avāpya |
āvedayāmi yad ahaṃ tava tan nidānaṃ
tatrāvadhehi mṛḍa mā kuru mayy avajñām || 2

Fleeing in utter panic from the disease
Of unstoppable rebirth, on reaching you,
Supporter of the moon, through good deeds
I'll declare the cause of illness to you
O Compassionate One pay heed to that –
Do not spurn me![31]

durvāsanāśatavaśād aśucitvam īkṣya
yā me haṭhāt kṛtavatī manasi praveśam |
sānekajanmamaraṇāvaṭapātanena
māṃ rākṣasīva bahu nātha tudaty avidyā || 3

Ignorance, she violently seized my mind
Seeing my evil in predilections vile.

Just like a demoness she pummels me
Often, causing me to tumble down
Into the pit of countless births and deaths

Kālidāsa, though less severe, partakes of this fundamentally tragic view of the world.

The curse is an omnipresent theme in the determination of tragic events in Kālidāsa's work. Durvāsas curses Śakuntalā so that Duṣyanta forgets her. Bharata curses Urvaśī so that she loses her divinity and descends to earth (though here it is a positive propeller leading to Urvaśī and Purūravas uniting rather than a negative force). The sage Tṛṇabindu curses Indumatī in her previous incarnation as the seductress nymph Hariṇī. Kubera curses the *yakṣa*, banishing him from his wife. The word uttered in anger is a narrative instrument evoking the story of Rāma and marking devastating turning points in the experiences of primary characters. In this way though, characters are portrayed, as they are in the *Rāmāyaṇa*, to be in a certain sense responsible for the fate they have to suffer. Śakuntalā's preoccupation brought on by love leads her to neglect her hospitality to Durvāsas, leading to his curse. Hariṇī's (Indumatī's) temptation of the sage Tṛṇabindu while he is attempting to meditate leads to his curse. The *yakṣa*, *svādhikārapramattaḥ* 'negligent of his responsibilities [to Kubera]', is banished by his master. Urvaśī, lost in love, makes a mistake in her speech on stage and so is cursed by Bharata. Kālidāsa's world is a veritable battlefield of offence and retaliation.

In the *Raghuvaṃśa* Kālidāsa creates meaningful links with epic tragedy in his version of the hermit's curse from the *Ayodhyākāṇḍa*:

diṣṭāntam āpsyati bhavān api putraśokād
antye vayasy aham iveti tam uktavantam |
ākrāntapūrvam iva muktaviṣaṃ bhujaṅgam
provāca kośalapatiḥ prathamāparāddhaḥ || *Raghuvaṃśa* M 8.79–80

'As I, so you shall die in misery
For your son in your twilight period!'
Said he just like a poison-spitting snake
When threatened. To him the Lord of Kośala
Who had made the first transgression spoke.

Even as he condenses the two statement *yad* … *evaṃ* ('since … thus') structure of Vālmīki's curse (see *Rāmāyaṇa* II.58.46, pp. 340–1) into one, he intones Vālmīki's words: *bhavān* echoes Vālmīki's *tvam*, *putraśokād* echoes *putraśokena*, *diṣṭāntam āpsyati* echoes *kālaṃ kariṣyasi*. What to Kālidāsa is truly interesting is

Daśaratha's responsibility: he ends his verse by reminding us that the king was the first to transgress. In so doing, he reminds us how tragedy in the epic model can be self-caused. Kālidāsa is deeply aware of the human capacity, however noble, to make mistakes, and *prathamāparāddhaḥ*, one who has offended first', is an adjective one can readily apply to all of Kālidāsa's curse-victims.

The above curse is in profound unison with another: the curse the sage Durvāsas places on Śakuntalā, which is in the same tradition of tragedy as retaliation:

vicintayantī yam ananyamānasā/
tapodhanaṃ vetsi na mām upasthitam |
smariṣyati tvāṃ na sa bodhito 'pi san
kathāṃ pramattaḥ prathamaṃ kṛtām iva || Śakuntalā D IV.1

Immersed in contemplating him
Your mind on no one else
You did not see me standing there,
Rich in ascetic powers.
That man won't remember you
Even when he's made aware
As a drunk forgets the things
He'd said in the beginning.

Both curses are in the *vasantatilakā* metre, with the first *pāda* ending in a past participle (*uktavantam/upasthitam*) referring to the curser. In terms of architecture the participle acts as a hinge for the two different sense units conveyed in each half of the verse. Importantly both verses contain an indication of the *aparādha*, the transgression underlying the curse, which imitates the structure of the epic *śāpa* wherein too the offence is stated along with stating the punishment. They also contain a simile: the *Raghuvaṃśa* verse contains an image of a snake, the *Śakuntalā* verse a drunk. Both similes are about speech uttered in some form of mental turmoil: in the first, the sage's words correspond with the poison of the snake whose ire is provoked; in the second Duṣyanta's words correspond with a drunk's. In this sense both curses expand on the idea of altered talk, or, in other words, the expression of the *anyathāvṛtti cetaḥ*.

On the other hand, while individual responsibility underlies the curse, for Kālidāsa fate is an entirely absurd entity. It represents the principle of natural chaos and natural cruelty in the universe, manifesting itself in human experience in the form of accidents, like fortune in the tale of Troilus and Criseyde. Its absurdity is no better illustrated than in the episode of Indumatī's death, when we find, to our and Aja's shock, that even flowers can kill. The instrument of death here is natural, wrought by *prakṛti* herself, just as fate is a natural tragic element in the world it governs: and in this way the garland is a symbol of fate. Here though we must add that toward the end of the *Ajavilāpa* the absurdity of the flower garland as an instrument of death is explained by the story of the curse by Tṛṇabindu, in which Hariṇī is cursed to dwell on earth 'only till the sighting of a celestial garland' (*āsuramālyadarśanāt*) (*Raghuvaṃśa* A 8.79). It is not fate, which is the cause here, we learn, but a curse in a former life. But at the time of its occurrence, it is interpreted by Aja in his lament as a moment of fate's inscrutable and all-powerful impulse at play. Its power can even challenge in these moments all other forces of causality, including *karma* and *īśvara*.

Aja's lament begins with a contemplation of the possible causes for the tragedy. These reveal how for Kālidāsa the lament is also a mode for engaging in questions about death and life. A contemplative philosophical 'pause', the lament in Kālidāsa's writings registers the *vimarśa* as a critical revaluation of one's existence and of the causal powers behind grief:

> *kusumāny api gātrasaṅgamāt prabhavanty āyur apohituṃ yadi* |
> *na bhaviṣyati hanta sādhanaṃ kim ivānyat prahariṣyato vidheḥ* ||
> *Raghuvaṃśa* A 8.44

> If flowers too can kill simply by touch
> Any other thing can be a weapon
> Alas, it seems, for fate about to strike!

For the lamenter, calamity is inauspicious, and so how can it be explained by such auspicious causal powers as the gods? The culprit for inauspiciousness is first and foremost some other entity, an anti-god – fate. One of the commentators on the *Raghuvaṃśa*, Aruṇagirinātha, indicates that the supremacy of Fate as a god-like entity is the key point of the verse, by commenting on how fate's desire indicated in the future participle *prahariṣyataḥ* is the cause of tragedy: 'The meaning is that the Desire [of fate] alone is the cause in the bringing about of the achievement of his wish. The unimaginable power of fate is suggested thereby' (| *ichaiveṣṭasādhanatvāpādane hetur ity arthaḥ* | *vidher ityacintyānubhāvatvaṃ dhvanyate* ||).

For Aja in this moment, fate is so powerful that it even causes flowers, simply by touch, to be an instrument of its will. Confused and in shock, he then disputes fate's power in tragedy, and he then gives second reason as to why death happens to some in an untimely manner. There must be a rational cause and not the inscrutability of fate, for as previous examples in the world show, his wife's death by flowers was imminent, for gentleness is slain by gentleness as the example of the lotus in frost proves:

athavā mṛdu vastu hiṃsituṃ mṛdunaivārabhate prajāntakaḥ |
himasekavipattir atra me nalinī pūrvadarśanaṃ matā || *Raghuvaṃśa* A 8.45

Death, or else, has tried to strike something
Gentle with only a gentle thing.
I hold as prior example the lotus
For which a shower of frost spells doom.

The text of the *Raghuvaṃśa* as read by the tenth-century commentator Vallabhadeva transmits a verse after this, missing in the version interpreted by Aruṇagirinātha, in which Aja postulates another possible alternative: the ripening of action in a previous birth (*karmavipāka*):

athavā suramālyarūpabhāg aśanir nirmita eṣa karmaṇā |
yad anena tarur na pātitaḥ kṣapitā tadviṭapāśrayā latā || *Raghuvamsa* V 8.47

Or else this lightning is the outward form
Of a divine garland by *karma* wrought,
For it felled not the tree but instead destroyed
Her, the vine, that sought shelter on my trunk.

Vallabhadeva interprets the garland as a special type of flower-lightning wrought by the power of karmic retribution: 'The sense is that this is not a flower, but a lightning bolt created by fate bearing the disguise of a divine flower-garland, since I, comparable to a tree, have not been brought down by it, and the vine that is Indumatī who took shelter in the trunk of my body has been destroyed. For, in general, it is the nature of a lightning bolt that it destroys [only one thing, that is,] the weight [resting] on top of the branches of a tree and not its trunk. And if one argues in this way, then what must be established is the fact that the garland is a lightning bolt. According to others, what must be established is the fact that the lightning is [a special kind of] a garland. It is well known that lightning has [the power] of crushing a tree. This, however, is another [type] of lightning, which due to the effect of previous action, destroyed the vine by avoiding the tree' (*nedaṃ puṣpam ity arthaḥ api tu vidhināiṣa divyamālākusumaveśadhārī vajraḥ sṛṣṭaṃ yad anena vṛkṣatulyo 'haṃ na pātitaḥ madaṅgaprakāṇḍāśritā cendumatīlatā vināśitā* | *aśaner hi prāyeṇaiṣa svabhāvo yad upariśākhābhāraṃ taror nāśayati na stambham* | *evaṃ ca vyākhyāne mālyasyāśanitvaṃ sādhyam* | *aśaner mālyatvaṃ sādhyam ity anye* | *aśaneḥ kila tarupeṣaṇaṃ prasiddham* | *ayaṃ punar anya evāśanir yat karmavaśāt taruṃ visṛjya latāṃ nāśitavān* |).[32]

The only way Aja sees out of this cycle of questions with no answer is to end everything. He tries to kill himself by wearing the garland but another absurdity presents itself: He remains alive, and, unable to explain this further, he says that contrariness is down to the will of God (*īśvarecchā*) like the accidental interchangeable natures of poison and nectar:

> *srag iyaṃ yadi jīvitāpahā hṛdaye kin nihitā na hanti mām |*
> *viṣam apy amṛtaṃ kvacid bhaved amṛtaṃ vā viṣam īśvarīcchayā ||*
> *Raghuvaṃśa* A 8.46
>
> If even this garland can annihilate,
> Placed on my neck it kills me not – oh why!
> We find in some examples poison too
> Behaves like nectar, while in some, nectar
> Is like poison, depending on God's will.

Finally, tragedy becomes simply *divaś cyutam* (something fallen from heaven), and the garland fallen from the instrument of Nārada in the air becomes a metaphor in the *Ajavilāpa* of such astral tragedy, governed by inscrutable powers in the sky that mechanize when the time is right.

> *krathakaiśikavaṃśasambhavā tava bhūtvā mahiṣī cirāya sā |*
> *upalabdhavatī divaś cyutaṃ vivaśā śāpanivṛttikāraṇam || Raghuvaṃśa* A 8.80
>
> Born into the Krathakaiśika line
> She became your supreme queen for long.
> When she felt the cause of her curse's end
> To fall from heaven, senseless she grew.

In Aja's *vilāpa* we find the exploration of a whole range of causes of an inexplicable death: fate, karma, the will of God and finally something driven by astral powers.

Among these overlapping threads of causes, fate is the preferred culprit for tragedy for Kālidāsa's sufferers of accidents. Thus, in *Śakuntalā*, Act V, at the moment when tragedy ensues, as Śakuntalā finds to her horror that the ring of recognition, whereby the king's memory could be restored, was lost: *ettha dāva vihiṇā daṃśidaṃ pahuttaṇā* ('Here fate has shown its lordship') (*Śakuntalā* D, Act V, p. 243). When we wonder why the jester who was witness to their marriage did not speak up to support her we learn in Act VI from Duṣyanta that Mādhavya was in fact not present at the rejection to stop the king, to which the jester comments, that among all other reasons: *avi a bhavidavvadā balavadi* ('Also fate is powerful' *Śakuntalā* D, Act VI, p. 279).

The power of fate is accused of being the culprit of separation also in the *Meghadūta*: 'Thus I, who through the power of fate am banished from my wife, have become your supplicant' (*tenārthitvaṃ tvayi vidhivaśād dūrabandhur gato 'haṃ*, 6); 'Or her left thigh which has been made to give up by the course of fate (*daivagatyā*) the net of pearls long familiar to it' (*vāmo vāsyāḥ kararuhapadair mucyamāno madīyair muktājālaṃ ciraparicitaṃ tyājito daivagatyā*, 93); 'the one far from you whose way is blocked by inimical fate (*dūravartī … vairiṇā vidhinā ruddhamārgaḥ*, 99) and 'cruel fate, the bringer of ends' (*krūras … kṛtāntaḥ*, 102).

And most famously *Meghadūta* 106, on the unpredictable mutabilities of life:

nanv ātmānaṃ bahu vigaṇayann ātmanā nāvalambe
tat kalyāṇi tvam api sutarāṃ mā gamaḥ kātaratvam |
kasyātyantaṃ sukham upanataṃ duḥkham ekāntato vā
nīcair gacchaty upari ca daśā cakranemikrameṇa || *Meghadūta* 106

Yes, I take care of myself, fair lady –
In many ways I look after myself.
So don't you worry too much about me!
No rule governs our miseries and joys
Once up, once down, like a chariot wheel our states!

Kālidāsa's revolving *cakranemi* (chariot wheel) of human existence reminds one of Aśvaghoṣa's *cakragati* (the motion of a wheel) in the *Saundarananda* (as it also does of the wheel of Lady Fortune in *Troilus and Criseyde*). They are metaphors of the lack of agency, of existence shaped by fate.

On the other hand, fate, though certainly the deified image of inauspiciousness and accident, the anti-god as it were in the epic and for Kālidāsa, who, as Eliot wrote in *The Mill on the Floss*, 'sweeps the stage in regal robes and makes the duller chronicler sublime', is equally pitted against other causal powers in the Indian view, including human will. All strands of causality overlap, and ultimately no answer to tragedy is found. Fate can only ostensibly be the engine of something horrific. Then we discover that actually a curse led to that tragedy. But that curse was not without rationale, for it was in retaliation to a crime perpetrated by the individual in a previous birth or in the present. And finally we realize that the crime committed was commanded by the gods – as in Kāma or Hariṇī's cases. *Vidhi*, *śāpa*, karma, *deva* – all play a part in shaping the complex, layered entity of tragedy in Kālidāsa's universe. No one in particular is responsible. For the Indians, tragedy is not a climactic punishment for humanity, who must hold its actions up to judgement like a criminal in the courtroom of existence's magisterial powers. It is inevitable in the journey of the human heart.

2

The map of melancholy: Lamentation and the philosophical pause

We see in needleworks and embroideries, it is more pleasing to have a lively work upon a sad and solemn ground, than to have a dark and melancholy work upon a lightsome ground: judge, therefore, of the pleasure of the heart by the pleasure of the eye. Certainly virtue is like precious odours, most fragrant when they are incensed, or crushed: for prosperity doth best discover vice, but adversity doth best discover virtue. Francis Bacon, Of Adversity.[1]

The joyous kāryas of the *Raghuvaṃśa* and the *Kumārasambhava*

The *Raghuvaṃśa* and the *Kumārasambhava*[2] are usually understood neither to be tragedies nor even to be slightly sad, like the contrasting and variegated embroidered cloth praised by Bacon. Both epic poems (*mahākāvyas*) are thought of as unequivocal portraits of prosperity, ending as they do with the continuity and success of the ancestral line, a cause for joy in the epic genre. The *kārya* for both, it can be said, is the drive for the attainment of a special offspring who is the harbinger of great things, which is the Fruit (*phala*) of the broader narrative design.

In the *Raghuvaṃśa*, where we have a series of heroes in what the tenth-century literary critic Bhoja regarded as a *saṃhitā* (collection),[3] one can say that the same *kārya* is collectively represented through multiple streams. We are shown the proliferation of Raghu's lineage, the unifying *kārya*, through the depiction of individual Fruits, or heirs. Most important among these are Dilīpa, Raghu, Aja, Daśaratha, Rāma, Atithi and Agnivarṇa, the narrative ending with the conception of Agnivarṇa's heir-to-be. Each individual fruiting contains its particular problems and turning points, and the whole development is an interweaving of all its parts, the single fruit of the Raghu family line in illustrious totality.[4] As argued by Dezső (2014), the *Raghuvaṃśa*, in spite of its much-commented upon unfinished sense, is thematically structured as a unity so that

> the concept of *puruṣavyasanas*, 'human vices' or 'passions' or 'addictions' is one of the organizing themes that comes into focus at key parts of the epic. Dilīpa, the first king portrayed by Kālidāsa, is free from these vices, but passionate about his kingly obligations; in the ninth canto, Daśaratha becomes absorbed in the diversion of hunting; and in the last canto, Agnivarṇa devotes his whole life to sexual gratification.[5]

In this light, the deeper *kārya* of the *Raghuvaṃśa* – the *kārya* underlying the *kārya* of heirs – would be an illustration of these rulers' attitudes towards two aims of man (*puruṣārthas*), religious piety (*dharma*) and eros (*kāma*) through the presentation of their individual obsessions.

In the *Kumārasambhava* the design of the chief plot is comparatively more straightforward. As indicated in the title, the objective is to achieve the birth of Skanda,[6] which will ensure the death of Tāraka, the demon usurping the powers of heaven or, according to another view,[7] the attraction of Śiva's heart. The development is devoted to how the *bīja* comes to fruition in the parentage of Skanda. Key to attaining the Fruit is to achieve the union of the gods Śiva and Pārvatī, prophesied to be parents to Skanda, which is celebrated in the epithalamion of the eighth canto. Nonetheless, emotionally the *kārya* is more complicated than that of the *Raghuvaṃśa*, for this is a long, delayed and difficult love in the making, made much more frustrating, for the greater part of the tale, by Śiva's utter lack of interest in Pārvatī.

Lamentation (vilāpa) and the 'tragic middle' in the *Raghuvaṃśa* and the *Kumārasambhava*

Neither narrative, in fact, proceeds to a joyous culmination without severe adversity. Here indeed is a case of Bacon's light superimposed and made all the more palpable against a dark background, of his idea that 'virtue is like precious odours, most fragrant when they are incensed, or crushed' since 'adversity doth best discover virtue'. All the various adversities within the narratives, be they to do with addiction and its effects as in the *Raghuvaṃśa* or with delayed love as in the *Kumārasambhava*, intensify and are focused into one climactic vision of reversal from which the transition into the joyful end commences. At the very middle of both narratives, the fourth Canto among the eight of the

Kumārasambhava and the eighth Canto of the nineteen in the *Raghuvaṃśa*, appear two momentous revelations of loss: the deaths of the god of love in the former and of Indumatī, the spouse of King Aja, in the latter. (One, the death of love, is indeed a literal 'incensing', wrought by the fire of Śiva's ire.)

These sudden deaths are then mourned by the respective lovers of the dead, whereby they confront 'the mystery of the cruelty of things' (Bhat 1974, p. 7). As such, their dirges (*vilāpas*) mark the point at which the supporting narratives, having left behind idylls erected, it seems to us, from a sense of filigreed perfection, sit only upon the barer edifice of a lone human voice. On the bareness of breakage, the plenitude of the second birth – as Bacon's lively work on a sad and solemn ground – depends.

The bereavement of Rati, the consort of Kāma the god of love, is shown in Canto 4 in three parts: her realization of Kāma's burning in three verses (*Kumārasambhava* 4.1–4.3), her lament in twenty-six (ibid. 4.3–4.29) and her dialogue with Spring announcing her intention to immolate herself in sixteen (ibid. 4.30–4.46). Aja's bereavement shares a similar structural division in Canto 8: the death of his wife Indumatī is shown first in ten verses (*Raghuvaṃśa* A 8.33–8.43), his lament in twenty-three verses (ibid. 8.44–8.67) and the sage's message of consolation and Aja's death in twenty-five (ibid. 8.68–8.93). The laments proper have a roughly similar numbers of verses. These are no inconsiderable explorations of death and its consequences, and they emanate unexpectedly from the centre of the two epics, holding our shocked attention for a considerable period of time during which we only hear the cry of complaint. The story, it appears to us, has now entered its winter, when nothingness, it seems, wields kingship over both action and moral development. A new reality now appears.

Purposes of the tragic middle

Both reversals are not asides but critical elements of the stories. In the *Kumārasambhava* the death makes the continuation of the *kārya* appear impossible. The only way whereby Skanda can be born is through the union of Śiva and Pārvatī. Since Śiva is the lord of asceticism, Kāma had been enlisted to stimulate passion between Pārvatī and the great ascetic god. At the failure of his project, and his incineration by Śiva, a mortified Pārvatī is carried away to her home by her father, and Śiva's single-mindedness to pursue celibacy becomes even more obdurate. So with the death of Kāma, the great erotic project is deflated, the fruit truly is lost at the end of Canto 3 and Rati's mourning in Canto 4 seems also to be the framing incantation for this disastrous turn of events.

In the *Raghuvaṃśa*, Aja's union with Indumatī is an invention by Kālidāsa, allowing him to construct in meticulous detail the vision of her death and its tragic repercussions. At her loss, Aja is so distraught that although he lives, it is only a half-life endured for the sake of his son Daśaratha, then still a boy. When Daśaratha reaches the age when he is able to take over responsibilities, Aja commits ritual suicide by drowning (preceded by preparatory fasting) in the confluence of two holy rivers, unable to continue living. Kālidāsa portrays the darkest malady of the soul, the death-wish, to be present in one of the most important kings of the Raghu line. If the various episodes in the *Raghuvaṃśa* can be thought as a single reflection on the nature of human kingship, then the episode with Aja shows an important aspect of it: human kingship is essentially fragile and impinged upon by mortality. The greatest wealth of kings, in Aja's case his conjugal love, is subject to diminishment, just as royal fortune, kingship's emblem of success, is fickle. And even the greatest king is not impervious to the consequences of grief on his soul.

In terms of broader design, the centring of estrangement and its effects in both episodes allow Kālidāsa to depict a nuanced and protracted *vimarśa* within the narrative. He thereby creates a philosophical pause within the progress of events: an obstacle causes such a pause, which in turn leads the afflicted character to psychologically confront the obstacle through intense, at times deeply philosophical, rumination. As argued in the previous chapter, the *vimarśa* generated by estrangement sets forth into budding activity a flurry of deliberations concerning the problem of agency (who is/are responsible for grief). Larger ideas behind the causality of suffering concerning fate, *karma* or the responsibility of gods are explored in the *Ajavilāpa* and also, as we shall see, in the *Rativilāpa*. In this sense, the *vimarśa* in the form of an elegiac voice creates a gnostic moment. From this pause, or in other words out of its ground, the story can grow, further renewed. If the narrative is to be seen as a metaphor for psychological growth, then this pause is a moment of maturation through a critical testing period in which the chief character faces the prospect of defeat.[8]

In particular, inasmuch as both deaths constitute a reversal for the characters of the two stories and form critical junctures impacting the narrative flow, they form something similar to Aristotelian anagnorisis, the violent thrusting forward of truth in the development of a narrative.[9] The truth Aja and Rati have to confront, as in turn do we, is the omnipresence of fatal calamity in the universe. Both episodes of confrontation with death are similarly imagined in

Raghuvaṃśa A 8.40 and in *Kumārasambhava* 4.1 as a *mohabhaṅga*, a change from ignorance to knowledge. This change is registered in the images of each confronting the corpses of their lovers, either whole, as in the case of Aja, or scorched to ashes in the case of Rati. Kālidāsa's presentation of 'the body revealed' in those two verses harmonizes with Aristotelian anagnorisis: it is a real *mohabhaṅga*, 'a breaking of delusion', for the bereaved lovers as they wake up from their swoon (to recollect Aristotle, anagnorisis is 'a change from ignorance to knowledge … [it] takes its finest form when it coincides with reversal', *Poetics*, p. 30). This awakening to knowledge is imagined as the lifting of a dark, heavy substance (*tamas*) for Aja and the removal of stupefaction (*moha*) for Rati. In Sanskrit material darkness and mental delusion can be the same thing, and this is evidently so for Kālidāsa: 'the king's darkness (*tamo*) departed by such means as fanning' (*nṛpater vyajanādibhis tamo nunude, Raghuvaṃśa* A 8.40a); 'then the wife of Kāma, the good woman, overcome by a swoon, helpless, was awoken' (*atha mohaparāyaṇā satī vivaśā kāmavadhūr vibodhitā, Kumārasambhava* 4.1). Subtler phonetic harmonies interweave the two revelations. The perfect verbal form *nunude* beginning the second quarter of *Raghuvaṃśa* 8.41 is mirrored in the adjective *vivaśā* opening the second quarter of *Kumārasambhava* 4.1 (this in fact gives the impression of a 'mock-perfect' in the reduplicated '*vi*'). The final word of those same *pāda*s in each verse is a past participle in the feminine (*saṃsthitā, Raghuvaṃśa* A 8.40b; *vibodhitā, Kumārasambhava* 4.1b).

The inclusion of the tragic permits Kālidāsa to explore, what I would like to call *alteritas*,[10] the very nature of being *anyathā* – a state of becoming not-oneself – by showing the nakedness of the soul when confronted with tragedy. By portraying Aja, who carries a portion of the divine as a dharmic king, and a celestial figure, Rati, as crippled by shock, Kālidāsa shows that in his universe cruelty affects and changes even the godlike and the gods. In this respect, Kālidāsa, even in preferring the world of the divine as subject matter, is fundamentally interested in exploring the human condition, and in doing so he can be regarded as a true humanist (in Canto 8 of the *Kumārasambhava*, the famous and infamous love scene between Śiva and Pārvatī, we are shown in the opening verses not a scene of consummately perfect lovemaking but a farce in which a bemused and awkward Śiva encounters a painfully shy and frightened virgin bride). A component of this state of *alteritas* is a sense of the universe's absurdity. At the time of their occurrence, both deaths appear absurd to Aja and Rati because of their inexplicability, and such is the most palpable effect of tragedy in human experience – when in our personal lives we encounter something tragic, we are often seized first by a queer sense of comic absurdity

('I can't believe it ... it can't be happening to me'). Rati points out the absurdity of Kāma's body, once the standard of beauty for lovers, now reduced to a pile of formless ashes. Aja points out the absurdity of the murderous ability of a flower garland that, fallen from the sky, is the cause of Indumatī's death (only Kālidāsa can invent so exquisite an instrument of death). As the audience, we partake of their shock. Kālidāsa forces on our experience a revelation of paradoxes: the absurdity of Kāma, the most beautiful of all gods, being 'bodiless' (*anaṅga*) in the *Kumārasambhava*, and the absurdity of the deathly potential of a *mṛdu vastu* (gentle object), the garland, in the *Raghuvaṃśa* A 8.45a.

In terms of metaphoric and thematic connections, the death-scenes allow Kālidāsa to explore shifting identities and role reversals. There are indications within the poems that Kālidāsa considered Aja and Indumatī to be figurative re-embodiments of Kāma and Rati. While Aja is consistently compared to Kāma and is held to be his earthly incarnation, Indumatī is paralleled in Rati. In *Raghuvaṃśa* M 6.2, Aja is likened to 'Kāma, his body restored to him by Śiva on accepting Rati's conciliations' (*rater gṛhītānunayena kāmaṃ pratyarpitasvāṅgam iveśvareṇa*). In 7.61 he is 'as beautiful as the flower-bowed god' (*kusumāstrakāntaḥ*). In 7.15, during Indumatī's courtly choosing of Aja from other suitors, Kālidāsa alludes to the idea of them being reincarnations: 'Surely these two were Rati and Kāma, for, among a hundred kings, this girl [Indumatī] went to [the one who was] only befitting of herself. Indeed the heart has knowledge of unions in previous births!' (*ratismarau nūnam imāv abhūtām rājnāṃ sahasreṣu tathā hi bālā* | *gateyam ātmapratirūpam eva mano hi janmāntarasaṅgatijñam* ||). The name Aja too resonates with Kāma's name Anaṅga, much used by Kālidāsa: *aja* means 'one with no birth' and by logical implication 'one with no body', while *anaṅga* means 'the bodiless one'. Kālidāsa is well known for creating thematic, metaphoric and structural harmonies within his works.[11] Kāma's death is metaphorically reversed in Indumatī's death. In the death of Kāma, the griever is Rati, and in reversing this configuration in the death of Indumatī, Kālidāsa symbolically creates an equilibrium in their experiences, which thereby interlock: as Aja, Kāma now experiences the grief of losing his beloved. All the experiences of Rati are reversed and replayed with Aja-Kāma as their experiencer. In this way Kālidāsa creates a tragic inversion, linking together the *Raghuvaṃśa* and the *Kumārasambhava* so that the two episodes of tragedy echo and are in unison with each other. Kāma and Rati can be thought of as the cosmic paradigms of Aja and Indumatī, and this synchronization of the tragic pattern can also be thought of as a possible motivation for the invention of the death of Indumatī and for Aja's lament in the *Raghuvaṃśa*.

Kinship between Aja's lament (Ajavilāpa) and Rati's lament (Rativilāpa)

The most evident equality between the two poems is in the sound. Both *vilāpas* are composed in the *viyoginī* metre (also called the *vaitālīyam*), comprising unequal quarters, the first and third of which are ten-syllabled while the second and fourth are eleven.[12] The impression on the ear of the entirety is of short sounds followed by a predominance of long sounds (--+ --+ -+- + | --+ +-- +-+ -+), yielding an overall rapid, rhythmic effect during enunciation: this sound-pattern evokes the gasping of crying, short breaths rapidly followed by long ones. The burst of longer sound in the form of the two heavy third and fourth syllables in the equal *pādas* replicates a longer wail within the more rapid and forceful syllables. The rhythmic quality of *viyoginī* also lends itself well to musical rhythm: in keeping time there will be found to be fourteen *mātrās* or beats (with a light syllable measuring one beat and a heavy syllable two beats) in the unequal quarters, and fifteen in the equal feet. This means that in musical composition, each verse quarter can span the sequence of a *tāla* such as the sixteen-beat *tīn tāla* from Hindustani classical music.[13] These indications allow the possibility that Kālidāsa's *vilāpas* in *viyoginī* were – or could have been – set to music and performed. This is unsurprising given the link between lamentation and music in Indian belief.

While there are doubtless many correlations that might be retrievable, below are discussed ten kinds of verses that interconnect both poems. I characterize their thematic concerns as follows:

(i) *mohabhaṅga* (the swoon broken, recognition, confrontation)
(ii) *vilāpavarṇana* (description of the lament)
(iii) *adbhutanirdeśa* (an indication of absurdity)
(iv) *utsūtratānirdeśa* (an indication of an anomaly)
(v) *dehivākya* (a statement about embodied beings)
(vi) *rahaḥsmaraṇa* and *kāmacihnāni* (a recollection of intimacy and signs of love)
(vii) *asamāptaparikarma* (a verse about an unfinished decoration)
(viii) *vācyanirdeśa* (an indication of censure)
(ix) *vidhyāropa* (attribution to fate)
(x) *maraṇecchā* (a death-wish)

These verses form the variegated and finely detailed topography of a map of melancholy, which even overlap in their artistic design: for, in the order of verses, many stanzas coincide closely. The contextual starting point for both laments is a verse about the breaking of a swoon. The description of Aja and Rati launching into their laments appears around three or four verses after this verse, an indication of absurdity five verses from the start of the lament, the verse about embodied beings after ten, the recollection of intimate moments after about seventeen, the verse about the unfinished decoration about twenty-one verses from the start of the lament. More of this kind of number-parallelism can be discerned. The laments thereby both form kindred landscapes of grief.

(i) The *mohabhaṅga* (the swoon broken)

The *Ajavilāpa* begins, on the surface, propitiously enough but descends rapidly into disaster. An ominous hint, though, to the ensuing grief is given in the comparison of a cloud of black bees surrounding the garland that crowns Nārada's lyre to collyrium-darkened tears, giving the impression that the lyre is crying.

> At a certain time, [Aja], father to a good son, roamed with his queen in the groves near the city after he had taken care of his subjects, like the companion of Śacī, the protector of the storm gods, roams in the Nandana garden. Then Nārada followed the path that turns towards the rising of the sun in order to play the *vīṇā* before the Lord who was ensconced in the holy ford Gokarṇa [in Karnataka], on the shore of the southern ocean. It is said that the swift wind stole the garland placed on top of his instrument, which was woven with flowers not from our world, as if in greed for its fragrance. The sage's instrument, covered by bees attendant on the flowers, appeared to be shedding tears sullied with collyrium, provoked by the insults of the wind. That celestial garland, surpassing the seasonal splendour of [earthly] plants with the abundant fragrance of its nectar, rested, alluringly, on the nipple of the queen's burgeoning breast. Growing agitated on seeing it partnered for a split second with her rounded breasts, she, the beloved of the best of men, like moonlight when the moon is stolen by darkness, closed her eyes. Falling, with her body cut off from its faculties, she caused also her husband to fall. Indeed the flame of a candle falls to the earth along with its oil-infusion. The birds dwelling in the lotus-pond frightened by the anguished cry of creatures surrounding the couple, wailed. (*Raghuvaṃśa* A 8.32–39)[14]

The preamble to the lament of Rati in Canto 3 of the *Kumārasambhava* also contains a sudden descent from idyllic and optimistic beginnings (for who has known Kāma to fail?). While the cries of the gods to restrain his anger resounded in heaven, a flame leapt out from Śiva's third eye burning Kāma so that nothing but ashes remained. Rati, unaware of her husband's death, fell into a deep and heavy paralysis (*Kumārasambhava* 3.72–73).

Immediately after their swoons, the corpses are revealed and the transition into the tragic is shown. The darkness that had shielded Aja and Rati fades and that brings a confrontation with truth:

nṛpater vyajanādibhis tamo nunude sā tu tathaiva saṃsthitā |
pratikāravidhānam āyuṣaḥ sati śeṣe hi phalāya kalpate || Raghuvaṃśa A 8.40

Fanning drove the king's darkness away
But she lay on the ground in that same state –
Remedies will only work
When a little life remains.

atha mohaparāyaṇā satī vivaśā kāmavadhūr vibodhitā /
vidhinā pratipādayiṣyatā navavaidhavyam asahyavedanam //
Kumārasambhava 4.1 //

Wishing to make her feel new widowhood,
Its pain intolerable, Destiny
Then roused the wife of Kāma, that good woman,
Who was helpless and in the grip of swoon.

As mentioned before, the revelation of the corpses of the beloveds precipitates the transition to the Trial and marks the commencement, following from confrontation, of stasis of external action and the ripening of internal reality.

(ii) The *vilāpavarṇana* (description of the lament)

The verses of revelation are immediately followed by images of Aja and Rati lamenting over the dead bodies of their beloveds. For Aja there remains the visible memory of his wife, her body. Kālidāsa describes her as 'the woman who was in the same state as a musical instrument that needed to be fitted with strings' (*aṅganām pratiyojitavyavallakīsamavasthām, Raghuvaṃśa* A 8.41a). With her, the stringless musical instrument, placed in his lap, he, a descendant of the Lunar dynasty, appeared 'like (*iva*) the moon at dawn (*uṣasi … candramāḥ*) as it carries a shadowy line in the shape of a deer (*bibhrad āvilāṃ mṛgarekhāṃ*)' (the moon is a symbol of the Lunar dynasty). (The scene cannot help but remind of the lineaments of Michelangelo's Pieta, with the tragic, stoic figure of Mary carrying the limp, dead body of Jesus, who like Indumatī, reborn in a glorious heaven, will be born again.) Yet the larger allusion, set off by *pratiyojitavyavallakīsamavasthām*, is of a musician before he sings, and in Aja's case, the song he will sing holding the body of his wife like a lyre is his lament.

For Rati there are only the ashes of her husband's once inestimably beautiful physical form, arranged in his shape. For a moment this tricks her into thinking that he is still alive (*Kumārasambhava* 4.3), before the realization that 'the form of the man on the ground was just the ash from the fire of the Slaying Lord's wrath' (*puruṣākṛti kṣitau harakopānalabhasma kevalam*). While there is no body for her to cling to, she rubs her husband's ashes on her breasts, closest to her heart, in an echo – even ironic given its futility – of Aja holding his wife.

For both – especially for Aja – the grief is physical:

vilalāpa sa bāṣpagadgadaṃ sahajām apy apahāya dhīratām |
abhitaptam ayo'pi mārdavaṃ bhajate kaiva kathā śarīriṣu || *Raghuvaṃśa* A 8.43

Lamented he, speechless in his grief
Forgetting his fortitude, although innate.
Iron too when heated softens and becomes pliant
What then can one say of living creatures?

atha sā punar eva vihvalā vasudhāliṅganadhūsarastanī /
vilalāpa vikīrṇamūrdhajā samaduḥkhām iva kurvatī sthalīm //
Kumārasambhava 4.4

Once again she grew disconsolate
Lamented she her breast covered in dust
Embracing fast the earth, her hair awry,
Making the woodland-beasts
It seemed just as miserable.

For Kālidāsa nature and forest animals are mirrors of human emotion: in *Raghuvaṃśa* A 8.30, the birds, like the other forest animals here, wail in empathy with Aja, and one is also reminded of the *Śakuntalā* in which forest animals such as the fawn and the baby lion at the end of the play, and plants such as the jasmine creeper and the mango tree, appear in perfect spiritual communion with vulnerable characters who are isolated from the social world.

(iii) An *adbhutanirdeśa* (indication of something absurd)

As discussed previously the opening verses of both laments, immediately after the previous introductory verses, point out absurdity and paradox:

kusumāny api gātrasaṅgamāt prabhavanty āyur apohituṃ yadi |
na bhaviṣyati hanta sādhanaṃ kim ivānyat prahariṣyato vidheḥ ||
Raghuvaṃśa A 8.44

If flowers too can kill simply by touch
Any other thing can be a weapon
Alas, it seems, for fate about to strike!

upamānam abhūd vilāsināṃ karaṇaṃ yat tava kāntimattayā /
tad idaṃ gatam īdṛśīṃ daśāṃ na vidīrye kaṭhināḥ khalu striyaḥ //
Kumārasambhava 4.5

Once the standard of beauty for lovers
In its store of loveliness your body
Is nought but ashes now, although I
Unscathed remain – women indeed are tough!

(iv) An *utsūtratānirdeśa*[15] (an indication of an anomaly)

After an indication of absurdity, both laments shift into a question about something unfair, a deviation from the appropriate (*utsūtratā*). For Aja, this question appears after a verse exploring the first among the two (in Vallabhadeva's version, three) reasons for the absurdity of the flower garland as a fatal instrument: gentleness can only by slain by gentleness, as examples in the world show (*Raghuvaṃśa* A 8.45).[16] The previous verse implies that Aja wore the fatal garland to kill himself and on seeing that he remained alive, to him an unfairness, he utters the following stanza, which posits the second reason in tragic occurrence – the will of God:

srag iyaṃ yadi jīvitāpahā hṛdaye kin nihitā na hanti mām |
viṣam apy amṛtaṃ kvacid bhaved amṛtaṃ vā viṣam īśvarecchayā ||
Raghuvaṃśa A 8.46

If even this garland can annihilate,
Placed on my neck it kills me not – oh why!
We find in some examples poison too
Behaves like nectar, while in some, nectar
Is like poison, depending on God's will. *Raghuvaṃśa* A 8.46 (see also Chapter 1, p. 85)

In the following way Rati too poses a question complaining of *utsūtratā* just after indicating the absurdity of the tragedy:

kva nu māṃ tvadadhīnajīvitāṃ vinikīrya kṣaṇabhinnasauhṛdaḥ /
nalinīṃ kṣatasetubandhano jalasaṃghāta ivāsi vidrutaḥ //
Kumārasambhava 4.6

I depended on you and you fled
Casting me aside: where have you gone

Having in a flash torn our partnership
Like a torrent rushes on breaking a dam
Throwing aside the lotus it supports?

Between the two verses, Aja's *utsūtratānirdeśa* is more a vehicle for the justification of the death (through his argument that poison behaves like nectar and vice versa according to God's will) than one expressing injustice and complaint. Rati's question is in contrast far more powerful in its expression of injustice. In this respect it seems that while Aja's habit of posing reasons to explain the tragedy is evidence of a nature quick to accept Fate, Rati's absence of justification evinces a more rebellious, forceful self-expression, which resists Fate's designs. This might partly be because of their different roles. As a king and upholder of the larger order of dharma, Aja has been trained no doubt since childhood to accept a higher force, and the idea of action 'for the sake of the greater good' has more customary hold over him. This may be less so for Rati, and hence her lament becomes, in contrast to Aja's, a more spirited expression of will as she rails and smites against the tyranny of the 'greater Good'.

Aruṇagirinātha, the fourteenth-century Keralan commentator to the *Raghuvaṃśa*, whose text we are principally following, describes the lament as 'an utterance of censure directed at oneself, at the Divine or at someone else' (*vilalāpeti | vilāpaḥ ātmanoḥ daivasyānyasya vā nindāvacanam |*). In this sense, the *utsūtratānirdeśa* verses become vehicles for articulations of free will. In a religious universe in which everything is determined, either by karma or by gods or by Aruṇagirinātha's 'someone else' (*anya*), and in which individual will is inevitably constrained, these *vilāpa*s project a vociferously independent human consciousness. In them, and in these verses of rebuke in particular, are angry voices, voices of dissent that challenge what is to be and what is said should be. As such these laments are spaces for the assertion of individualism.

(v) *dehivākya* (a statement about embodied beings)

Both laments next move onto verses containing a statement about *dehin*s, embodied beings. This statement appears in the final *pāda* of both verses.

surataśramasambhṛto mukhe dhriyate svedalavodgamo 'pi te |
atha cāstamitā tvam ātmanā dhig imāṃ dehabhṛtām asāratām ||
Raghuvaṃśa A 8.50

Even the perspiration on your face
From the labour of our love-play remains,

But you have gone together with your soul:
Shame on the mutability of creatures!

paralokanavapravāsinaḥ pratipatsye padavīm ahaṃ tava /
vidhinā jana eṣa vañcitas tvadadhīnaṃ khalu dehināṃ sukham //
Kumārasambhava 4.10

Though to the afterlife you're newly gone
I will take your path for Fate deceives
This world where pleasure is no more
Indeed all creatures' pleasure lay in you.[17]

There are other, subtler connections. The structure of the third quarters (*atha cāstamitā tvam ātmanā*, *Raghuvaṃśa* A 8.50c; *vidhinā jana eṣa vañcitas*, *Kumārasambhava* 4.10c) is the same, both being statements about the death of the beloved. In the case of Rati's lament, she implies her husband's death by saying that the world has been tricked by Fate – meaning that because of Kāma's death, the world, dependent on Kāma for its pleasures, can never find any joy and, in this sense, has been duped by Fate.[18] The first quarter of the verse in Aja's lament presents an illusion of life, what one might call a *jīvitabhrama*: the drops of sweat on Indumatī's face still fresh after their recent lovemaking give the impression to Aja that she is alive, the passive present tense *dhriyate* (remains) conveying the impression of life continuing. In reality the verse is about the newness of the death. A similar indication that the death has just occurred is created in the first quarter of the corresponding verse in Rati's *vilāpa* through her description of Kāma as a newly arrived dweller in the afterlife (*paralokanavapravāsinaḥ*). Here too one can say there is a *jīvitabhrama* through Rati's imagining death as Kāma settling into a different place.

(vi) *Rahaḥsmaraṇa* and *kāmacihnāni* (a recollection of intimacy and the signs of the beloved)

The laments contain sections recollecting the couple's secret lovemaking, what can be described as a *rahaḥsmaraṇa* (recollection of lovemaking) and other signs of the beloved (*kāmacihnāni*) that endure, though the lover does not. Kālidāsa's language of love comprises a miscellany of erotic signs and emblems that, like the ring in the *Śakuntalā*, trigger memories, which become more powerful than the reality of love itself.

In the *Raghuvaṃśa* the *rahaḥsmaraṇa* verse tells us about Indumatī's girdle (*raśanā*), a metaphor of privacy in a very literal sense as it sits next to and holds together the garments covering her genitals. The erotic identity of the belt is further implied by the fact that its jingling loops dangling low around the waist, the posterior and sexual organs, draws attention to them. No doubt given this powerful erotic indication, the *raśanā* verse became a subject of great interest in the transmission of this poem, yielding significant variants. Vallabhadeva reads,

> *ghanacārunitambagocarā raśaneyaṃ mukharā tavādhunā |*
> *gativibhramasādanīravā na śucā nānumṛteva lakṣyate || Raghuvaṃśa* V 8.59

> Now quiet that your restless walk has died
> Your jingling belt has seemed to die with you
> On your dense and pleasing buttocks through grief.[19]

Aruṇagirinātha, later than Vallabhadeva by three hundred years, reads a more puritan version:

> *iyam apratibodhaśāyinīṃ raśanā tvāṃ prathamā rahassakhī |*
> *gativibhramasādanīravā na śucā nānumṛteva lakṣyate || Raghuvaṃśa* A 8.57

> Your foremost friend in acts of lovemaking,
> Now quiet that your restless walk has died
> Your girdle appears to have died with you
> While you lie in the sleep of no waking.

What remains unchanged though is the second sentence, with its contrastive power to the first, whatever its variants. Here the immersive lovemaking of the first sentence is inverted in the tragedy of the silent belt and the implication, evoked through the personification of the belt as a friend who has killed herself in grief, of Aja's own death-wish, which will be expressed more clearly later. The double negative emphatic in force (Vallabhadeva glosses: *na na jñāyate api tu jñāyata eva*) conveys, through a secondary projection (in the form of the personified belt), Aja's own conviction in dying. Eros and death sit side by side.

These are then followed by verses that closely parallel the signs of the beloved verses in *Meghadūta* 101 in which the conceit is that of the lover's body parts left behind in aspects of nature:

> *kalam anyabhṛtāsu bhāṣitaṃ kalahaṃsīṣu madālasaṃ gatam |*
> *pṛṣatīṣu vilolam īkṣitaṃ pavanādhūtalatāsu vibhramaḥ || Raghuvaṃśa* A 8.58
> *tridivotsukayāpy avekṣya māṃ nihitāḥ satyam amī guṇās tvayā |*
> *virahe tava me guruvyathaṃ hṛdayaṃ na tv avalambituṃ kṣamāḥ ||*
> *Raghuvaṃśa* A 8.59

> Though keen on heaven, you *did* think of me

And left behind these qualities in nature:
In the female cuckoo your cooing speech,
In the female goose, your slow, drunken gait
In the spotted antelope your rolling eye
In wind-stirred vines your coquettishness.
They however fail to bear my heart
Whose hurt is powerful while you're not there.

In Rati's lament too, emblems of the natural world become tokens of the lover:

haritāruṇacārubandhanaḥ kalapuṃskokilaśabdasūcitaḥ /
vada saṃprati kasya bāṇatāṃ navacūtaprasavo gamiṣyati //
Kumārasambhava 4.14

Say – who'll hold now as arrow the fresh bud
Of mango with its pretty green-red stem
The cuckoo's cooing heralds its arrival.

alipaṅktir anekaśas tvayā guṇakṛtye dhanuṣo niyojitā /
virutaiḥ karuṇasvanair iyaṃ guruśokām anuroditīva mām //
Kumārasambhava 4.15

The row of bees you used so many times
As bowstring with their pitiful humming
Seems to weep with me filled with heavy grief.

This is followed by the 'recollection of intimacy' (*rahaḥsmaraṇa*) verse:

śirasā praṇipatya yācitāny upagūḍhāni savepathūni ca /
suratāni ca tāni te rahaḥ smara saṃsmṛtya na śāntir asti me //
Kumārasambhava 4.17

Remember I, O Love, your trembling prayers
With your head bowed down, your embraces
And our private lovemaking – and then
I lose my peace!

In the next verse, Rati describes a *kāmacihna* similar to Indumatī's belt:

racitaṃ ratipaṇḍita tvayā svayam aṅgeṣu mamedam ārtavam /
dhriyate kusumaprasādhanaṃ tava tac cāru vapur na dṛśyate //
Kumārasambhava 4.18

Passion-adept, the ornament that you
Made for my limbs with seasonal flowers
Stays, though I can't see your handsome body.

Dhriyate, 'stays', echoes *dhriyate* in *Raghuvaṃśa* A 8.50.

For Kālidāsa, a lover's personhood is relayed through 'knowledge symbols', *abhijñās*. In the *Meghadūta*, the verses of the *yakṣa*'s message which describe his city, Alakā, his conjugal home and his beloved (*Meghadūta* 73 ff), are crafted through a language of symbols: his house is characterized by, among other things, a coral tree tended by his wife, a gate and an exquisite gem-encrusted pool. These signs are called *abhijñas* by Vallabhadeva in his commentary introducing verse 73. In fact beginning with this signage for the house, the rest of the *Meghadūta* is all about a setting forth of *abhijñāḥ* for the cloud, the central part of which concerns the state (*avasthā*) of his wife in the depths of sorrow (ibid. 78–93). The real issue here is how the cloud shall recognize his lover correctly. As such love in Kālidāsa is about the process of knowing and a 'how to know', one can even say, about an epistemology (how is the cloud to know the lover?) of love. Similarly here too in both laments, the epistemology of love – its knowledge-tokens in the form of *kāmacihnas* and *rahaḥsmaraṇa* – becomes a central expression of consciousness and personhood.

(vii) *asamāptaparikarma* (a verse about an unfinished decoration)

Following on from the verses about the signs of love, the laments complain about an unfinished adornment undertaken by the lovers in play. We can recall the one in the *Ratvilāpa* from before:

vibudhair asi yasya dāruṇair asamāpte parikarmaṇi smṛtaḥ /
tam imaṃ kuru dakṣiṇetaraṃ caraṇaṃ nirmitarāgam ehi me //
Kumārasambhava 4.19

Come back to me!
On my left foot daub the final paint-marks.
While yet undone its ornamentation,
The cruel gods recollected you just then.

The verse, as argued previously, had echoes of the unfinished make-up in *Saundarananda* 6.13. The unfinished adornment of the left foot is further paralleled in the unfinished play-belt (*vikalpamekhalā*) of flowers:

tava niśvasitānuvādibhir bakulair ardhacitāṃ samaṃ mayā |
asamāpya vikalpamekhalāṃ kim idaṃ kinnarakaṇṭhi supyate ||
Raghuvaṃśa A 8.62

O melodious lady, why do you sleep

Your play-belt made of heaped flowers, that we
Had stacked together with *bakula* blooms
As fragrant as your breath, left unfinished?

This belt of flowers evokes the unfinished flower adornment (*kusumaprasādhanam*) of *Kumārasambhava* 4.18. Unfinished flowers or make-up is a symbol of unfulfilled eros – one of the central concerns of Kālidāsa, explored in full narrative form for most part through the tales of Śiva and Pārvatī and Śakuntalā and Duṣyanta. Here too it appears as a reminder of the unfinished nature of love, an image of absence and yet too of persistence.

(viii) *vācyanirdeśa* (an indication of censure)

Both poems include an indication of social censure were the respective lovers to commit suicide. The type of censure in the event of suicide differs for the two. Rati is afraid that people would rebuke her for having survived even for a moment and for not having followed her husband immediately in his death. For Aja, the censure would be the opposite – that he *did* follow his wife in death. The apprehension of such censure is outlined as the reason for their continuing to live, even though they may privately wish to die. The struggle between the individual and the social, lies at the heart of Kālidāsa's world.

pramadām anu saṃsthitaḥ śucā nṛpatiḥ sann iti vācyadarśanāt |
na cakāra śarīram agnisāt saha devyā na tu jīvitecchayā || *Raghuvaṃśa* A 8.70

'Though a king, he followed in death
A woman!' Anticipating censure
From the public of this kind, the king
Did not burn on the fire with his queen,
But never from a wish to stay alive.

Aja's fear of *vācya* is paralleled in Rati's anxieties concerning public *vacanīya* in:

madanena vinākṛtā ratiḥ kṣaṇamātraṃ kila jīviteti me /
vacanīyam idaṃ vyavasthitaṃ ramaṇa tvām anuyāmi yady api //
Kumārasambhava 4.21

O Love were I to follow you in death
Long will this censure stay regarding me –
Though separated from Kāma, Rati,
It's true, remained alive for a moment.

Note that both *vācya* and *vacanīya* are gerunds. Strictly speaking they have a future sense, meaning 'to be said', which indicates that both Rati and Aja see such censure of suicide as inevitable rather than possible.

(ix) *vidhyāropa* (attribution to Fate)

As argued in the third chapter, the *Ajavilāpa* registers Kālidāsa's concern with agency and subjective responsibility through arguments Aja engages in concerning the roles of fate, the will of God and personal responsibility. Kālidāsa's own view on agency is one of complex subjectivity, in which various agencies overlap and cannot be distinguished. When no single cause is to be found, fate is made into the single, governing tragic agent, but it remains at the same time a synecdoche of complex causation, underpinned by the self, someone else and the gods. I have discussed most of the verses in the *ajavilāpa* (*Raghuvaṃśa* A 8.38, 8.67 and 8.91) in which Aja's lament becomes a rumination on complex causality in Chapter 1, pp. 77–85, but in this context I shall mention one, leading up to Aja's lament. This verse, about Indumatī's dying, also contains an image of Aja's fall. It represents Kālidāsa's view of Tragedy as something in which more than one entity is implicated in the descent to the nadir.

vapuṣā karaṇojjhitena sā nipatantī patim apy apātayat |
nanu tailaniṣekabindunā saha dīpārcir upaiti medinīm || *Raghuvaṃśa* A 8.38

With her senseless body falling she caused
Her husband too to fall with her – 'tis true,
A candle-flame shall tumble to the earth
Taking its droplet of sustaining oil.

The verse is written differently in the older text of the *Raghuvaṃśa* read by Vallabhadeva, providing details about Aja's loss of consciousness in a compound that attunes more closely with the details provided for Rati's swoon in the *Kumārasambhava*. This verse, as argued by Goodall, preserves the original reading (comparing feminine *sā* with the neuter *-arcis*) later corrected and emended by transmitters:[20]

samam eva narādhipena sā gurusammohaviluptacetasā |
agamat saha tailabindunā navadīpārcir iva kṣites talam || *Raghuvaṃśa* V 8.39

With the king, his mind robbed by heavy swoon,
She descended to the surface of the earth,

Like a newly lit lamp-flame burning bright
Falls to the earth with its drop of oil.

The compound describing his 'consciousness robbed by a heavy swoon' (*gurusammohaviluptacetasā*) harmonizes with the description of Rati's swoon: 'by a swoon, powerful through acute shock, that removed the capabilities of her faculties' (*tīvrābhiṣaṅgaprabhavena vṛttiṃ mohena saṃstabhayatendriyāṇām*, *Kumārasambhava* 4.73ab). *Guru* (heavy) resonates with *tīvra* (powerful). The words *saṃmoha* used for Aja and *moha* for Rati even more closely accord (*tamas* is used later for Aja's swoon, hence here it does seem to be a conscious phonetic reminder of Rati's swoon). Vallabhadeva's verse, in presenting the power of Aja's *sammoha*, is in much clearer apposition with the *Rativilāpa*.

What remains unchanged in both early and late versions is the image of the flame and the oil falling in unison to the earth. This conveys the importance of the image itself for transmitters – tragic rupture sets off a chain of interrelated falls, so that to ascertain a single cause to the fall becomes nigh impossible, which remains thereby ultimately sourceless.

Similarly, the lament of Rati too is a reflection on subjectivity within the causation of grief. Fate too, as for Aja, is the most recurrent trope of complex agency in the articulation of questions about subjectivity. As such, as in the *Ajavilāpa*, here also we find a *vidhyāropa*, an attribution to fate in the causation of grief.

vidhinā kṛtam ardhavaiśasaṃ nanu māṃ kāmavadhe vimuñcatā /
anaghāpi hi saṃśrayadrume gajabhagne patanāya vallarī // Kumārasambhava 4.31 //

Sparing me when Kāma he destroyed
Truly, Fate has half destroyed my life
Because a vine will also fall though blameless
When an elephant fells the tree supporting it.

Here the final sentence about the fall resonates with the metaphor given for Indumatī falling: the oil drop (*tailaniṣekabindu*) in the *Raghuvaṃśa* and the tree (*druma*) in the *Kumārasambhava*, the supports, mutually harmonize, while the flame (*dīpārcis*) and the vine (*vallarī*) – the things supported – correlate. Moreover, the half-death (*ardhavaiśasam*) that Rati mourns appears too in Aja's complaint (*Raghuvaṃśa* A 8.46). That both Aja and Rati 'fall' physically and emotionally when their spouses 'fall' shows the closeness of their union, like that between flame and fuel.

(x) *maraṇecchā* (a death-wish)

The latter state leads to an all-consuming wish for suicide in both lamenters, held back from fruition only by a fear of public rebuke in Aja, while in the case of Rati it is actually put into action, in spite of her fear of rebuke.

tasya prasahya hṛdayaṃ kila śokaśaṅkuḥ
plakṣaprarohaḥ iva saudhatalaṃ babādhe |
prāṇāntahetum api taṃ bhiṣajām asādhyaṃ
lābhaṃ priyānugamane tvarayā sa mene || *Raghuvaṃśa* A 8.91

They say he could not bear the knife of grief
That broke his heart as a growing shoot
Of a fig tree crumbles a plastered wall.
He deemed that knife, although it brought his death,
Incurable through drugs, to be a gain
In hastening his journey to his dear.

Indeed the chapter ends with Aja committing ritual suicide:

samyagvinītam atha varmaharaṃ kumāram
ādiśya rakṣaṇavidhau vidhivat prajānām |
rogopasṛṣṭatanur durvasatiṃ mumukṣuḥ
prāyopaveśanamatir nṛpatir babhūva || *Raghuvaṃśa* A 8.92

Advising the Crown Prince who'd reach the age
To wear an armour, was suitably trained
In the lawful protection of his subjects,
The king resolved to fast until his death,
His mortal frame with ailments indisposed.
Craving freedom from his unhappy lot.

tīrthe toyavyatikarabhave jahnukanyāsarayvor
dehatyāgād amaragaṇanālekhyam āsādya sadyaḥ |
pūrvākārādhikacaturayā saṅgataḥ kāntayāsau
līlāgāreṣv aramata punar nandanābhyantareṣu || *Raghuvaṃśa* A 8.93

He freed his body in a sacred place
Where the Gaṅgā and the Sarayū meet,
Where commingled are their holy waters.
Instantly, a celestial place he gained
Among the gods. In pleasure palaces,
In the groves of Nandana he rejoiced

Again united with his love more splendid
Than her old embodiment Hariṇī.

In the *Kumārasambhava* the wish for suicide is also put into action. Between 4.32 and 4.39, Rati asks Kāma's best friend, Spring, to prepare a funeral pyre for her so that she could immolate herself.

tad idaṃ kriyatām anantaraṃ bhavatā bandhujanaprayojanam /
vidhurāṃ jvalanātisarjanān nanu māṃ prāpaya patyur antikam //
Kumārasambhava 4.32

Thus at once fulfil this obligation
To a dear friend by making wretched me
Reach my spouse by bestowing me to Fire.

She advises him about the post-mortuary rites (*Kumārasambhava* 4.33–4.38), before the celestial voice from heaven stops her with the consolation that she will be reunited with her husband after Śiva and Pārvatī are married.

In this way for Kālidāsa, suicide is not a stray wish but the only resolution to being trapped in a vortex of spiralling unanswerable questions.

The map of melancholy

Had William James, to whose idea of the second birth I am indebted, read these laments he might well have held them to be utterances of the sick soul, like Marcus Aurelius's squealing sacrificed pig. On the other hand, complaints in the Indian tradition are not merely expressions of sickness. Aruṇagirinātha understands the elegiac voice of the lamenter to cause a purificatory transformation, a *saṃskāra*. So powerful is this transformation that it affects even trees.

The verse prompting such a comment on the transformational effect of the *vilāpa* on even the botanic world is *Raghuvaṃśa* A 8.68:

vilapann iti kosalādhipaḥ karuṇārthagrathitaṃ priyāṃ prati |
akarot pṛthivīruhān api srutaśākhārasabāṣpadūṣitān ||

The King of Kosala thus singing his lament
Imbued with plaintive meaning for his dear
Made even the trees grow soiled with their tears:
Drops of sap that trickled down their branches.

Aruṇagirinātha comments:

> *yataḥ sthāvarāṇām api caitanyamayatvena darśanaśravaṇādimattayā mahābhāratādiṣu sayuktikaṃ pratipāditatvāt sukhaduḥkhānuvedhas sulabhaḥ | … api śabdas tu pṛthivāruhāṇām arvāksrotastvāt tamomayatvena virodhaṃ dyotayan vilāpasya prabalasaṃskārādhāyakatvena tatkāryakaruṇāvedhasya sarvaviṣayatāṃ dyotayati |*
>
> Since even stationery things possess consciousness, as [we are told that] they have vision, hearing etc. in such works as the *Mahābhārata,*], [their] empathy in happiness and grief [imagined by Kālidāsa] is entirely feasible (*sulabhaḥ*) because it can be demonstrated with arguments … The word 'even' (*api*), while it illuminates an incongruity in trees being depressed because of their streaming fluids, shines light on the fact that trembling in pity, the purpose of a lament, can occur in anything. This is because it is the nature of a lament to instil a powerful purificatory process (*saṃskāra*).

Aruṇagirinātha is perhaps the first to see the lament as an aesthetic ritual, a performance much like a lament we might hear in opera (I think here of Desdemona's "Willow Song" in Verdi's *Otello*), which induces a powerful transformation that is psychical, emotional, knowledge-related and located in consciousness.

In this way, the moment of the Trial in epic poetry with its roots in the confrontation with cruelty, represents, as I have said earlier, a philosophical pause, and this is to be found registered by the lament. The philosophical pause is an active, multifarious moment, a landscape of infinite variety. Through a preoccupation with the process of knowing and its elements – knowledge-tokens in the form of *kāmacihnas* and *rahaḥsmaraṇa* – Kālidāsa's laments concern an epistemology of love; through an acknowledgement of absurdity, *alteritas*; through complaints of aberrations, and dissent against fate, free will; in images of love-play, stalled and frozen as if in paintings of still life, interruption and persistence; in questions with no answers, vortex; and finally, through grieving as purification, *saṃskāra*. In all these ways, Kālidāsa's map of melancholy is a rumination of consciousness and personhood.

3

On losing and finding love: Conflict, obstacle and drama

Brutus used madness as a cloak to conceal the sword of his purpose, the dagger of his will, but the Hamlet madness is a mere mask for the hiding of weakness. In the making of fancies and jests he sees a chance of delay. He keeps playing with action as an artist plays with a theory. He makes himself the spy of his proper actions, and listening to his own words knows them to be but "words, words, words." Instead of trying to be the hero of his own history, he seeks to be the spectator of his own tragedy. He disbelieves in everything, including himself, and yet his doubt helps him not, as it comes not from scepticism, but from a divided will. De Profundis, p. 477.

Divided heroes in the *Śakuntalā* and the *Vikramorvaśīya*

Two of Kālidāsa's plays, the *Śakuntalā*[1] and the *Vikramorvaśīya*, share a similar tragic middle. In them embedded crisis is shown as the breakdown of epistemological capacity in the hero, *nāyaka*, similar to the 'divided will' Wilde sees in Hamlet. This leads to an estrangement that affects not just the 'divided' character but equally his beloved and that has ramifications in the social world of duty in which he is embedded. Clarity in perception for the two *nāyaka*s in these plays entirely collapses during the Trial. For both Duṣyanta in the *Śakuntalā* and Purūravas in the *Vikramorvaśīya*, these experiences of estrangement take the form of a sudden decline into a confusing state of not-knowing, from which they have to learn how to make sense of the world and to relearn how to live (such is exactly the challenge as many sufferers of severe mental health difficulties say they face). For Duṣyanta the return to epistemological clarity, or knowing clearly, brings with it a deeper tragedy: the painful burden of knowing what he had done and an arduous coming-to-terms with that knowledge. Let me first start with the *Śakuntalā*.

The tragic middle in the *Śakuntalā*

There is no happy ending to the *Śakuntalā*.[2] In his introduction to the edition and translation of the Kashmiri recension of the play, S. Vasudeva has pointed out the structural inversion guiding its development: 'It would be a mistake to assume … that the "Recognition of Shakúntala" concludes with a banal happy ending … We start with what might be called an *idyll*. This is reversed to *not-idyll*. *Not-idyll* is countermanded, but the end-result is not a reversal back to *idyll* … but a strange, ambivalent situation *quasi-idyll*.'[3]

The plot of the *Śakuntalā* indeed is structured by such a strange chiasmus. We begin in Act I with a description of the fortuitous meeting of the nymph's daughter Śakuntalā and King Duṣyanta, who is out on a hunt in the forest with his comic sidekick Mādhavya. Act II shows Duṣyanta's love for Śakuntalā and we learn of his opportunity to remain in the hermitage to protect the ascetic's sacrifices; in Act III, we witness their love-sickness and are informed of their intimate tryst in the groves of her father Kaṇva's hermitage, where animal and human are shown to cohabit and commune in trust and fraternity. In Act IV, we learn of the *gāndharva* marriage (performed secretly and requiring no ritual) between them, that Duṣyanta has left to return to his duties as king and that he promises to send for his new wife. Śakuntalā, lost in reverie of her departed beloved, incurs the curse of the irascible sage Durvāsas, whereby Duṣyanta forgets her. The curse can only be broken on his seeing a 'knowledge token', a signet ring given by Duṣyanta to his wife, called variously 'the jewel of recognition' (*abhijñānābharaṇa* Act IV), 'ring' or 'ring bearing the owner's name' (*aṅgulīyaka*, *nāmamudrā* Act VI), seal (*mudrā*) or '[instrument of] recognition (*ahiṇṇāṇam*/*abhijñānam* [Act VI])'.

At this point the idyll of the trustful relationship is broken by forgetfulness, and the king's loss of memory precipitates a tragic series of events, all of which concern the breakdown of knowing and how to know and those who suffer from becoming unknown. Śakuntalā loses the awareness-provoking ring on her way to the king's palace, and, as in Canto 4 of the *Kumārasambhava* (discussed in Chapter 2), the joyful reunion truly seems to have become impossible. In Act V in an arduous and embarrassing courtroom scene, Śakuntalā, pregnant with her husband's child, is repudiated publicly by him. In Act VI Duṣyanta recovers his memory when the ring of recognition is fortuitously recovered from the body of a fish. But even with the departing of 'non-knowledge' and with knowledge regained, all is not set right. The primary idyll is not restored but shattered. A period of remorse spanning six years follows, in which Duṣyanta learns to live with the knowledge of what he has done. Shamed by his repudiation of his wife, he sinks into abject despondency and withdraws from the world. He is invisibly observed at this point by the nymph Sānumatī, a friend of Śakuntalā's mother, who critically evaluates his behaviour, much as a judge would, to ascertain the veracity and depth of his grief. In Act VII, which returns us structurally to the beginning of the play, Duṣyanta, on his way home after having defeated demons, stops in the hermitage of Mārīca and Aditi, the parents of the gods, where Śakuntalā has been raising her son as a single mother for the past six years. He is reunited with her and with his child and everything once lost in the middle returns to him. The play ends joyfully – or apparently so.

The quasi-idyll Vasudeva talks about is a sense of things irrevocably changed at the end. Surely Duṣyanta having first lost his memory and then having grieved for six years on finding it, to the point where we suspect in Act VI that he even begins to go mad, was not the same man he was in the beginning? Surely Śakuntalā, accused of being a harlot by her husband, abandoned by her adoptive family and forced to raise her child on her own, even though in the shelter of Mārīca's hermitage, is not the happy innocent of the start of the play?

In the *Śakuntalā* the tragic middle begins when Duṣyanta stops knowing his wife, his past and himself, a perceptual crisis that leads inexorably to a second, now truly painful, estrangement, from his true love and from his son. These two processes of estrangement, the first from the mind leading to the second from love and duty, turn around a single pivot of knowing, which forms the central theme of the play. It is symbolized in the ring, the concrete form of correct knowledge, and also of love – the two are synonymous in the play – and its circuitous journey from the king to Śakuntalā to the fish's stomach to the fisherman and back to the king again represents the convoluted journey taken by knowledge in the play.

Moreover, the mutual resonances between the preceding and succeeding acts in the play isolate and offset the fourth act, in which the curse is uttered and the downward spiral to the courtroom repudiation is set into motion. As pointed out by Johnson,[4] developing older arguments made by Gerow,[5] each act in the *Śakuntalā* evokes another, either repeating events or inversing them, so that they are mutually interwoven. While the first and the last acts replay a pattern in which Duṣyanta enters a sage's hermitage after an expedition and encounters

Śakuntalā, the third and the fifth acts are in contrapuntal association with each other, the former showing the two romancing and thereby love-in-union, the latter revealing the two in conflict and love thwarted. Act II is where Duṣyanta and Mādhavya converse about the former's love for Śakuntalā, a pattern revisited in Act VI, in which Duṣyanta is again in conversation with the buffoon about Śakuntalā and his longing for her.

Within this intermesh, the autonomous hinge is the fourth act, which does not interlock with the others in any evident way.[6] Opening with the sage's curse, its amelioration through the intervention of Priyaṃvadā and Anasūyā, this act presents a heart-rending 'cutting of the umbilical cord'. This begins with the outing of Śakuntalā's secret marriage, her blessing by her father Kaṇva, the wedding party's preparations for the journey to the palace and her painful farewell to the comrades of her childhood idyll. The trees and forest deities grant of their own accord the auspicious adornments (*maṅgalasamālambhanam*) for the new bride (IV.5). The close link between Śakuntalā, emblem of the earth – just as is Sītā her archetype[7] – and the forest, which forms the other great love story in the play, is emphasized in the fourth act. There is a strong impression throughout of heavy, wounding loss in her departure from the green world of her childhood. This is summoned in a verse Kaṇva sings to the trees of the hermitage grove:

pātuṃ na prathamaṃ vyavasyati jalaṃ yuṣmāsv apīteṣu yā
nādatte priyamaṇḍanāpi bhavatāṃ snehena yā pallavam |
ādye vaḥ kusumaprasūtisamaye yasyā bhavaty utsavaḥ
seyaṃ yāti śakuntalā patigṛhaṃ sarvair anujñāyatām || *Śakuntalā* IV.9

To her spousal home departs Śakuntalā
Who drank not water before you had drunk
Who, though fond of ornamenting, never
Plucked your foliage since she was fond of you
For whom your first bloom marked a festival –
All consent to give her leave to depart!

As the forest trees and the hermitage divinities (*tapovanadevatāḥ*) give her leave, Śakuntalā's sentient green world, which is shown to have succoured and nourished the innocent and the good – the primal idyll with which we start the play – will vanish from view and be replaced by anti-nature, the court where the 'divided will' of the king will repudiate her. The advent of this tragic middle has the same independent, self-complete quality of the laments in the *Raghuvaṃśa* and the *Kumārasambhava*.[8] In their positioning, they form what could be detachable centres that can be experienced on their own merits.

Within the history of the interpretation of this play, this ambivalence has not gone unnoticed, but its importance nevertheless tends to be underplayed. Rāghavabhaṭṭa, commentator to the Devanāgarī *Śakuntalā*, had characterized the tragic content of the *Śakuntalā* in terms of the narrative junctures found in the field of aesthetics, seeing the fourth till the middle of the fifth acts, the point at which Śakuntalā lifts her veil as constituting the Embryo (*garbha*). He explains in his commentary that in the junctures prior to Act IV the possibility of success had been put forward, but after the curse of Durvāsas success is thwarted. Success becomes possible only after Durvāsas, placated by Śakuntalā's two friends, grants the remedy in the form of the ring of recognition.[9] From the *sandhyaṅga* (a constitutive limb of the Embryo) of 'disclosure' (*ākṣipti*), that is, the confrontation in which Śakuntalā lifts her veil and the king fails to recognize her, and the scene in Act VI, in which the king's grief is portrayed, is a manifestation of the Trial (*vimarśa*). Gerow in an analysis of Rāghavabhaṭṭa's application of the *sandhis* to the plot of *Śakuntalā* says about this part of the play:

> In the *vimarśa saṃdhi* (5.19 through act VI) "love," refined through the hostility of asceticism, becomes its very opposite: despair (love in separation); and heroism also (in a form thereto apposite), in effect, disappears; the King ceases to be a dharmic hero, withdraws from the affairs of state in utter depression and loss of identity. Śakuntalā is not present after 5.29/30 during this *saṃdhi*: her assumption to heaven serves both to express the existential bereavement of the King, and poetically, her "non-being": as complete as is the King's, though somewhat more metaphorical.[10]

Gerow sees the Trial as inverting two interrelated themes within the play, love and duty (*dharma*): 'Here both love and duty (*dharma*) have become their emotional opposites: despair and faiblesse which, curiously, are one.'[11] On the other hand, even while noticing its presence, Gerow sees the only reason for such reversal to be logical consequentiality: the bereavement in the middle is the logical consequence of previous actions; it is removed in Act VII by an undoing of the inversion:

> This is interesting in our sequence of *saṃdhis* for one reason only: it is now clear, in effect *demonstrated* (in the logic of the emotions) that love and duty have *both* disappeared *because of each other*: love because of a failure in *dharma* (both the King's and Śakuntalā's); *dharma* because of a failure in love (both the King's and Śakuntalā's). It is this certainty, now a *reciprocity* between the two emotional modes, that marks the *vimarśa* … The only thing we must *do*, is make that reciprocity positive, and the play will be over.[12]

The relation between dharma and love in turn serves to create an emotional tension between the two predominant *rasa*s in the play, *śṛṅgāra* (the erotic) and *vīra* (the heroic).[13] In addition to seeing the tragic middle as establishing structural reciprocity between love and dharma (the loss of one leading to the loss of the other, both later reinstated in the dénouement), Gerow also sees this part of the play as a way to evoke emotions connected with separation, fear, anger and the *rasa* of pity (*karuṇarasa*), 'the mode of sympathy for the lost and for great enterprises foundering'.[14] Nonetheless, Gerow's view of what happens in the *Śakuntalā*'s Trial explains *vimarśa* simply as a structural 'step' to a happy outcome (much in the vein of those interpreters criticized by Abhinavagupta, who explained the Trial as a limb to the body of the story). In doing so, he overlooks the full phenomenological implications of embedded conflict and separation. How does Duṣyanta feel during the amnesia and his later depression? How does the world process Duṣyanta's experience? How did Śakuntalā feel? How are the characters fundamentally altered? In his interpretation (following Rāghavabhaṭṭa's), the content in the middle is entirely subordinated to a formalist understanding of structural outcomes and teleological harmonization.

In contrast to Gerow, and throughout this book, I see dramatic *vimarśa*, what I call the tragic middle, in the *Śakuntalā*, and also elsewhere in Kālidāsa, as a study of consciousness that in certain cases can even stand apart as an independent work. It is true that structurally its constitutive elements in the *Śakuntalā*, the curse and the forgetfulness, serve as internal cogs in the plot-machine as it were to establish the emotional conflict between heroism-duty and eros-love, as Gerow argues (ibid., p. 570). On the other hand, when seen and experienced in its *independence* – as an articulation and exploration of human subjectivity and as an exploration of the relation of consciousness to itself, others and the world – it is much more: it is a study of a severe human crisis in knowing. This study has deep philosophical underpinnings, for it evokes, as I have argued below, the Naiyyāyika understanding of *vimarśa* as doubt (*saṃśaya/sandeha*, one of the sixteen categories of the knowledge-process). In the *Śakuntalā*, tragedy, disruptive, doubt-ridden and estranging, ensues when there is a rupture in clear awareness. From the very beginning the theme of awareness – how to know correctly and the suffering caused by not knowing correctly and by then knowing correctly – runs through the play. In what follows I shall identify the various ways whereby the thematic centring of awareness is achieved.

The knowledge of the heart

Śakuntalā's grief results from the breakdown in Duṣyanta of his ability to perceive clearly because of Durvāsas' curse. When his normal perception is occluded in this way by a fault (*doṣa*) – the gap in his memory – there are ample indications in the play that he could have relied on the deeper clearer knowledge of the heart that underlies the miasma caused by dysfunctional faculties. When direct perception and verbal testimony, the means of correct knowledge, are shown to fail in the courtroom scene, the apprehension of this inner awareness, manifesting itself in the king and Śakuntalā herself (as premonition) often in the form of the throbbing of a vein, the quivering of an eye or intense inexplicable feelings of dejá vu, could have helped the king to reclaim awareness and do what was right.

Throughout his time in darkness, this intuitive knowledge is shown to surface a number of times.

(i) At the beginning of Act V, before the debacle of the courtroom scene, in the depths of the forgetting-curse, he hears a song sung by one of his wives, Haṃṣapadikā, which metaphorically foretells, through the image of a bee having left a mango flower for a lotus, what will happen later, his rejection of Śakuntalā. On hearing the song in the background he is privately startled, as recognition stirs, and he asks himself 'why indeed on hearing such a song do I feel a powerful yearning, even without separation from a beloved?' (*kiṃ nu khalu evaṃvidhārtham ākarṇyeṣṭajanavirahād ṛte balavad utkaṇṭhito 'smi, Śakuntalā* V, p. 160). His consciousness altered by the plaintive song, he sings a verse in response (famously used in the ninth century by the literary critic Abhinavagupta in his commentary to the *Nāṭyaśāstra* to explain aesthetic experience), in which he tries to explain to himself the sense of longing when seeing a beautiful object or hearing pieces of music through the argument of past-life memories:

ramyāṇi vīkṣya madhurāṃś ca niśamya śabdān
paryutsuko bhavati yat sukhito 'pi jantuḥ |
tac cetasā smarati nūnam abodhapūrvaṃ
bhāvasthirāṇi jananāntarasauhṛdāni || *Śakuntalā* V.2

Seeing charming things, hearing honeyed notes
When even the happy hungers for more
Remembers he for sure unconsciously
Friendships from other lives abiding in his heart.

Even as he explains away the inexplicable alteration in his mood through the excuse of loves in other lives, he unconsciously interprets, as indeed we do as an audience, Haṃsadīpikā's song as an allegory that refers to him and his actions. And yet, the explanation of *janāntarasauhṛdāni*, friendships from other lives, does not console him. The feeling of distress does not leave him. Even after singing the verse the stage direction is, 'he remains in agitation' (*iti paryākulas tiṣṭhati*). Some kind of doubt (*saṃśaya*) troubles him.

We are shown that there is the potential in the king to move forward from the indeterminate (*nirvikalpa*) perception that his amnesia has thrust him into towards an awareness that grasps all particulars. The *abodhapūrvaṃ smaraṇam*, 'unconscious remembrance', discussed in *Śakuntalā* V.2 of a past experience imprinted in consciousness resonates with the idea of knowledge based on memory called *pratyabhijñā* – re-recognition, in fact, a better, truer, knowledge of something already known, through remembering something from the past – a stage of perception described in Nyāya, one of the earliest traditions of logic in India and one that was contemporaneous with Kālidāsa.

In Nyāya texts, *pratyabhijñā*, recognition, is a form of direct perception (*pratyakṣa*), 'an understanding of something predicated upon a past state. For, in the direct perception called Recognition, a previous experience, though in the past, concretely flashes forth' (*atītāvasthāvacchinnavastugrahaṇam | pratyabhijñāpratyakṣe hi atītāpi pūrvāvasthā sphuraty eva |*).[15] It is also described as 'direct perception of [knowledge] relating to a previous state penetrating [lit. plunging] into the present context' (*atītāvasthāvacchinnasya vartamānabhedāvagāhi pratyakṣam*),[16] an 'illumination of something brought near [to the faculties]' (*upanītabhānam*), 'whose nature concerns such things as the particular property of the thing brought near'; it is 'connected to experience' (*pratyabhijñāyām upanītatattādiviṣayakatvarūpam upanītabhānam ānubhāvikam iti bodhyam*);[17] 'moves towards a definitive knowledge' (*pratigatā abhijñām iti pratyabhijñā*);[18] and is 'characterized by awareness produced through a latent impression in consciousness [from a past life] activated by the senses' (*tallakṣaṇaṃ tu indriyasahakṛtasaṃskā rajanyajñānatvam*).[19] In a similar text we read: 'This pot is that very thing which I had earlier experienced – a recognition, having its origin in the senses, enabled by latent impressions produced by experiences in a previous state is such' (*sā ca yathā sa evāyaṃ ghaṭaḥ yo mayā pūrvam upalabdhaḥ ity ākārikāpūrvāvasthānubhavaja nitasaṃskārasahakṛtendriyaprabhavā pratyabhijñā*);[20] 'or for example, if someone appears directly before [one], it is a realization through connection [with a past experience] that 'This person Caitra, in front of me, is that very one!' (*yathā vā sa evāyaṃ caitraḥ iti pratisaṃdhānenābhimukhībhūte vastuni jñāna*).[21]

The return of the king's memory is in fact called something similar to *pratyabhijñā*. Sānumatī, the nymph who judges the king's penitence in Act VI, describing the now fully recovered king, calls this state *paḍiboho* in Prakrit (Skt: *pratibodhaḥ*, *Śakuntalā* Act VI, p. 220), 'awakening'. The prior knowledge of his love for Śakuntalā, abiding in his emotional memory (*bhāvasthiram*), in spite of the distortion in his mental clarity, is awoken *abodhapūrvam* (unconsciously) when he hears the song. In Kālidāsa's plays, songs, wafting from offstage, often have this capacity to trigger *pratyabhijñā* – they serve to allegorize characters and events, and offer, much in the way of the Greek chorus, an incisive comment on human nature and action. Here we associate the king with the fickle bee. In fact the bee becomes a metaphor for the king in the play and its dalliance with a flower a metaphor of his relationship with Śakuntalā. Such is also the way songs are used in the *Vikramorvaśīya*, for instance, in Act IV in which songs about the king elephant in distress mirror Purūravas's condition.

I cite three more instances in the play, in which this type of *paḍiboho*/*pratyabhijñā* – the intuitive re-awareness of the heart based on memory (*saṃskāra*) – stirs in the consciousness of the king even when he is in the grip of the curse. The point is that the king is always shown to be subconsciously aware, and such recognition is always latently active, even when superficially he is unaware.

(ii) When Śakuntalā lifts her veil in the court to show the king her face, the king doesn't recognize her – a moment an Indian scholar of *pramāṇa* (proof of knowledge) might say was the failure of *pratyakṣa*, direct perception, for some traditions such as the Mīmāṃsā, the best evidence of truth. The fact/knowledge needing validity for the king is his marriage with Śakuntalā. The only proof that Kālidāsa implies could have been valid at this point when even direct perception had failed because of amnesia, was the inner knowledge of the heart (Pkt: *hiyaya*). On the other hand, this too is *ācchādita* – veiled – in the king by the curse. However, it is not fully veiled, for, even at this point, in which the king is dense with forgetfulness, it is shown distinctly in the play that an inner knowledge shines through, for, on seeing her face, the king intuits – or re-recognizes – a prior knowledge, prompting him to say in confusion:

idam upanatam evaṃ rūpam akliṣṭakānti
prathamaparigṛhītaṃ syān na vety avyavasyan |
bhramara iva vibhāte kundam antastuṣāraṃ

na ca khalu paribhoktuṃ nāpi śaknomi hātum || *Śakuntalā* V. 19

Unable am I to love or to leave,
Vacillating if I'd previously known
This gorgeous vision thus before my eye
Whose inner resplendence is flawless.
Like am I a bee dallying at dawn
Over a jasmine bloom with gleaming dew.[22]

Perhaps heartened by this confusion in the king (this might be easily shown by the actors), Śakuntalā hesitates to reveal the signet ring which the king had given her when he left, presumably because she wants to know that the king's love, being true and firm, would not require external prompts. She does not know of the curse of forgetfulness, which her friends have kept hidden from her. When still the doubt (*āsaṅka*) in Duṣyanta is not assuaged, and she sees that he is a changed man – of 'divided will' – Śakuntalā reaches out for the symbol of knowledge that would readily correct everything. But finding it lost, she realizes that the moment of the alteration is complete. In the absence of the best proof of love, she reaches desperately to cherished memories of their courtship and wedding, to what in fact should have been the most infallible proofs of their relationship. She offers in other words verbal testimony (*śabdapramāṇa*) of the validity of their marriage. She relates an incident when he had teased her by calling her 'of the same smell/sort' (*sagandha*) as forest animals, since a young fawn would drink water from her, though he would not drink the same from him (*Śakuntalā* Act V, p. 184). The incident in fact does much to show the integrity of Śakuntalā, who is one with the forest and whom its beings naturally trust, and it shows Duṣyanta as an outsider to this world and the one to be wary of. However, even after hearing proof of an intimate past experience, which in her eyes should have served as strong evidence of their relationship, the king appears to remain doubtful. The courtroom scene thematizes the testing of truth, first through direct perception, then through testimony of prior experience, the failure of these means of testing knowledge and the triumph of doubt (Skt: *saṃśaya*, Pkt: *āsaṅka*) over the truth.

(iii) When Śakuntalā expresses her anger at his confusion and at his suspicion that she was trying to get him to raise another man's child, by calling him *anajja* (ignoble), once again the play shows the king to feel the latent knowledge of the heart to cast his action into doubt. He calls himself 'one of conflicted knowledge' (*sandigdhabuddhi*):

'Rendering me one of conflicted knowledge, her anger appears to be genuine' (*sandhigdhabuddhiṃ māṃ kurvann akaitava ivāsyāḥ kopo lakṣyate*).

He follows this with a verse in which the certainty of his doubt is shaken by the power of Śakuntalā's anger and in which we might even read a confession of his guilt:

mayy eva vismaraṇadāruṇacittavṛttau
vṛttaṃ rahaḥ praṇayam apratipadyamāne |
bhedād bhruvoḥ kuṭilayor atilohitākṣyā
bhagnaṃ śarāsanam ivātiruṣā smarasya || *Śakuntalā* V.23

The furrowed eyebrows of this red-eyed girl
Snap in ire like the bow of Kāma
Broken in fierce wrath while only I,
My thought cruel because of forgetfulness,
Refuse to believe our secret affair.

This is a strange verse. By acknowledging that he could be 'one whose thought is cruel because of forgetfulness' (*vismaraṇadāruṇacittavṛttau*) and by noticing that the full force of Śakuntalā's ire was directed solely at him and not at someone else – and therefore that there surely must be an underlying cause to this – he begins to admit the truth of their love, though the condition of being *sandigdhabuddhi* remains dominant. On the other hand, the statement also invites us to think of another possibility: did he know all along as he had in the version of the story in the *Mahābhārata* I.62–9, a possible source for Kālidāsa, that she was speaking the truth?[23] There he had feigned not knowing his wife, as he was afraid the court, unfamiliar with her, would accuse him of being a ready cuckold. Could he, by pretending to be forgetful, be testing her, to see if she was faithful to him, and had not had a child with another man after he had gone?

Again, in another moment of conflict, the king weighs his options:

mūḍhaḥ syām aham eṣā vā vaden mithyeti saṃśaye |
dāratyāgī bhavāmy aho parastrīsparśapāṃsulaḥ || *Śakuntalā* V.29

Is it that I'm mad or does she dissemble?
With doubt as this is it better to be
Someone who leaves his wife or tainted grows
By leaving his touch on another's wife?

(iv) In this confrontation, played out with the flavour of an opponent challenging a defendant in a philosophical work, there is only one valid proof for the marriage. The pre-eminence of the heart as an instrument of true knowledge is highlighted in the end of the courtroom scene: the king even with his knowledge befuddled feels his conscience tell him that he knows and trusts this woman:

kāmaṃ pratyādiṣṭāṃ smarāmi na parigrahaṃ munes tanayām |
balavat tu dūyamānaṃ pratyāyatīva māṃ hṛdayam || *Śakuntalā* V.31

I am certain I cannot remember
Marrying the sage's child as she describes,
But powerfully does my trembling heart
Appear to reassure me that she's correct.

In this way the entire story from the curse onwards is, as implied in the title itself, about the troubled, delayed unfolding of *pratyabhijñā* – the luminous recognition of something already known. Its evocation is not shown in earlier versions of the story (see *Awareness and the ring* below) in contrast to its centrality here, which suggests that an awareness of the philosophical understanding of memory-based knowledge lies just below the surface. *Pratyabhijñā* is so central to the story that the process does not end even when the king remembers in Act VI, but continues: the king is shown to grapple with the knowledge returned to him and the new person that he must confront, that is, himself.

Not knowing correctly and doubt in the *Śakuntalā*

The epistemological process, to which Kālidāsa, given his Sanskrit education, would have doubtless been exposed in his youth, is in the background of the poet's thought in its conceptualization of awareness in the play (just as, e.g. Boethius's *Consolation of Philosophy* for Chaucer's conceptualization of Time and free will in *Troilus and Criseyde*). On the other hand, Kālidāsa, the true artist, wears his learning lightly, and we shall be disappointed were we to try and find a crude exemplification of epistemological categories. Rather, the emphasis on the knowledge-process dramatized in the play holds an implicit and subtle conversation with traditions of logic and theories of knowledge prevalent in India since at least the time of Gautama's *Nyāyasūtra* (*c.* second century BCE).

The theme of the importance of true knowledge is particularly, and peculiarly, brought out in descriptions of states of doubt and forgetting.

This is gently introduced in the very beginning: Priyaṃvadā playfully accuses Śakuntalā, in the first act, of forgetting her beloved jasmine tree called

Vanajyotsnā (Radiance of the Forest) (*Śakuntalā* Act I, p. 28). Vanajyotsnā is in fact a metaphor for Śakuntalā, who retorts to Priyaṃvadā's accusation by saying that were she to truly forget the plant, she would be forgetting her own self (*tadā attāṇaṃ vi visumarissaṃ* (ibid.): The jest of the jasmine being forgotten becomes a symbolic reference to the heroine being forgotten later.

The king's forgetfulness and its consequence, doubt regarding Śakuntalā, appear much later though, in the Trial which coincides with Act V, and in fact Kālidāsa shows in this act a close relationship between tragic *vimarśa* and *saṃśaya*, 'doubt', the latter (activated by the amnesia-curse) generating the former and also structurally coming to fullness in the former. Let us revisit the verse, which registers the moment the king acknowledges he is 'one of conflicted knowledge' (*sandigdhabuddhi*):

idam upanatam evaṃ rūpam akliṣṭakānti
prathamaparigṛhitaṃ syān na vety avyavasyan |
bhramara iva vibhāte kundamantas tuṣāraṃ
na ca khalu paribhoktuṃ nāpi śaknomi hātum || *Śakuntalā* V.19

The words *vimarśa* and *saṃśaya* are used interchangeably in Nyāya, in which doubt in logical argument is called *vimarśa* (contradictory knowledge) and may arise due to five reasons:

Nyāyasūtra I.I.23:

samānānekadharmopapatteḥ vipratipatter upalabdhyanupalabdhyavyavasthātaś ca viśeṣāpekṣo vimarśaḥ saṃśayaḥ |[24]

Doubt (*saṃśaya*) is the 'contradictory apprehension about the same object' (*vimarśa*) which 'depends on the remembrance of the unique characteristic of each' (*viśeṣāpekṣā*). The [doubt] may be due to: 1) the 'apprehension of common characteristics' (*samānadharmopapatti*), 2) the 'apprehension of the unique characteristic' (*anekadharmopapatti*), 3) 'contradictory assertions about the same object' (*vipratipatti*), 4) the 'irregularity of apprehension' (*upalabdhyavavasthā*) and 5) the 'irregularity of non-apprehension' (*anupalabdhyavyavasthā*). (Gangopadhyaya 1982, pp. 32–3)

Duṣyanta's doubt in 5.19 – 'is [this beauty] someone I had first married or not?' *prathamaparigṛhītam syān na vā* – depends on a definitive characteristic (*viśeṣa*) – a clinching factor – for resolution, and one might consider the conclusive *viśeṣa* in this case to be the ring. The doubt is due to both *vipratipatti* (contradictory assertion), as a bee unable to decide whether to leave or stay in the flower that has been made more alluring through its dewdrop, and *upalabdhyavyavasthā* (lack of settlement concerning understanding).

When the curse lifts in Act VI and he remembers the truth, the Trial becomes characterized by his depressive deliberations: such thoughts of failure had been considered by Udbhaṭa to form the *vimarśa's* core nature. In expressing these thoughts Duṣyanta acknowledges that his doubt arose through a state of erroneous perception (he does not know yet about the curse). The verses in which he conflates forgetting with perceptual *saṃmoha* (literally delusion, in this context, error) are all in Act VII, the conclusion, and details clarifying the nature of that state of mind and its attendant regret are provided.

This *sammoha* is imagined as darkness:

> *smṛtibhinnatamaso diṣṭyā pramukhe sthitāsi me sumukhi |*
> *uparāgānte śaśinaḥ samupagatā rohiṇī yogam ||* *Śakuntalā* VII.22

> Through luck, Beauty, you stand before me,
> My darkness now shattered by remembrance.
> Just like the constellation Rohiṇī
> At eclipse's end is joined with the moon.

Relating this darkness (*tamas*) to error (*sammoha*), Duṣyanta asks Śakuntalā after their reconciliation:

> *sutanu hṛdayāt pratyādeśavyalīkam apaitu te*
> *kimapimanasaḥ saṃmoho me tadā balavān abhūt /*
> *prabalatamasām evaṃprāyāḥ śubheṣu hi vṛttayaḥ*
> *srajam api śirasy andhaḥ kṣiptāṃ dhunoty ahiśaṅkayā //* VII.24

> O fair-bodied lady, pluck from your heart,
> The thorn of my denial. Then, a mighty
> Error had possessed me of feeble mind.
> Often thus the deeds towards the righteous
> Of those with darkness heavy in their minds.
> For fear of snakes the blind will cast away
> Even a garland fallen on their head.

In a similar verse spoken afterwards, the king again describes his previous deed as a fault of error (*moha*):

> *mohān mayā sutanu pūrvam upekṣitas te*
> *yo baddhabindur adharaṃ paribādhamānaḥ /*
> *taṃ tāvad ākuṭilapakṣmavilagnam adya*
> *bāṣpaṃ pramṛjya vigatānuśayo bhaveyam //* *Śakuntalā* VII.25

O Fair-limbed one, in error first had I
Scorned the gathered teardrop troubling your lip
Let me be free of ruefulness today
Wiping the moisture on your curling lash.

Later, in VII.31, he uses an analogy to precisely describe the process of the alteration of the mind:

yathā gajo neti samakṣarūpe tasminn apakrāmati saṃśayaḥ syāt |
padāni dṛṣṭvā tu bhavet pratītis tathāvidho me manaso vikāraḥ ||
Śakuntalā VII.31

Is it an elephant or is it not?
Just as there may be such uncertainty
Though one may visibly be passing by,
But knowledge dawns on seeing its pug marks –
Of such a kind was my mind's alteration.

In the next verse, the sage Mārīca, in whose hermitage the reconciliation occurs, summarizes for Śakuntalā the process of the king's knowledge-loss as follows:

śāpād asi pratihatā smṛtirodharūkṣe bhartary apetatamasi prabhutā tava eva /
chāyā na mūrchati malopahataprasāde śuddhe tu darpaṇatale sulabhāvakāśā //
Śakuntalā VII.32

When hard your husband, his memory blocked,
You were scorned by him, because of the curse.
Now, when departed his mind's murkiness,
You're the one who holds power over him
When soiled a glass, reflections do not show
When clear the surface, they're easily viewed.[25]

These verses, in which the king describes the darkness of his forgetfulness as *sammoha* or *moha*, are reminiscent of descriptions of perceptual 'error' (*mithyājñāna/bhrānti*) in epistemology. In order to show the resonance of cognitive error with the process whereby Duṣyanta's perception is shown to be inaccurate, I cite below a classic example from the commentary of the Mīmāṃsā philosopher Śabara to Jaiminī's *Mīmāṃsāsūtra* (*c.* fourth century CE):

How is [the truth] to be known when a person believes to be seeing silver if s/he cognizes a silver object even when the object is mother-of-pearl? For, when there is a conjunction [of the senses and the mind] with something else [and not the actual object], a rectifying knowledge (*bādhakaṃ* … *jñānam*) arises,

> [namely] that this is not so, this is [in fact] an error in cognition (*mithyājñāna*); while the opposite scenario (*viparītam*) [correct knowledge – this is mother-of-pearl] occurs when there is a conjunction [of the eye and the mind] with that [very object].
>
> [However] how is [knowledge] understood [to be right] before the arising of a rectifying knowledge, if there is no distinction between correct and false knowledge at that very moment [of perception]? When the mind is afflicted by such things as hunger or the senses by night-blindness, etc., or external objects by minuteness, etc., then there is an error in perception. When [these things are] unimpeded, there is correct knowledge. For, the cause of knowledge is the conjunction between senses, mind and object; ... A defect internal to that [conjunction of the three] is the cause of error. For, defective knowledge is false. How is one to understand that that was an error? [It is understood] by the perception of right knowledge (*saṃpratipatti*) when the fault disappears (*doṣāpagame*). [But] how can one understand that there is defective knowledge or correct knowledge? Were we to investigate carefully and not find a fault, in the absence of proof we should understand that the knowledge is not defective. Thus, that very cognition is erroneous and not something other, where there arises a [secondary, rectifying] cognition that 'this is false' and/or the faculties involved in which are defective.[26]

The analogies in *Śakuntalā* VII.24 and VII.31 closely ally with the discussion on incorrect knowledge. Śabara discusses two steps in arriving at correct perception after making an error: (i) on seeing mother-of-pearl one thinks it is silver, an example of 'false knowledge'; (ii) a secondary, corrective knowledge, 'this is in fact mother-of-pearl not silver', arising afterwards, contradicting and overturning the false knowledge, called *bādhakajñāna* (falsifying knowledge). In fact it is only when such a secondary knowledge arises that one can label the previous knowledge, otherwise valid in Mīmāṃsā, as erroneous. The cause of the false perception is a defect in the sensory nexus, which generates direct perceptual awareness.

In *Śakuntalā* VII.24 we find an example of error that tallies with the erroneous perception of mother-of-pearl as silver: the blind man unable to tell that what hit his head is a garland thinks it is a snake and throws it away. The blind man's inability to see also coincides with perceptual *doṣa* that impedes direct perception and generates error.

Śabara's discussion of a double process of perceiving incorrectly and then rectifying oneself on careful examination aligns with the analogy of overcoming error made in *Śakuntalā* VII.31 – thinking that something is not an elephant when it actually is (*mithyājñāna*) and then, on perceiving the footprints (*padāni*), correcting oneself and arriving at a secondary knowledge (*bādhakajñāna*) – 'yes it is in fact an elephant'. The king's description of the process of forgetting Śakuntalā and then remembering her aligns with such a concept of false perception (*mithyājñāna*) – 'Śakuntalā was not my wife' – overturned later by true knowledge – 'Śakuntalā is my wife and I love her' – once he has been presented with the appropriate evidence (the ring).

In *Śakuntalā* VII.32, the mind in amnesia is compared to a mirror whose surface is dirty with dust. This resonates with the discussion about the causes of such *mithyājñāna*. The thing perceived in the mirror, which is a metaphor for *manas* (the mind), is blocked because of a *doṣa*, a flaw on the surface of the mirror – the dust. Śabara says that the thing thwarting correct knowledge might be some kind of obstructive flaw within the nexus of things involved in perception, namely, the mind, the object and the faculty of perception. He says that such things as hunger can afflict the mind, or darkness the senses, or the object being minute in its perception. These flaws (*doṣas*) can corrupt perception. When the flaw is removed (*doṣāpagame*), one arrives at clarity of perception. When that happens the connection between the mind, the object and the faculties of perception is unimpeded and valid. Only when the things involved in perception are defective, and when there is a secondary knowledge produced later correcting the flawed knowledge, is the first knowledge understood to be false. In the case of the *Śakuntalā*, this entire perceptual process leading to re-recognition, comprising the arising of flaws in perception due to the impediment of the amnesia-curse and its subsequent removal, is thus dramatized: the king's repudiation is shown as the outcome of wrong perception caused by a *doṣa*; the *doṣa* for the king is the forgetting-curse, the dust as it were, tarnishing the surface of his mind, the mirror, and this, when removed (*doṣāpagame*), leads to a secondary knowledge, the re-recognition of his true love, his son and himself. This secondary knowledge overturns and falsifies his previous error and leads to a deeper state of awareness than he had previously experienced, even prior to his amnesia. So, Duṣyanta's forgetfulness is not presented as an innate defect in character in the manner of hamartia in Greek tragedy – as it is in the *Mahābhārata* – but as an externally caused flaw obstructing the senses and occluding clear awareness. What is interesting is that in recasting Duṣyanta's forgetfulness as a perceptual error rather than a moral deficiency, Kālidāsa makes Duṣyanta's experience of *saṃmoha* analogous to mental health issues characterized by incorrect judgements in patients who are unable to cognize accurately (such as, e.g. paranoia, or obsessive-compulsive disorder).

True awareness in the play, which is self-awareness, is conflated with knowing and reclaiming love. While the tragic middle shows the disjunction between the two – in losing his memory of love, Duṣyanta also loses knowledge of himself– in Act VII Kālidāsa is concerned with re-establishing this connection through the reunion of Śakuntalā and Duṣyanta. Once this connection is made, its positive and auspicious fruit is shown in the acknowledgement of Sarvadamana as Duṣyanta's offspring and heir in the ritually sacrosanct, celestial context of Hemakūṭa, the abode of the parents of all the gods, Prajāpati and Aditi. Given the function of the final act in bringing everything together, there is a metaphoric summary as it were of the central theme at the very beginning: When this act begins the central theme of the true nature of things revealing themselves is represented in the description of the descent of the chariot. As the chariot carrying the king descends from higher to lower levels, from the celestial to the aerial, to the earthly, more and more is revealed to the king. When Mātali the charioteer and the king have descended from the path of the *parivaha* wind, one of various types of winds above cloud-level, the king sees the horses tinged by lightning and the *cātaka* birds escape through chariot wheels. Then the king sees the mountains loom up and the earth seeming to drop down and other things become clearer – the canopy of leaves, then the tree trunks, then the rivers 'whose waters were [previously] invisible because of their state of being thin (*tanubhāvanaṣṭasalilā*)' and finally the earth: everything acquires gradual manifestation (*vyaktim*) as things are brought near (*upanīta*) to the faculties, just as the play dramatizes a process of *vyakti*.[27]

But such a description also contains the idea of reality appearing otherwise, the key theme in the *Śakuntalā*: for the chariot, even when it has descended to the ground, appears to the king not to have descended because, as he remarks, it does not make contact with the earth: 'Hovering above it, its wheels are soundless, there is no dust in the front, and Mātali does not pull back the reigns' (*Śakuntalā* VII.10[28]). To see reality otherwise is the aspect of perception that is central to the play.

Awareness and the ring

The main symbol of awareness in the play is the signet ring – in William Jones's 1870 translation of the play into English the subtitle even reads 'Or, the Fatal

Ring' –the object, which on becoming lost perpetuates the tragic middle and, on being found, begins the onset of Duṣyanta's remorse, one of the critical emotional experiences of the play. Through this remorse, the journey progresses to the happy end. It thereby is the engine for the tragic in the *Śakuntalā*. Within an earlier prototype of the story of Śakuntalā and Duṣyanta in *Mahābhārata* I.62–69, the trope of the ring is not present. Duṣyanta, an ambiguous lothario, seduces Śakuntalā, fathers her child, abandons her and then in cowardice rejects her when she brings his son to his court. Upon hearing a heavenly voice asking him publicly to accept his son, he does so, explaining to Śakuntalā that he had known all along that he was the father of her son, but had wanted to avoid the censure of the court.[29] On the other hand, the ring as proof of identity is used in a story very similar to that of the *Śakuntalā* from the Buddhist *Kaṭṭhahārijātaka*.[30] A king of Benaras, Brahmadatta, meets a beautiful woman in the forest picking up sticks, and attracted to each other, their relationship grows intimate. The future Bodhisattva is conceived immediately, and on being told of the imminent birth, the king gives the woman a signet ring with the order that if the child is a boy, the woman is to bring him to his palace. When the boy is grown, the woman takes him to the palace and shows the king the ring as asked. But the king denies the boy is his. The woman flings the boy up into the air, praying for a miracle that he will stay suspended in ether if her words were true. The boy, a divine being, miraculously sits cross-legged in mid-air and sings to his father to rear him. The king is convinced and joyfully accepts mother and boy. He grows up to be King Kaṭṭhavāhana.[31]

Given that no Sanskrit translation of this story existed contemporaneous to or prior to Kālidāsa (Āryaśūra did not translate the *Kaṭṭahārijātaka*) we cannot know for certain if Kālidāsa was aware of this story or not. However it shows that a version, and possibly even more versions, of a similar story with a ring that was involved in deciding contested paternity did exist in Indian culture from at least the second century BCE (the *Vessantarajātaka*, as discussed in Chapter 1, pp. 62–4, is represented in carvings from Bharhut). Kālidāsa, possibly familiar with extant paradigms of the story, could have combined the version as recorded in the *Mahābhārata* and the Buddhist story recorded in the *Kaṭṭhahārijātaka* together. In any case, the theme of awareness, especially identity/self-awareness, the very thing signified by the ring, is something that is uniquely developed with careful detail in his interpretation. Neither earlier version, Buddhist or Brahmanical, represents the long-drawn-out process of knowing and the king's remorse on knowing, which form the central problem and conflict of Kālidāsa's reception. In other words, Kālidāsa seizes the opportunity to develop a tragic middle of psychological depth and philosophical richness that was potential but either absent or superficial in the known forms of the story circulating in the culture.

In Act VI, the dramatization of the king's remorse, the symbolism of the ring as 'awareness/identity' is even more sharply visible: the king compares himself with the ring, and the parallelism between the two is expressed in VI.13. Addressing the ring, he asks rhetorically: 'How did you, leaving that hand [Śakuntalā's], whose fingers are curved and delicate, become submerged in water?' (*kathaṃ ny taṃ bandhurakomalāṅguliṃ karaṃ vihāyāsi nimagnam ambhasi*). Immediately after this, he answers the question, positing, in self-rebuke, a homology between himself and the ring: 'Surely, something unthinking may not observe merits– why [then] did I reject my beloved!' (*acetanaṃ nāma guṇaṃ na lakṣayen mayaiva kasmād avadhīritā priyā* ||). The implied answer is that he too, like the ring, was *acetanam* (unthinking/heartless).

Perceiving reality

Act VI of the *Śakuntalā* is a crucial act, for here we find, after the preamble (*praveśaka*) showing the recovery of the ring, a presentation of the king's remorse, the real test of his love. Duṣyanta, even after recovering his memory on finding the ring, is not let off 'scot-free': he has to be emotionally tested in the way Śakuntalā was in the previous act. None of the other versions of the story show the penitence of the king – the king quickly accepts his marriage and things are righted – but this grieving, indeed, is critical for the progression of Kālidāsa's story. For, observing his remorse invisibly is an *apsaras* called Sānumatī, friend of Śakuntalā's mother, who is the judge of the king's grief, and also a representative of the audience, rejoicing at the king's deserved torment (*immassa saṃdāvena ahaṃ ramāmi*) just as the spectator does, and commenting on what transpires. She will later report all this to Śakuntalā to console her.

Sānumatī learns that the king in his grief has interdicted the customary spring festival, that he cannot sleep at night and confuses the names of his wives. Then enters the king in a disconsolate manner, and there follows a rich portrayal of his state: he has abandoned his special adornments, he wears only a single gold bracelet on his left forearm (an echo of the *yakṣa* in the *Meghadūta* whose gold bracelet slips on his forearm due to his lack of eating); his lower lip is crimson with his hot sighs, his eyes gape in stress-induced insomnia (*Śakuntalā* VI.6).

The king's grief is shown as a state of severe mental alteration. This is unbecoming, as Mādhavya later comments, for good men should be like mountains (*Śakuntalā*, p. 218), and yet for Kālidāsa it is critical that the king is thus *anyathā*. One can imagine this process of grieving in the same terms that Aruṇagirinātha describes the lament of Aja (see Chapter 2, p. 108), as a purificatory ritual burning and testing the soul, only after which largesse will return. Its traumatic intensity is shown without excisions. He acknowledges his mistake and expresses regret:

prathamaṃ sāraṅgākṣyā priyayā pratibodhyamānam api suptam |
anuśayaduḥkhāyedaṃ hṛtahṛdayaṃ samprati vibuddham || *Śakuntalā* VI.7

At first it stayed asleep though being roused
By my beloved with the deer-like eyes
But now this wicked heart awakes to grief.

He reflects on his period of forgetfulness and laments on the transitory nature of love:

svapno nu māyā nu matibhramo nu kliṣṭaṃ tu tāvat phalam eva puṇyam |
asaṃnivṛttyai tad atītaṃ ete manorathā nāma taṭaprapātāḥ || *Śakuntalā* VI.10

Whether a dream, a phantasm, a flaw
In my perception or a karmic fruit
Whose fund of merits became diminished -
Love has passed me by never to return.
My wishes moulder like a riverbank.

Being *anyathā* - inhabiting *alteritas* - grants him a new, kinder, philosophical insight into things. In this sense his remorse is ennobling.

At this moment in order to cure the 'Śakuntalā-sickness' (*sauntalāvāhi*), Mādhavya brings a painting of Śakuntalā for the king, which he gazes upon in a bower of vines. From this moment, the idea of perceiving reality, gradually developed through descriptions of the king's misery, crystallizes in a very clear way. While the king watches Śakuntalā in the painting, he is watched by Sānumati hidden on stage, and both levels of watchers comment on what they see - this becomes a metaphor of perception itself, represented in the flesh, embodied on stage before the audience.

During this moment of 'perception embodied' the king provides another metaphor of error, describing his amnesia as a mirage:

sākṣāt priyām upagatām apahāya pūrvaṃ
citrārpitāṃ punar imāṃ bahu manyamānaḥ |
srotovahāṃ pathi nikāmajalām atītya

jātaḥ sakhe praṇayavān mṛgatṛṣṇikāyām ||*Śakuntalā* VI.16

My love I first discarded when she stood
Right before my eyes, and later, when
I found her in a portrait, highly valued!
O Friend I passed a watery river
And grew infatuated with a mirage!

This verse introduces what will be concretely shown later in this act – the confusion between illusion and reality.

The implication that he is going mad is clearly manifested when he becomes so lost in loving spectatorship of the painting that he even thinks the bee hovering over her face is real, and the *vidūṣaka* makes frequent snide asides that his friend is deranged. But in actual fact, the act shows the king's clarity of perception, his *pratyabhijñā*, which appears as madness to his observers.

With Sānumatī watching eagle-eyed in secret, we find the trial scene (*vimarśa*) of Act V replayed here (the king now is on trial), and she interprets Duṣyanta's behaviour not as deranged but as perfectly appropriate. As the audience we are guided by Sānumatī's judgement, which is unwaveringly critical and fair. After the king reveals how the ring was lost – which she did not know about – a change in her originally scathing opinion is wrought: (*ado evva tavassiṇīe saundalāe adhammabhīruṇo immassa … kahaṃ via edaṃ*, *Śakuntalā* Act VI, p. 224). She continues to test his words to see if they express appropriate grief (*sarisaṃ … aṇavelavassa a*, ibid., p. 228). Then she considers the farce with the bee, seeing it as a powerful sign of his love (*ahaṃ pi dāṇiṃ avagadatthā … esī*, ibid., p. 236). The importance of this show of terrible heartache is that it leads to the observation: 'Unprecedented is this path of grief contradicting what happened and what followed' (*puvvāvaravirohī apūvvo eso virahamaggo*, *Śakuntalā* Act VI, p. 236). This in turn allows her to conclude that he is to be exonerated of his mistake (*savvahā pamajjidaṃ tue … sauntalāe*, ibid., p. 239). When she realizes that he is married to Vasumatī, the first wife, she still does not grow angry with him, because she felt he respected his first love even while attached to another (*aṇṇasaṃkantahiaao vi … eso*, ibid.).

While the king and his sidekick are spectators of the painting, which represents what has already happened (the first act, in which Śakuntalā, tormented by a bee, was spied on by the king), Sānumatī's role is as the philosopher perceiving the evidence (*pramāṇa*) at hand and making appropriate conclusions. In this way there are various types of perceiving and reality levels going on here. There is a perception of what happened in the form of the painting. There is the king perceiving the perception of what happened. There is Sānumati perceiving the king perceiving the perception of what happened. And finally we as an audience perceive these different processes of perception in totality.

A 'madman' sings and dances: The tragic middle in the *Vikramorvaśīya*

The hero who endures an experience of *alteritas* is central also to the *Vikramorvaśīya*. This short five-act play is a benign romance, but nevertheless, Act IV contains a vision of grief and mental breakdown similar to that envisaged in the *Śakuntalā*. Here, though, the heartbroken hero becomes a madman – overlapping, as argued below, with the figure of the seemingly mad poet – who sings and dances.[32]

Again the tragic middle comes without warning: in Act III the Fruit seems to have been accomplished as the secret love affair conducted between the king and the nymph behind the back of the chief queen ends with the queen's acceptance of her rival. The king wins Urvaśī, all parties are happy and this is where the play could have ended. Nevertheless, calamity unfolds in Act IV, in a scene probably invented by Kālidāsa for it is not depicted in earlier extant versions of the legend.[33] In harmony with the conception of tragic causation in Kālidāsa's works, the reversal of fortune is incurred by the character who is to some degree personally responsible for the tragedy. We learn from two friends of Urvaśī, Citralekhā and Sahajanyā, that while sojourning on Gandhamādana Mountain near the banks of the Mandākinī, Purūravas admired the daughter of a Vidyādhara, Udayavatī. Urvaśī grew irate and ran into the grove of Skanda, forbidden to women, and there she turned into a creeper. The only remedy for this is a jewel born from the red lac of the goddess Gaurī's feet. Purūravas is so anguished he roams about the grove in shock searching for Urvaśī, with no idea that a remedy exists – as in Act VI of the *Śakuntalā*, the tragic middle is an act of repentance. Purūravas, despite being a great and noble king, must show remorse for his action – the jewel does not come to his possession so readily – and the interlude where he is lost and disoriented in the wilderness shows, it seems, his penitence. On the other hand, fate's role in the bigger design is also underlined: in introducing the act, Sahajanyā says *bhavidavvadā ettha balavadī* (in this case, 'What is to be (fate), is powerful') and on hearing Urvaśī's change of form: *savvadhā ṇatthi vihiṇo alaṅghaṇīyaṃ ṇāma* (Surely, there is nothing that fate cannot transgress!, *Vikramorvaśīya* IV,

p. 88). The inclusion of this act – otherwise entirely dispensable in a play that could naturally have ended happily – can be explained by its thematic centring of several aspects already seen in other works of Kālidāsa: the heartfelt penitence of the hero, which in turn becomes a mark of his nobility; human consciousness in profound alteration; the necessity for characters to undergo a period of Keatsian 'negative capability' – 'when man is capable of being in uncertainties, Mysteries, doubts, without any irritable reaching after fact or reason';[34] and the power of fate in suddenly altering individual destinies, even those of divine beings and rulers. This act contains elements from both the *Śakuntalā* and the *Meghadūta*.

(i) The separation between the lovers will be resolved through a magical jewel (the *saṃgamamaṇi*, 'jewel of union', like the ring of the *Śakuntalā*) – and this ornament is the key to resolving the tragedy. Kālidāsa is fond of such keys in his plays, and he uses them as a game of 'lost and found'. The jewel is lost somewhere in the grove of Kumāra, where Urvaśī is transformed into a creeper, and there is little hope of Purūravas, the hero, finding either. Part of the whimsy to Kālidāsean tragedy is that the ornament, symbolic of knowledge-returned, is hidden in places where it is impossible to find, and the play, after the commencement of tragedy, is about the mission to find the key, so that union may take place and knowledge may return. Like the ring of recognition, the jewel returns in the second half of the plot, this time to bring about a critical turn of events. Just as the ring is swallowed by a fish, the jewel is carried away by a vulture. Its retrieval – when Āyus shoots the vulture (Act V) – brings with it recognition and another *saṃgama*: as the ring had returned memory for Duṣyanta, here the jewel brings recognition of Purūravas's son. The jewel is brought back to the king with a message from Āyus written on the arrow, identifying himself as Urvaśī's son. As such the jewel of union turns into a knowledge-instrument – an *abhijñānam* of identity – in the final act. Both ring and jewel are visually connected with the owner's name in the two plays. Both knowledge-instruments are in turn connected with losing and finding children. While the retrieval of the ring in the *Śakuntalā* precipitates the movement towards reunion for Duṣyanta with his family, in the *Vikramorvaśīya*, the jewel reverses this process: knowledge precipitates the separation of family, as union with Āyus is the harbinger of the end of Urvaśī's curse and her return to heaven (this though does not ultimately occur due to Indra interceding in the final act to modify the curse, enabling Urvaśī to remain on earth). In this way in both plays symbols of knowledge work in carefully deliberated ways to manoeuvre plot and unite the central theme of the process of knowledge. Knowledge in turn is intertwined with love.

(ii) This theme is evoked also in another way through gesture (*anubhāva*). The king has feelings of intuitive premonition, as in the *Śakuntalā*: in *Vikramorvaśīya* III.9 Purūravas interprets the throbbing of his right arm as consolation that he will be with Urvaśī.

(iii) Both Duṣyanta and Purūravas are so anguished by the separation that they appear mad to the outside world. Once again knowledge returned through the retrieval of an object symbolic of *pratyabhijñā* brings the cessation of madness. This retrieval brings a second Trial. The joy of reunion with Urvaśī in the grove is only temporary for Purūravas, as in the final act the jewel will reappear to threaten estrangement. For Duṣyanta finding the ring brings with it a period of profound guilt. The symbol of knowledge does not grant instant resolution but a long and laboured movement towards resolution filled with tension for the lovers.

(iv) The theme of mistaken perception (*mithyājñāna*) also appears in the *Vikramorvaśīya*: in verses IV.50–55 Purūravas thinks the river is actually Urvaśī transformed, and he even begins to feel ardour for it:

> *imāṃ navāmbukaluṣāṃ srotovahāṃ paśyatā mayā ratir upalabhyate | kutaḥ |*
> *taraṅgabhrūbhaṅgā kṣubhitavihagaśreṇiraśanā*
> *vikarṣantī phenaṃ vasanam iva saṃrambhaśithilam |*
> *padāviddhaṃ yāntī skhalitam abhisaṃdhāya bahuśo*
> *nadībhāveneyaṃ dhruvam asahanā sā pariṇitā || Vikramorvaśīya* IV.52
>
> 'While gazing on this river, muddy with fresh water, I feel desire! Why?
> Scurrying in her steps while dragging foam
> Like a raiment loosened in vexation,
> A row of bobbing ducks her girdle string,
> Undulating waves her play of eyebrows,
> This river *is* my jealous lady hexed
> Fixated on my many sins she goes!

The compound *kṣubhitavihagaśreṇiraśanā* ('with a row of bobbing ducks for her belt') recalls the Nirvindhyā River in the *Meghadūta*, described as *vīcikṣob-hastanitavihagaśreṇīkāñcīguṇāyāḥ* 'having for a girdle a row of birds crying out because of the agitation of the waves' in *Meghadūta* 28. Rivers in Kālidāsa are often imagined as attractive women, but the conceit here is not just an amorous flight of fancy but a real *bhrānti* – an error of perception.

After superimposing his beloved's qualities on the river in error, and singing the verse to the river, he sings a *kuṭilikā* in Prakrit with which he tries to conciliate his angry beloved. The farce ends only in verse IV.55 when, on seeing the river is unresponsive to his placations, he realizes that it is not Urvaśī.

(v) At the same time, there is also an indication of correct knowledge in the form of *pratyabhijñā* as in the *Śakuntalā* – on seeing the creeper, Urvaśī, transformed towards the end of the act, such *pratyabhijñā* stirs. He recognizes, correctly this time, qualities of his beloved in the vine and his search ends. In fact here, almost the same introductory dialogue used with the river is spoken:

aye kiṃ nu khalu kusumarahitām api latām imāṃ paśyatā mayā ratir upalabhyate | athavā sthāne mama mano ramate | iyaṃ hi –
tanvī meghajalārdrapallavatayā dhautādharevāśrubhiḥ
śūnyevābharaṇaiḥ svakālavirahād viśrāntapuṣpodgamā |
cintāmaunam ivāsthitā madhulihāṃ śabdair vinā lakṣyate
caṇḍī mām avadhūya pādapatitaṃ jātānutāpeva sā || Vikramorvaśīya IV.66
yāvad asyāṃ priyānukāriṇyāṃ latāyāṃ pariṣvaṅgapraṇayī bhavāmi |

Ah! While gazing on this vine, why oh why do I feel desire, even though it is without blossom? For this –
Slim vine is my angry girl remorseful
After tossing me when I fell at her feet –
In petals bedewed with droplets of rain
Her lower lip with teardrops washed appears,
She's shorn of jewels since her flowering
Has ceased because her time for fruit has ceased,
Quiet in pensiveness without humming bees. *Vikramorvaśīya* IV.52
I wish passionately to embrace this vine who resembles my beloved!

Immediately after this, greatly agitated by this inner knowledge of his love, he embraces the vine, which turns into Urvaśī. Recognition takes place in this episode too and ends the search (*anveṣaṇa*) for the beloved.

Imagination and reality are shown to blur here, as they do in the *Śakuntalā*, but in a fully creative way. Illusion – which in *Śakuntalā* VI.16, referred to as a *mṛgatṛṣṇikā*, a 'mirage', misleads and leads to suspicion, as in the example of the blind man tossing away the garland – is the very essence of the imagination here in the *Vikramorvaśīya*. Purūravas in many ways enacts the figure of the poet in a joyful play of fancy: he informs and fills other bodies and loses his sense of self in the process of investing in other natures. It is tempting to think once again of John Keats: 'A poet is continually in for – and filling some other body.. the poet has no identity' (Letter to Richard Woodhouse, 1818).[35] Imagination here empathises completely with its object of study so that self-identity becomes dissolved. Only the jewel of union reconnects the hero once again to the dissolved self. Purūravas's madman is in fact the singing poet in deepest sympathy with and immersion in his subject. Moreover, parallels with the *Meghadūta* can be seen here too. The verse about the grief-stricken vine recalls *Meghadūta* 79–80, in which the *yakṣa* describes his beloved, waiting for him in Alakā in dejection, with almost the same words and concepts: thin (*tanvī*), of little speech (*parimitakathām*) and of altered appearance (*jātām anyarūpām*), like a lotus pond afflicted by frost.

The types of mental alteration the heroes of the two plays undergo are slightly different: while Duṣyanta's amnesia is called *sammoha* or *moha* and is characterized by error and doubt in his behavior, and while his later depression (*anutāpa*) is marked by guilt, Purūravas's alteration is called an *unmāda* 'up-madness/mania' and it is a joyous intoxication, akin to that of an ecstatic fakir or, even, through the various verses he sings to flora and fauna, a singing poet whose self has merged intensely with his subject. This is the state inhabited by the *yakṣa* of the *Meghadūta*. Grief in its severity turns into a withdrawal from the world and is powerfully altered into its stark opposite – an ecstasy centred in communion with nature. Purūravas and the *yakṣa* are both child-like in their delirium (and such is their charm as characters). But it is the severity of their grief that has pushed them into behaving like children (on the other hand one might argue that while the *yakṣa* is always hopeful, Purūravas is not). As Act IV progresses, its conception of the anguished lover begins to resemble the *Meghadūta* even more closely: like the *yakṣa* speaking to the cloud, the king talks to a range of *cetana*s and *acetana*s, beings and things, the peacock, the cuckoo, the *haṃsa*, the *cakravāka* bird, the elephant, a mountain, a river and an antelope. In this respect, one can argue that Purūravas's grief is more powerful than Duṣyanta's. Duṣyanta withdraws from the world – he neglects attending the court for instance – but he does not alter to such a degree. Purūravas becomes in his anguish the opposite of what the heroic *nāyaka* should be – there is a Dionysian essence and flamboyance to his personality in Act IV that Duṣyanta never has. On the other hand the tragic middles in both plays are concerned with the anti-hero, be it the anti-hero as the 'hero in conflict' – the *sandigdhabuddhi* – in the *Śakuntalā* or the anti-hero as the 'madman' – the *unmāda* – in the *Vikramorvaśīya*: embedded in these stories of inevitable union and harmonization are stark inversions and disruptions, not just to plot but to the hero himself.

This though is an inversion that is entertaining and celebratory in spectacle. Setting apart the act from the rest of the play is its musical nature (hinted at in the very beginning with the episode of Bharata's curse [see Chapter 1, pp. 60–1]). The actor playing the king is constantly in motion, often collapsing in a swoon, and in full flight of song on stage, and the entire act can be seen as an extended lament interspersed with dancing. From time to time, songs about a distraught king elephant float from backstage that echo what is transpiring onstage and provide the act with a harmony, creating a parallel sonic narrative. The king elephant looking for his beloved is a continuous metaphor for Purūravas, threading the entire act. Within the tragic middle, they form triggers of *pratyabhijñā* for the audience, who recognizes in the elephant the king's own state. A number of terms for dancing or song appear here (it would be interesting to see how, after a careful understanding of what the musical terms denote, the act when set to music and choreography might appear). Purūravas's madness is a tour de force in performance – traipsing about the stage, falling into fainting fits, singing beautifully and behaving comically, he momentarily becomes the *vidūṣaka*, the buffoon for the audience.

There are other links with the *Śakuntalā*. Urvaśī and Purūravas meet in Act II, which is a condensation of what happens in the third act of the *Śakuntalā*. While she watches in hiding, Purūravas discusses with the *vidūṣaka* his love for her. Urvaśī then writes him a love letter and when he has read it, she reveals herself to him. In much the same way, in Act III of the *Śakuntalā*, Duṣyanta, like Urvaśī, had secretly witnessed Śakuntalā's declaration of love for him to her friends, and after she has composed a letter incised on a lotus leaf declaring her love, he reveals himself to her. Act V, the final act in the *Vikromorvaśīya*, presents the loss of the 'jewel of union', when a vulture flies away with it. It returns with an arrow bearing the name of Purūravas's son Āyus, whom Urvaśī had hidden from the king, as the sight of his son would lead to the end of her curse on earth and would bring about her separation from him. This act contains a union between father and son, king and heir. The sudden loss and return of the topos of union and the meeting of Purūravas with his son closely aligns with the final movement of the *Śakuntalā*, in which the ring had been lost by sheer accident and then returned by accident too, leading to the meeting of the father and son in the final act.

The verses sung by the king contain many of the elements that form the topography of the map of melancholy in the *vilāpa*s of the *Raghuvaṃśa* and the *Kumārasambhava* (see Chapter 2, pp. 87–108 for a discussion of the ten elements of the map of melancholy). Verse 4.10, and its introductory comment, in attributing causality to fate and pointing out fate's absurdity, contains both a *vidhyāropa* and an *adbhutanirdeśa*:

aye parāvṛttabhāgadheyānāṃ duḥkhaṃ duḥkhānubandhi | *kutaḥ* -
ayam ekapade tayā viyogaḥ
priyayā copanataḥ suduḥsaho me |
navavāridharodayād ahobhir
bhavitavyaṃ ca nirātapatvaramyaiḥ || *Vikramorvaśīya* IV.10

'Alas, for those whose fortune (*bhāgadheya*) is adverse, grief follows upon
grief! Why?
At one and the same time here come -
This parting from my beloved
That I find intolerable
And days that will turn delightful
With no heat, now new clouds arrive.

Verse 4.15, in which Purūravas mistakes the red buds of the banana flower for Urvaśī's eyes, contains the topos of the lover seeing signs of the beloved (*kāmacihnas*) in nature:

āraktarājibhir iyaṃ kusumair navakandalī salilagarbhaiḥ |
kopād antarbāṣpe smarayati māṃ locane tasyāḥ || *Vikramorvaśīya* IV.15

Its blossoms streaked with red,
Their centres full of water,
This young banana tree brings to my mind
Her eyes tearful in anger.

The theme of 'how is my lover to be discovered' and the indication of *abhijñas* – knowledge tokens that track her path – also appear. In IV.17 Purūravas mistakes a glade with *indragopa* insects to be the green garment covering her breasts, which recalls both of the *Meghadūta*'s signs for knowing the lover provided by the *yakṣa* to the cloud (see Chapter 4, pp. 154–5), and the *Śakuntalā*'s mistaken perception:

upalabdham upalakṣaṇaṃ yena tasyāḥ kopanāyā mārgo'numīyate |
hṛtoṣṭharāgair nayanodabindubhir
nimagnanābher nipatadbhir aṅkitam |
cyutaṃ ruṣā bhinnagater asaṃśayaṃ
śukodaraśyāmam idaṃ stanāṃśukam || *Vikramorvaśīya* IV.17

I've got the signs! Through these I can infer the path she took in anger!
Here – the raiment on her breast as green
As a parrot's belly that she'd flung down
Surely in anger when it slowed her gait,
Stained with tears that smudged her lips' ruddiness,
Shed by my lady with the deep set-navel.

When he bent down to pick up the scarf, he noticed that it was grass covered with *indragopa* insects: Imagination and reality blurred, one of the themes of the *Meghadūta* too, finds evocation here. The epistemology of love – the importance of finding and knowing the lover correctly – is central to resolving the 'divided will' in the hero in both the *Śakuntalā* and the *Vikramorvaśīya*, but its way is fraught with reversal and delay.

These thematic concerns, found also in other grieving voices in Kālidāsa's works, interconnect the sung verses dispersed in the act into a single lamentation. Their presence indicates that the process of grieving is constructed in a manner similar to that of the mourners in the *Raghuvaṃśa* and the *Kumārasambhava* (see Chapter 2, pp. 99–102). Adding greater depth and detail to this portrayal of grief is the king's physical transfiguration. He faints, weeps, babbles incoherently (at one point he keeps repeating 'she is angry') and sits on his knees. While he is in the throes of misery, the forest shelters him. This bond between man in grief and nature recalls *Madrīvilāpa*, where Madrī too, torn apart by woe, runs out into the forest in search of her children (see Chapter 1, pp. 64–7). In fact, the image of Purūravas going mad in the forest cannot but remind us forcibly of the *Madrivilāpa* section of the *Viśvantarajātaka*, and a close analogy between the two grieving figures lost in the wilderness can be discerned. Purūravas could well be the dramatized male counterpart to Madrī. Except here Purūravas entertains us. His sorrow is mitigated – undercut – by the buffoon's facade: because his sorrow is also performance. Madrī only mourns. Her grief, given its privacy, its a-theatricality, is never undercut by paradox but remains true to its very essence.

4

The altered heart: Anguish, entreaty and lyric

I am in love with moistness.

George Eliot, *The Mill on the Floss*, p. 10

The *Meghadūta* as a lament

Kālidāsa's *Meghadūta*,[1] the *Cloud Messenger*, in spite of its great fame[2] contains a trope that may have been found problematic by the great literary critic Bhāmaha, who flourished prior to 700 CE.[3] The respected author of the influential *Kāvyālaṅkāra*, a treatise on literary tropes, finds the use of such insentient things as a cloud, winds, the moon, bees, *hārīta* and *cakravāka* birds and parrots as messengers to exemplify 'unreasonableness' (*ayuktimat*), a literary defect (*doṣa*) aspiring poets ought to avoid. For, how could inarticulate, inaudible things moving about in a remote place possibly carry messages to others? (*Kāvyālaṅkāra* 1.42–3).[4] Due to its use of this illogicality the *Meghadūta* may be considered faulty. On the other hand, Bhāmaha provides an important caveat in verse 1.44, which says that the topos of an insentient messenger is perfectly appropriate for learned poets to use if the speaker of the message behaves like a madman out of intense longing for his beloved.[5] In other words, the madness in the hero adds passion and lyricism to the composition when its source is the power of his love for someone else.

Kālidāsa himself implies that the *yakṣa*, asking the cloud to carry his message, acts insane but he argues that it is in fact the fire of his grief in separation that makes him behave so:

dhūmajyotiḥsalilamarutāṃ saṃnipātaḥ kva meghaḥ
saṃdeśārthāḥ kva paṭukaraṇaiḥ prāṇibhiḥ prāpaṇīyāḥ |
ity autsukyād aparigaṇayan guhyakaṃs taṃ yayāce
kāmārtā hi praṇayakṛpaṇāś cetanācetaneṣu || *Meghadūta* 5

Vast the gulf between a cloud, a mass
Of smoke, light, wind and water, and the content
Of messages, conveyed by beings alone
By faculties of sense! Unmindful through
His longing the *yakṣa* made his plea to the cloud.
For love-sick souls wretchedly solicit
The living and the lifeless in their grief.[6]

Vallabhadeva, apparently keeping Bhāmaha's caveat in mind, further emphasizes that love is to be blamed here, and not the *nāyaka* himself for his aberrant behaviour, thus removing any hint of there being a flaw in the composition: 'How then did he [the *yakṣa*] not realize this [the gulf between them]? To explain this he [Kālidāsa] says: "It is because those who are 'tortured by love', afflicted by the net of passion, become 'wretched in soliciting' with entreaties, etc. 'the sentient and insentient'", such as lions and trees. For, they are incapable of discriminating an object [worthy of conversing with] from one that is not – through such an implication, the poet obviates a flaw [of illogicality] on his part' (*kathaṃ tarhy etad asau na vimṛṣtavān ity āha | yasmād ye kāmārtā madanavāgurāpīḍitās te cetanācetaneṣu siṃhapādapādiṣu praṇayakṛpaṇāḥ prārthanādīnā bhavanti | na hi te viṣayam aviṣayaṃ vā vivektuṃ samarthā iti bhaṅgyā kaviḥ svadoṣaṃ nirasyati* |).

In addition to *Meghadūta* 5d, one may consider *Meghadūta* 109c, in the final verse of the *yakṣa*'s message, in which, circularly tying up his argument with the beginning, the *yakṣa* reiterates that the reason for his message is the depth of his despair:

snehān āhuḥ kim api virahahrāsinas te hy abhogād |

Indeed, those who are emaciated with grief declare their affections however they can for they are without enjoyment.

Moreover, given the existence of a Pāli prototype (discussed later), and examples in the *Rāmāyaṇa* and the *Mahābhārata*, there seem to have been other earlier poems of the *Meghadūta*'s ilk,[7] in which non-humans associated with love are asked to be carriers of love poems, usually recited by a male lover in distress out of concern for the loved one. The wind, the moon, a bee or various types of beautiful birds may have been entreated by the separated lover to be a messenger in these other types of poems prevalent in a period before Kālidāsa, when the scope of amorous expression, experiential states and their imaginative exploration seem to have been remarkably rich and free. The *Meghadūta* is the earliest known self-standing example in Sanskrit of this genre later called the *sandeśakāvya* or *dūtakāvya* (messenger poetry).

Certainly, Kālidāsa, though at pains it seems to justify the *yakṣa*'s apparent insanity, appears to have been fond of the trope of the male lover talking to nature like a madman. Usually the context is separation in love. Such is evidenced in *Vikramorvaśīya* Act IV (discussed in a previous chapter), in which the aggrieved *nāyaka*, separated from his beloved, is in poetic conversation with the woodlands, soliciting forest creatures, clouds, mountains and rivers to tell him the whereabouts of Urvaśī, inhabiting a disconcerting, and even somewhat comical, state of *alteritas*. The anthropomorphizing of nature bears an illustrious pedigree in Indian history. Speaking animals at least, if not clouds, were popular in Indian literature for a very long period, appearing in the Buddhist stories of the past lives of the Buddha – in which he is frequently an animal – and most famously (in as much as it is widely translated) in the *Pañcatantra* (*c.*300 CE)[8] in which they predominate, illustrating topics of governance. It seems that the love-crazed speaker declaiming to the natural world had waned in popularity by the time of Bhāmaha – and even by Kālidāsa's time – at which point stricter expectations of amorous psychology prevailed, prompting Kālidāsa to point out the faulty perception of his protagonist in verse 5 and Bhāmaha to caution against the use of this topos, excepting in contexts of love-in-separation. The hint of criticism that madness was unsuitable, even emasculating, for the hero, implicit in both Kālidāsa and Bhāmaha, continued well into the modern period. De summarizes such opinions (ultimately rejecting them) – 'It has been urged that the temporary character of a very brief separation and the absolute certainty of reunion make the display of grief unmanly and its pathos unreal' (De 1957, p. xxxi).

In light of this early history that regards tragic separation as the exception to what is otherwise a fault I would like to see the *yakṣa*, as Vallabhadeva did, first and foremost as a tragic character, not as someone who is *ayuktimat* 'illogical', and the psyche of dejection to form the true wellspring of his message. Adopting Bhāmaha and Kālidāsa's own rationale, Vallabhadeva argues that the *yakṣa*'s unreasonableness is the very evidence of the power of his grief. Grief through love-in-separation is a central emotional concern of the *sandeśakāvya* genre.[9] Such is registered, as argued by Warder (1972, III, p. 146), even by the *Meghadūta*'s metre *mandākrāntā*: 'a long drawn out, nostalgic rhythm of 17 syllables to the line, perfectly suited to the emotion expressed by the *yakṣa* in his isolation. Each line begins with four long syllables, followed by five shorts leading into three successive syncopations. The first four syllables (which are followed by a caesura) suggest the feeling of longing or yearning, the series of shorts intensify this by suggesting an outward rush of anxious feeling and the syncopations heighten it further with their uncertainty ending in suspense.'

Following Kālidāsa's own rationale in this crucial verse, 5d, and in 109c, and in harmony with Vallabhadeva, I would like to interpret the *Meghadūta* as a lament: an entreaty (*yācñā*) of a *kāmārta*, a being tortured by love. It is, along with perhaps the other poems in this genre, a study of the psychology of grief in love, rather than a portrayal of illogicality. That the genre of this type of message-poem, delivered to animals or to things to console a separated lover, was called a *vilāpa* even in Pāli literature further strengthens the argument (see the discussion of the *Kāmavilāpajātaka* above). The speaker is so tortured in love, and the implication is also that he is so isolated, that he solicits anyone and anything to transport his message to his far-off beloved. The *Meghadūta* is a poem born out of desperation and loneliness.[10] The point is not *unmāda*, insanity – as Mallīnātha had felt (*tatrāpy unmādāvasthā*) – for any person suffering from the severe loss of a loved one might be made to feel insane. The point is the delicate nature of loving human hearts that can so easily be tipped by circumstances into abject, and unhealthy (*asvastha*) melancholy, but which, with an endurance also natural, can rise back to equanimity, as we see in the case of the *yakṣa* at the end of his message.

What sets the *Meghadūta* apart though from many other laments is its hopefulness, a frail yet resilient shoot breaking forth from desperation toward the prospect of union. In this regard unlike other *vilāpa*s, such as the *Ajavilāpa* and the *Rativilāpa*, the *Meghadūta* is not a complaint. Its tone, instead of being one of dissatisfaction with things as they are, is characterized by an imaginative projection of what might be (most passionately exemplified in the *aṅgenāṅgaṃ* verse). As argued by Wezler, interpreting the meaning of a genre Vallabhadeva calls *kelikāvya*, the poem is an exercise in *keli*: 'a term used to denote a particular phase in the development of love for another person, viz. that characterized by a constant dwelling of one's imagination on the beloved, the imaginative "play" with her or him' (Wezler 1998, in *Meghadūta* V, p. xii). Moreover, the psychological-poetic device used to engage in this *keli* is a substitution of identity: the lamenting voice in the imaginative play of union with the beloved substitutes itself with something else. In personifying the cloud, the *yakṣa* speaks vicariously of himself – such that cloud and *yakṣa* are really one and the same character. Through the identity of the cloud, the poet engages in an act of *upādāna*, taking for himself what he cannot really have: for instance, when the cloud is described to cavort and flirt with rivers personified as enchanting women, we find a substitution – a metaphor – of the *yakṣa*'s own desire for sexual union with his wife. The pained ardour of the speaker infuses everything he imagines the cloud will see with signs of separation that are the externalized forms of his own anguished consciousness.

The onward advancement of this entreaty characterized by the play of metaphoric substitution seems to me to encapsulate the stages of a psychological process of healing – the working-through of human consciousness coming to terms with grief through intense imaginative focus on seeking out and confronting the absent lover. As such, I read it almost as a diary of the journey of a human mind encountering, through words intended only for a special listener, a reality it cannot face alone. The process comes to an end with acceptance – unlike the ceaseless *cakranemi* of grief in Loṣṭaka's *Dīnākrandanastotra*, here grief arrives at a resolution.

The *Meghadūta* as the tragic middle made independent

The *Meghadūta* suggests a resolution through hints within the broader story of which it is a part. In verse 1, for example, where the subject of the poem is introduced in what is known as a *vastunirdeśa* (an indication of the topic) we learn of the background of the story, that the *yakṣa* had been cursed by his master Kubera because he had grown intoxicated with his own authority and banished as a result to Citrakūṭa, the place of Sītā and Rāma's year-long banishment from Ayodhyā. Verses 2–5 describe the *yakṣa*'s state of alteration through grief: we learn that he has spent a few months at Citrakūṭa (Vallabhadeva glosses this as seven or eight months) and has grown so thin in his grief that his armlet keeps slipping down. On the final day of Āṣāḍha he encounters a cloud that, like a playful elephant, bumps up and rolls against the mountain peak. He meditates upon the cloud and then addresses his message to him, and the rationale for this is provided in 5d. In verse 107, we learn that the *yakṣa*'s curse will end 'when Viṣṇu has arisen from his sleep' (Vallabhadeva says this is the bright twelfth day of Kārttika) and that there are just four months left till reunion. Describing the broader lineaments of a framing plot in a few brief strokes was a device that was recognized as part of the modus operandi of narrative poetry: in *Vakroktijīvita* 4.18, Kuntaka says that the *Kirātārjunīya* indicates the plot of the entire *Mahābhārata* in three verses: one describing the spy's message to Yudhiṣṭhira – marking the beginning of the great war, one telling of Draupadī's anger – the causal force behind the battle, and, lastly, one narrating Vyāsa's prophecy about the eventual victory (*Kirātārjunīya* 1.3ab, 1.46cd and 3.22cd), even though Bhāravi's work begins in medias res.[11] In the same way, one can argue that those six verses in the *Meghadūta* (1–5, 107) clarify the entire contextual setting despite the *Meghadūta* beginning in the middle of things. In this way, though the *Meghadūta* may seem free of plot – pure lyric as it were – it nevertheless evokes with clarity the flavour of a narrative (and the journey of the cloud further consolidates this impression with its progressive development of a *yātrā*). As such, the *yakṣa*'s message, it is implied, comes in the middle of a bigger story. One may even imagine it to form the moment of *vimarśa*, were the *Meghadūta* showcased in cantos as a *mahākāvya*, or dramatized in scenes on stage. In fact one can argue further that so interested is Kālidāsa in the tragic middle in the *Meghadūta*, that the other stages of plot, though intimated, appeared to him to be extraneous and that they are subsumed within a deeper, richer and lengthier exploration of character and psychology. The *vilāpa* of the *yakṣa* is independent but it could well form the middle section of a larger elaboration of the five junctures. In the *Meghadūta* the concern of narrative is completely inward – external reality has become compressed into the reality of the *yakṣa*'s inner state, which is as dynamic, as lively, as energetic and as colourful as any external progress of action. One can never complain of being bored by the *Meghadūta*: the *yakṣa*'s imagination presents an adventure traversing a colourful canvas of lands and a cornucopia of novelties. There is always a 'what happened next' to the cloud. The quality predominating the *Meghadūta* is that of fine detailing, of worlds leading to other worlds. In this poem the interior universe of the mind, what is hidden, replaces the great *mahākāvya* where, as in the Victorian novel of Eliot, objective reality wields supremacy.

My arguments concerning the quasi-*mahākāvya* quality to the *Meghadūta* must be read within the framework of historical debates concerning the *Meghadūta*'s ambiguity of genre. One camp, to which Mallīnātha, one of the commentators of the *Meghadūta* belonged, following Daṇḍin seemed to have considered it a *mahākāvya* (*atra kāvye tatra tatra naganagarārṇavādivarṇanā saṃbhavān mahākāvyatvam* | *Meghadūta* M, p. 2), while another, exemplified by the critic Viśvanātha, considered it a *khaṇḍakāvya* a fragmentary poem (*idaṃ ca khaṇḍakāvyam iti darpaṇakṛdādayaḥ* | *Daṇḍimatānusāriṇas tu mahākāvyam eva manyante* | (*Meghadūta* P, p. 1). An even earlier school, exemplified by Vallabhadeva, rejected both and considered it something called a *kelikāvya*, interpreted by Wezler as an erotic fantasy. All these genres can be easily applied to the poem. What is clear though is that the narrative element was noticed by most of these critics as a stand-out feature of the poem, and even if envisaged as an exercise in amorous *keli*, there is still the sense of dynamism and storytelling in the fantasy involving the beloved. My understanding of the *Meghadūta*, in a further interpretation of *kelikāvya*, is as a 'mock-epic', a genre in which, it seems, while hints were made about a framing plot, the reflective and the lyrical, subjectivity and personhood, found greater expression than what was allowed in either drama or a poem in cantos in which formulaic plot advancement overshadowed character study. A comparison may be found, for example, in Chaucer's dream poem *The House of Fame*, a fantasy about a journey and an encounter. It may be conjectured that Kālidāsa took as his originating germ the well-known idea of a lament comprising the trope of the message found in earlier literary examples in India and turned it into a trompe-l'oeil of an epic poem, using the formal grandeur of the latter to exploit the psychological possibilities afforded by the tragic core of the original to their fullest.

'Internally liquid': Cloud and *yakṣa* as one

In their liquid-like mutability, subject to the waxing and waning of quintessences – emotions for the *yakṣa*, water for the cloud – the *yakṣa*'s psyche and the changeling cloud, once an elephant (2, 51, 78), a touchstone with an oily streak (37), a staircase for Gaurī to descend (60) or a staring eye (59), become mutual mirrors for each other. The overlap between the cloud and the *yakṣa* is thematically registered in a number of equivalent compounds, mostly permutations around the word *antas*, 'inside', with another word corresponding to a fluid essence. These thematically connect the poem and are: *antarbāṣpa* (tearful), referring to the *yakṣa* in verse 3, *antaḥsāram* (with internal essence) describing the cloud in verse 20, *rasābhyantara* (internally fluid) referring to the cloud in verse 28, *antastoya* (internally fluid) again referring to the cloud in verse 64 and *ārdrāntarātmā* (one whose nature is moist [with compassion]), referring to any compassionate person in verse 91. A congruent formulation *upacitarasāḥ* (they in whom fluid/emotion is abundant) appears right at the very end of the message in verse 109, whereby the *yakṣa* alludes to himself through an axiom about all separated lovers. These words emphasize that just as the important thing about the cloud is not its appearance but its inner nature, so the richness of the *yakṣa* lies inward, in his emotional landscape.

In the first verse where the *yakṣa* is described consanguineously with the cloud, confronting the cloud and overcome in grief, he is said to have become one of altered heart. The compound is first used here in association with the *yakṣa* describing him to be tearful.

tasya sthitvā katham api puraḥ ketakādhānahetor
antarbāṣpaś ciram anucaro rājarājasya dadhyau |
meghāloke bhavati sukhino 'py anyathāvṛtti cetaḥ
kaṇṭhāśleṣapraṇayini jane kiṃ punar dūrasaṃsthe || *Meghadūta* 3

Before the bringer of the *ketaka*
With difficulty stood Kubera's serf
And strangled by his tears (*antarbāṣpaḥ*) he prayed for long –
Even the hearts of happy souls transform
On seeing clouds – then what more can one say
Of lovers in some country far away
Pining to clasp the necks of beloved ones?

When the *yakṣa* imagines the cloud to have arrived at the Vindhya mountain, depleted from shedding his essence, he describes it as pausing to replenish itself over the Revā river, and now a similar construction is used to describe the cloud filled with water:

tasyās tiktair vanagajamadair vāsitaṃ vāntavṛṣṭir
jambūṣaṇḍapratihatarayaṃ toyam ādāya gaccheḥ |
antaḥsāraṃ ghana tulayituṃ nānilaḥ śakṣyati tvāṃ
riktaḥ sarvo bhavati hi laghuḥ pūrṇatā gauravāya || *Meghadūta* 20

With all rain ejected, fill to the brim
With her water, bitter with the rut-fluid
Of wild elephants, its torrent checked
By Jambū trees on her banks, then go forth!
O Cloud, when you are full of inner essence (*antaḥsāram*),
The wind will fail to equal you in might!
For all depleted lightly taken are.
The rich and full are taken seriously!

While Vallabhadeva glosses 'with internal essence' (*antaḥsāram*) as 'being replete' (*paripūrṇaṃ santaṃ*), Dakṣiṇāvarta, the thirteenth-century commentator of the poem, glosses *antaḥsāram* as indicating 'the fact that the cloud contains water' *(abhyantarajalatvam)* and, also 'the fact that it possesses inner strength' *(abhyantarabalatvam)* (*Meghadūta* D, p. 17), the latter of which is repeated by Mallīnātha (*antaḥ sāro balaṃ yasya*, *Meghadūta* M, p. 13). The word *ghana*, 'dense/substantial', a common word for cloud, complements *antaḥsāram*, both of which are contrasted by the axiom about emptiness in the final quarter. When we think about the *yakṣa*, *antaḥsāram* can mean possessing a number of inner quintessences: inner strength, certainly, as he shows forbearance and patience in his time of separation, and also, emotional richness, or love, or compassion, mark his character. Drinking a river's water is a metaphor, as we shall see below, for lovemaking. The cloud becomes filled with inner essence after this. In the *yakṣa*'s case – or in the case of any languishing lover – lovemaking will rejuvenate and fulfil his empty, yearning heart after a long period of separation.

Another verse, arguably one of the most sensuous in the *Meghadūta*, appears in the set of verses describing the great city of Ujjayinī, which the *yakṣa* imagines the cloud to pass over in his northward ascent. Here he imagines the cloud alighting on the river Nirvindhyā, and because the cloud is now thin with the shedding of rain, the *yakṣa* urges him to drink the river's waters, and to become thereby *rasābhyantaraḥ*, 'one whose interior is filled with liquid'.[12] The compound could also be a metaphor for a lover: 'one whose interior is filled with erotic emotion'. The cloud is imagined as the male lover making love to the river, a drunk lady stumbling (thus Vallabhadeva points out the river's *kāminīsādharmya* – its 'co-identity with a woman in love'), flashing her navel, her girdle jingling charmingly, and thereby being suffused by ardour for her.

vīcikṣobhastanitavihagaśreṇikāñcīguṇāyāḥ
saṃsarpantyāḥ skhalitasubhagaṃ darśitāvarntanābheḥ |
nirvindhyāyāḥ pathi bhava rasābhyantaraḥ saṃnipatya
strīṇām ādyaṃ praṇayavacanaṃ vibhramo hi priyeṣu || *Meghadūta* 28

Alighting on the river Nirvindhyā –
Her girdle string a row of bobbing birds
Cacophonous as bells on rolling waves
Alluring in her stumbling as she glides
The grotto of her navel she displays –
Grow brimful of the nectar of her love (*rasābhyantara bhava*).
First, a lady tells her love through flirting.

The image in verses 20 and 28 foreshadows another of the cloud making love to the river by drinking her waters. This appears in verses 40–1, and the river is the Gambhīrā river near Ujjayinī. It is here in fact, nearest to the place the *yakṣa* seems to most love, that the cloud grows the most passionate. In drinking her waters the cloud is imagined as a lover disrobing his beloved:

gambhīrāyāḥ payasi saritaś cetasīva prasanne
chāyātmāpi prakṛtisubhago lapsyate te praveśam |
tasmāt tasyāḥ kumudaviśadāny arhasi tvaṃ na dhairyān

moghīkartuṃ caṭulaśapharodvartanaprekṣitāni || 40
tasyāḥ kiṃcit karadhṛtam iva prāptavānīraśākhaṃ
hṛtvā nīlaṃ salilavasanaṃ muktarodhonitambam |
prasthānaṃ te katham api sakhe lambamānasya bhāvi
jñātāsvādaḥ pulinajaghanāṃ ko vihātuṃ samarthaḥ || *Meghadūta* 41

Though you may not, your naturally fair
Shadow-self (*chāyātmā*) shall fall on Gambhīrā's
Pellucid waters, entering it seems
Her flawless heart: do not therefore let down
Her flashing eyes, the leaping fish as white
As water lilies, in your stoicism.

Daintily it seems she holds the robe –
The sheet of water where the cane reeds grow,
The smoothly undulating banks, her hips,
Freed by the cloth of blue that you disrobe.
O friend, your onward journey then
Will be reluctant while you hang on her.
For who on relishing her inner taste (*jñātāsvādaḥ*)
Can leave his lady with hips like riverbanks?

Jñātāsvādaḥ 'having known her taste' is a re-rendering in one sense of *rasābhyantaraḥ*, 'containing fluid', *āsvāda* aligning closely with *rasa*, *jñāta* with the idea of containment in *abhyantaraḥ*. Once again this could be a description of the *yakṣa* as a lover. Indeed one is tempted to read a resonance of the *yakṣa* in *chāyātmā* (*Meghadūta* 40b) when the latter is interpreted literally as 'shadow-self': 'in the pelucid waters of the Gambhīrā river (*gambhīrāyāḥ payasi saritaś … prasanne*), even your shadow self (*chāyātmāpi*), beautiful by nature (*prakṛtisubhago*) will gain an entrance'. Once again he seems to be talking about himself here, *vyājena*, in disguise. In this way, in the most erotically charged descriptions of the cloud with rivers, the *yakṣa* imprints a double identity.

The next verse appears in the series about the cloud's journey over Alakā, the land of the *yakṣa*, beyond the Himālayas. Here in describing the magnificent palaces of the residents of the city, the *yakṣa* correlates them with the cloud in various ways, and in one such correlation, the luminous, bejewelled floors of the palaces are seen to be cognate with the clear, liquid-filled body of the cloud.

vidyutvantaṃ lalitavanitāḥ sendracāpaṃ sacitrāḥ
saṃgītāya prahatamurajāḥ snigdhagambhīraghoṣam |
antastoyaṃ maṇimayabhuvas tuṅgam abhraṃlihāgrāḥ

prāsādās tvāṃ tulayitum alaṃ yatra tais tair viśeṣaiḥ || *Meghadūta* 64

Where through these qualities the palaces
Become your equal in every respect:
You for wife have lightning, they, ladies smart;
You a rainbow, colourful paintings they;
For music they have drums struck thunderously;
A deep and pleasing thunder is your voice;
With inner fluid (*antastoyam*) you, they bejewelled floors;
Their turrets touch the sky while you are tall!

Antastoyam is a mirror for both *antarbāṣpa* first associated in the sense of 'tearful' with the *yakṣa* and for *rasābhyantara* and thereby interconnects all three. To be full of water and to be full of tears are apposite images in the *Meghadūta*.

When the *yakṣa* describes his anguished wife lying desolate in their home in Alakā, another construction of the same type is used in the sense of a compassionate person:

sā saṃnyastābharaṇam abalā pelavaṃ dhārayantī
śayyotsaṅge nihitam asakṛd duḥkhaduḥkhena gātram |
tvām apy asram navajalamayaṃ mocayiṣyaty avaśyaṃ
prāyaḥ sarvo bhavati karuṇāvṛttir ārdrāntarātmā || *Meghadūta* 91

That weakened woman will make even you
Shed a fresh tear-droplet I'm certain
Her dainty body shorn of all her jewels
Cast more than once in anguish on her bed –
They who have moist quintessences often
Are fully disposed to compassion.

Finally, in the last verse of the *yakṣa's* message, the image of a 'vessel replete with fluid' is brought up to refer again to those susceptible to intense feelings of love-in-separation, and, analogously, to describe himself:

etasmān māṃ kuśalinam abhijñānadānād viditvā
mā kaulīnād asitanayane mayy aviśvāsino bhūḥ |
snehān āhuḥ kim api virahahrāsinas te hy abhogād
iṣṭe vastuny upacitarasāḥ premarāśībhavanti || *Meghadūta* 109

Thus knowing me to be of healthy mind
By disclosure of special memories
Mistrust me not O dark-eyed girl because
Of nasty things that people say such as

'Those wan in separation proclaim their love
Haphazardly.' They abundant in
Emotion (*upacitarasāḥ*) grow suffused in love
For their dears, when absent their company.

All these synonyms for the cloud, the *yakṣa* and finally for any kind and sensitive person, meaning 'internally moist', could apply equally to either character: in the *yakṣa*'s case they would mean tearful, or even compassionate (filled with the liquid of kindness; having a soft heart) or even aroused; in the cloud's case they would mean filled with rain. At each key moment in the movement of the poem these descriptions are summoned, first when the *yakṣa* is just about to start his message, then when he imagines the cloud to pass over and commune with, the great rivers of central India, the Narmadā and the Nirvindhyā, then in Alakā the *yakṣa*'s homeland, when he imagines his wife, the intended recipient of his message, and finally when he concludes his message. Forming a link tying together the entire poem, they remind us at every poetic turning point of the chief theme: that the fluid nature of the cloud, itself malleable and formless, and the sensitivity of the grieving lover's psyche – or of any compassionate being (as 91cd says) – itself changeable from minute to minute like liquid, are one and the same. The moisture that they carry, rain and emotions, are both their secret wealth and their burden.

In this connection, one is tempted to speak of another evocative image in the poem: that of moonstones (*candrakāntāḥ*). In imagining his hometown Alakā, the *yakṣa* says that it is:

yatra strīṇāṃ priyatamabhujāliṅganocchvāsitānām
aṅgaglāṇiṃ suratajanitāṃ tantujālāvalambāḥ |
tvatsaṃrodhāpagamaviśadai ścotitāś candrapādair
vyālumpanti sphuṭajalalavasyandinaś candrakāntāḥ || *Meghadūta* 67

Where, dangling from the lattice curtains,
Moonstones trickle liquid when moonbeams shine
Brightly on them when your cover has gone,
And wash away with sprays of gleaming drops
The weariness of lovemaking from limbs
Of panting wives clasped tight by their lovers.

The moonstone was thought to secrete water when moonlight falls on it, its opalescent luminosity possibly evoking this belief. It is an image that summons up the idea of the *antastoya*, the liquid-filled cloud and the sentiment-laden *yakṣa*, and in fact, a moonstone looks very much as if it contains water, like a cloud, or even a blue sky with wisps of cloud. As such it can be seen as a metaphor for both the *megha* and the *yakṣa*.

In pithy aphorisms (*subhāṣitas*), popular with Sanskrit poets, clouds are often metaphors for great altruism. This altruism then is the key characteristic of the *yakṣa*, who in thinking only of consoling his grieving love reaches out to the northward-travelling cloud. Kālidāsa chooses to merge a symbol of munificent compassion with his speaker, making a compassionate core, rather than any other heroic quality, such as boldness, the type and test of his nobility.

Love messages and 'insentient' messengers in earlier poetry

The trope of the insentient aerial messenger appears in several examples of Indian literature in contexts, excepting one, of separated lovers. There are two speaking geese in the *Chāndogyopaniṣad* IV.1.1–5,[13] who deliver the news of sage Raikva to King Jānuśruti Pautrāyaṇa; the impaled man who asks a crow to deliver a message of comfort to his wife in the Pāli *Kāmavilāpajātaka*;[14] Rāma's message to Sītā, carried by Hanumān, the monkey able to fly, in the *Yuddhakāṇḍa* of the *Rāmāyaṇa* (*Rāmāyaṇa* VI.101.1–43), which, inscribed into the *Meghadūta* in verse 97 (noticed by the commentarial tradition[15]), is a narrative template explicitly foregrounding the *Meghadūta*; and the match-making goose in the Nala and Damayantī story in the *Mahābhārata* (*Mahābhārata* III.50.19–31).

Among these, the dying man in the Buddhist *jātaka* and the *yakṣa* are similar in that they are anonymous characters, rather than exalted heroes as in the congruent examples from the Brahmanical tradition. In fact *yakṣas*, though partially divine, are not particularly hallowed creatures in some literature. In Āryaśūra's eighth birth story of the Buddha on Maitrībala the righteous, charitable and gentle king, five *yakṣas* (like the *Meghadūta*'s *yakṣa* banished from their kingdom by Kubera) are portrayed as ill-intentioned, avaricious creatures. Compared to dangerous spirits called *piśācas*, they wish only to feast on the blood and flesh of the compliant king, only much later to feel their conscience pinch at Maitrībala's whole-hearted charity and serenity allowing them to do so (*Jātakamālā* of Āryaśūra, pp. 41–52). Disguised as *brāhmaṇas*, their true visages, when revealed, are said to be monstrous: their mouths horrific with pointed teeth, their fierce eyes squinting and blazing yellow, their noses flat, wide and misshapen, their hair and beard reddish like burning fire (*ity uktvā daṃṣṭrākarālavadanāni dīptapiṅgalakekararaud ranayanāni sphuṭitacipiṭavirūpaghoṇāni jvaladanalakapilakeśaśmaśruṇi* ...

vikṛtabhīṣaṇāni svāny eva vapūṃṣi pratyapadyata, ibid., p. 44). Given such demonic associations in Buddhist literature at least, the *yakṣa* may seem to be a startling choice for the role of a lyrical lover, a far cry not just from the ideal hero but even from an ordinary human being. On the other hand Āryaśūra also describes his malevolent *yakṣas*' limbs 'dark as water-filled rainclouds' (*sajajaladharāndhakārāṇi*, ibid.). One is tempted to think of this as a subtle poetic bridge to the *Meghadūta*.

The parallel worth studying in detail though may be glimpsed closer to home, in Kālidāsa's own work the *Vikramorvaśīya*, in the depiction of Purūravas deranged in the forest in Act IV. The act instantiates in miniature all that is quintessential about the *Meghadūta*, and it is possible that they were written as companion pieces, the former either anticipating the *Meghadūta*, following shortly after it or even composed at the same time. The analogy, rather than being incidental, is made evident from the very beginning of the act. Purūravas enters the stage 'with madness' (*sonmādo rājā*) and chases after a cloud, mistaking it for a *rakṣas* carrying away his beloved. The personification of the cloud, reinforced by his ensuing interaction with it, cannot but help recall the *Meghadūta*. Realizing he had been mistaken – in another example of *mithyājñāna* corrected by rectifying knowledge – Purūravas sings the following verse, indicating his flash of clarity. Here the *yakṣa*'s cloud finds clear allusion:

navajaladharaḥ saṃnaddho'yaṃ na dṛptaniśācaraḥ
suradhanur idaṃ dūrākṛṣṭaṃ na nāma śarāsanam |
ayam api paṭur dhārāsāro na bāṇaparamparā
kanakanikaṣasnigdhā vidyut priyā mama norvaśī || *Vikramorvaśīya* IV.7

Here's a fresh cloud girt for rain, not a mad night-ghoul
Here's an outstretched rainbow, not a bow for arrows,
This too a fierce shower, a flood of arrows – no!
This – lightning like a shining gold-streak on touchstone,
Not my dear Urvaśī slick with *datura* paste.[16]

The comparison of lightning to a gleaming streak of gold left on a dark touchstone, *kanakanikaṣasnigdhā vidyut*, an especially striking conceit, is echoed also in verse 37 of the *Meghadūta*, in the context of the beloved Ujjayinī. In this case even the same words are used thus:

gacchantīnāṃ ramaṇavasatiṃ yoṣitāṃ tatra naktaṃ
ruddhāloke narapatipathe sūcibhedyais tamobhiḥ |
saudāminyā ***kanakanikaṣasnigdhayā*** *darśayorvīṃ*
toyotsargastanitamukharo mā sma bhūr viklavās tāḥ || *Meghadūta* 37

There, at night reveal the earth with lightning
Like a shining gold-streak on a touchstone
For ladies hurrying to their lovers' homes
On highways gloomy with a black so thick
One can almost prick it with a needle.
When you rain, don't thunder – they are timid!

The contrastive play between light and dark, central to the vision of clouds in both works, the dark bodies of which enhance and make jewel-like all other colours, is heightened by the image of the touchstone. Purūravas's realization that the *rakṣas* is actually a cloud is, nevertheless, followed by an address to it. He asks it, as if it were a person, to restrain its angry rainfall as it spreads across the sky, and he politely solicits it again, saying that if it should find Urvaśī, he would bear all its thunderous activities (IV.11). This is a plea that resonates with the solicitation of the *yakṣa*, which too is a request to the cloud for a favour. His allusion to the 'time of clouds' (*jaladharasamayaṃ*, *Vikramorvaśīya*, p. 93) suggests that the season is meant to be the monsoon – again in harmony with the *Meghadūta*. The culmination of his address is a verse in the *Meghadūta*'s own metre, the *mandākrāntā*:

vidyullekhākanakaruciraṃ śrīvitānaṃ mamābhraṃ
vyādhūyante niculatarubhir mañjarīcāmarāṇi |
gharmacchedāt paṭutaragiro bandino nīlakaṇṭhā
dhārāsāropanayanaparā naigamāś cāmbuvāhāḥ || *Vikramorvaśīya* IV.13

Flashing with golden lightning streaks, the sky
Is my glorious heraldic canopy,
The blooming sprays of mango pine that tremble,
The regnal yak-tail whisks that fan my person,
Peacocks, crying out at summer's passing,
Panegyrists praising me through singing
Busy in bringing their cargo of rain,
The monsoon clouds become my royal merchants.

This could almost be the *yakṣa* speaking a verse in the *Meghadūta*, and the image of the cloud as merchant transporting goods is particularly apt for the messenger's role envisaged for the cloud in the latter work. But this soliloquy to the cloud is continued with soliloquys to other forest creatures, each given up by Purūravas in exasperation before moving onto the next auditor, so that the entire act is structured as a series of failed solicitations for the beloved's whereabouts. At the same time they are laments in the spirit of the *Meghadūta*, to aspects of the natural world. Moreover, also in a departure from the *yakṣa*, Purūravas speaks additionally in Prakrit, the register generally reserved for women and side characters in drama, in a marked change for a Sanskrit *nāyaka* who usually only speaks in Sanskrit. First he laments to a peacock, asking it where Urvaśī is (*Vikramorvaśīya*, pp. 96–7), then a cuckoo (ibid., pp. 97–9), the Mānasa-bound cranes (ibid., pp. 99–102), then a *cakravāka* (ibid., 103–5), a honey bee (ibid., p. 106), the king of elephants (ibid., pp. 106–7), a mountain (ibid., pp. 108–9), and finally, in desperation, a black antelope (ibid., pp. 112–13). By the end he is so desolate he pleads with the antelope to rescue him 'from the ocean of separation from Urvaśī' (*tahavirahasamuddantare uttārahi maṃiṃ*, ibid., p. 113) by telling him he had seen his beloved. Many of these characters take centre stage in the visionary encounters of the *Meghadūta*: peacocks, the birds of the monsoon, are everywhere (such as *Vikramorvaśīya* IV.21–2), while elephants and Mānasa-bound birds appear too.

The topos of the hero appearing to be mad originates in Rāma distraught in the *Rāmāyaṇa* III.58.1–34: this likely had an imaginative hold over Kālidāsa in his portrayals of the love-deranged hero, his usual equanimity inverted. Many of the stages of derangement overlap: before he discovers his grass hut bereft of Sītā, stolen away by Rāvaṇa, Rāma's left eye trembles; he stumbles and trembles in panic. He interprets the signs of his physical unease as omens. Finally discovering the empty hut, compared to a lily pool in winter deserted by the lotus-loving Goddess Lakṣmī, he roams about the woods 'like a madman' (*unmatta iva Rāmāyaṇa* III.58.33c) 'intent on the search for his beloved' (*kāntānveṣaṇatatparaḥ Rāmāyaṇa* III.58.33d). He lamented again and again (forms of *vi-lap* 'to lament', which Kālidāsa uses abundantly, are employed to describe his crying), and distraught, he goes through various possibilities where Sītā could be. 'Drowned in grief that was like a sea of mire' (*śokapaṅkārṇavaplutaḥ Rāmāyaṇa* III.58.11d), he speaks to the Aśoka, the Kadamba, the *bel*, the Arjuna, the Kakubha, the Tilaka, the date-palm and the Jambū trees, then to a deer, an elephant and a tiger, and finally his brother Lakṣmaṇa to ask if they had seen Sītā. The details invested in Rāma's pain and his stark emotional inversion resonate with Purūravas's and the *yakṣa*'s experiences of grief and madness.

The tragic middle in the *Meghadūta*

From verse 70 onwards, the section commentators later than Vallabhadeva often organized under a second part concerning Alakā, the land of the *yakṣa*, appears a gradual telescoping of perspective, bringing into focus external signs (*abhijñas*, *lakṣaṇas*) of the *yakṣa*'s house: an *aśoka* tree with blood-red flowers, a saffron tree, a *mādhavī* vine under the awning a red amaranth tree (75), a golden bird-perch resting between them with a peacock (76), then the house itself with a conch shell and a lotus near the entrance (77), a sapphire-tipped play-hillock on which the cloud is asked to rest, then a window, and finally inside the window, the *yakṣiṇī*. On the one hand, the listing of these special memories, or knowledge-tokens, is crucial for the *yakṣa* to prove to his wife that, though distraught, he in fact remembers clearly (this will be made clear in verse 109). On the other hand, through this meticulous telescoping of perspective, we are led into the central point of the entire poem: a vision of the grief-stricken wife. This is the culmination of the *yakṣa*'s imagination, the dark abyss as it were of his anxiety, from which once again there will be an emotional ascent initiated by the message of consolation he imagines uttered by the cloud from verse 98 onwards: here too we find that the portrayal of grief is centred. It marks the moment of confrontation, when the *yakṣa*'s mind finally seizes the thing that causes its anguish. This portrayal, imagined by the *yakṣa*, contains metaphors of death. Love is absent. In his mind, his wife's appearance has altered like a lotus pond afflicted with frost (pp. 79–80):

tanvī śyāmā śikharadaśanā pakvabimbādharauṣṭhī
madhye kṣāmā cakita hariṇaprekṣaṇī nimnanābhiḥ |
śroṇībhārād alasagamanā stokanamrā stanābhyāṃ
yā tatra syād yuvativiṣaye sṛṣṭir ādyeva dhātuḥ || 79

tāṃ jānīyāḥ parimitakathāṃ jīvitaṃ me dvitīyaṃ
dūribhūte mayi sahacare cakravākīm ivaikām |
gāḍhotkaṇṭhāguruṣu divaseṣv eṣu gacchatsu bālāṃ
jātāṃ manye śiśiramathitāṃ padminīṃ vānyarūpām || *Meghadūta* 80

There, the lady who is slender and dark,
Pointed her teeth, ripe *bilva* fruits her lips,
Trim-waisted, having eyes like a startled deer's
A deep-set navel, heavy hips that cause
A languid gait, and breasts that make her stoop,
Of womenkind, the Maker's chief creation.

Know that reticent woman to be
My second self – a lonely *cakravākī*
When I her companion am far away.
When days pass by intense with grim longing,
My dear girl must have altered, fancy I,
Like a lotus pool blighted by the frost.[17]

The first two words *tanvī śyāmā* recollect the description of (Urvaśī transformed into) the thin wan vine in *Vikramorvaśīya* IV.66 (see Chapter 3, p. 134), and in fact *śyāmā* can also mean 'green-lady'.

The final quarter of the second verse contains a poetic fancy, in which a certain change in the beloved woman is illuminated. In *Meghadūta* 80, the *yakṣa* fancies the *yakṣiṇī* to be transformed like a verdant pond blighted by winter. In the *Vikramorvaśīya* verse, Purūravas imagines the vine to be his angry Urvaśī who is now silent because of her remorse at rebuffing his placations. Two senses of the same past participle *jāta* are used, creating a further mutual link: the participle is used transitively to mean *abhavat* (she became/turned into) in *Meghadūta* 81 and passively in the *bahuvrīhi jātānutapā*, 'she in whom remorse is born' in *Vikramorvaśīya* IV.66, as an adjective for *anutāpa*. The vine bereft of flower is paralleled in the *utprekṣā* (fancy) of the lotus pond in winter: both meaning that beauty has withered in the winter of depression. Both heroines are imagined by their lovers to be silent in their grief, this suggested by the vine due to the absence of the buzzing of bees (*parimitakathāṃ*; *cintāmaunam … āsthitā*).

In *Meghadūta* 80, the isolated *yakṣiṇī* is likened also to a solitary *cakravāka* bird. The *cakravāka* bird, the *Tadorna ferruginea*, roams in pairs but in poetic imagination at least is thought to spend the night in lonely separation from its mate. Thus in Sanskrit poetry it is a symbol of love-in-union and of love-in-separation. As observed by the fourteenth-century commentator Padmasarasvatī, (*Meghadūta* P, p. 126) both similes of adverse transformation (the dead lotus pond and the single female *cakravāka*) allude to the *Sundarakāṇḍa* of the *Rāmāyaṇa* (V.14. 30), in which the *cakravākī* and the lotus pond appear as symbols of Sītā:

himahatanalinīva naṣṭaśobhā
vyasanaparaṃparayā nipīḍyamānā |
sahacararahiteva cakravākīva
janakasutā kṛpaṇāṃ daśāṃ prapannā || *Rāmāyaṇa* V.14.30

The daughter of Janaka grew miserable
Like a lotus pool blighted by frost
Her beauty gone; with constant grief tortured
Just like a *cakravākī* reft of mate.

Apart from the two images of desolation, syntactically there are a few more interlocking elements with the epic precedent: *kṛpaṇāṃ daśām prapannā* ('attained a miserable state') correlates with *jātāṃ anyarūpām* ('became one of altered appearance'), and both past participles are used as transitive verbs, while *vyasanaparamparayā* ('by continuous longing') is analogous with *gāḍhotkaṇṭhāguruṣu* ('heavy with intense longing'), both being described as the causes for their haggard, care-worn appearance.

Having summoned in subtle form the vision of grieving Sītā as a backdrop for the *yakṣiṇī*, the *yakṣa* goes on to describe with greater detail the misery of his subject. He carefully constructs his wife's experience of grief, engaging in an extended *tarka* (process of conjecture) on how she might behave. Developing the inventory of signs set forth previously, he lays out the clues of his wife's desolation whereby the cloud will know her: her unkempt, rough hair tied in a single braid, her eyes – which it seems from 92d are blue in colour – swollen, her face cupped by her hands, she will be lost in reverie, exhibiting forgetfulness, suffering from insomnia, inhabiting an in-between state between sleep and wakefulness, and moreover, her ornaments rejected, thin in body, she will be abstaining from wine.

nūnaṃ tasyāḥ prabalaruditocchūnanetraṃ bahūnāṃ
niḥśvāsānām aśiśiratayā bhinnavarṇādharauṣṭham |
hastanyastaṃ mukham asakalavyakti lambālakatvād
indor dainyaṃ tvadupasaraṇakliṣṭakānter bibharti || 81
āloke te nipatati purā sā balivyākulā vā
matsādṛśyaṃ virahatanu vā bhāvagamyaṃ likhantī |
pṛcchantī vā madhuravacanāṃ śārikāṃ pañjarasthāṃ
kaccid bhartuḥ smarasi nibhṛte tvaṃ hi tasya priyeti || 82
utsaṅge vā malinavasane somya nikṣipya vīṇāṃ
madgotrāṅkaṃ viracitapadaṃ geyam udgātukāmā |
tantrīr ārdrā nayanasalilaiḥ sārayitvā kathaṃcid
bhūyo bhūyaḥ svayam api kṛtāṃ mūrchanāṃ vismarantī || 83
śeṣān māsān gamanadivasaprastutasyāvadher vā
vinyasyantī bhuvi gaṇanayā dehalīdattapuṣpaiḥ |
saṃyogaṃ vā hṛdayanihitārambham āsvādayantī
prāyeṇaite ramaṇaviraheṣv aṅganānāṃ vinodāḥ || *Meghadūta* 84

No doubt her cupped face is like the moon
Diminished when its radiance is worn out
By you approaching. Partially it shows
Through hanging hair; eyes with fierce weeping puffed,
Through hot sighs her lips have changed their hue.
Soon you will see her giving gods their gifts
Or engaged perhaps in drawing a picture
Of my body thin in separation,
Conjured up in her imagination,
Perhaps she asks the dulcet-voiced mynah
She keeps in a cage: 'Do you remember

Master, gentle one? You were his darling.'
Or keeps the *vīnā* on her lap good sir,
Its garment covered over all with dust
Keen to sing the song bearing my name
With difficulty stretches out its wires
Slippery with the water from her eyes
But over and over again forgets
The melody that she herself had set.
Or counting out the flower offerings
At the entrance ranged upon the floor
A record of the final months she keeps
Begun on the day of my departure,
Or tastes our union in her fantasy –
Such are women's sports in separation.

Since, his wife will be most tormented in the dark hours of the night, he asks the cloud to deliver his message to her at that time. Behold her then, he tells the cloud, in 86c, the verb for 'behold' *paśya* connecting the extended imagery of the *yakṣiṇī* that stretches as a delicate, riverine enjambment, into verse 89.

ādye badhvā virahadivase yā śikhādāma hitvā
śāpasyānte vigalitaśucā yā mayonmocanīyā |
sparśakliṣṭām ayaminakhenāsakṛt sārayantīṃ
gaṇḍābhogāt kaṭhinaviṣamād ekaveṇīṃ kareṇa || 85
savyāpārām ahani na tathā khedayed viprayogaḥ
śaṅke rātrau gurutaraśucaṃ nirvinodāṃ sakhīṃ te |
matsaṃdeśaiḥ sukhayiym ataḥ paśya sādhvāṃ niśīthe
tām unnidrām avaniśayanāsannavātāyanasthaḥ || 86
ādhikṣāmāṃ virahaśayane saṃnikīrṇaikapārśvāṃ
prācīmūle tanum iva kalāmātraśeṣāṃ himāṃśoḥ |
matsaṃyogaḥ katham upanamet svapnojo 'pīti nidrām
ākāṅkṣantīṃ nayanasalilotpīḍaruddhāvakāśam || 87
niḥśvāsenādharakisalayakleśinā vikṣipantīṃ
śuddhasnānāt paruṣam alakaṃ nūnam āgaṇḍalambam |
nītā rātriḥ ksaṇa iva mayā sārdham icchāratair yā
tām evoṣṇair virahaśayaneṣv asrubhir yāpayantīm || 88
pādānindor amṛtaśiśirāñ jālamārgapraviṣṭān
pūrvaprītyā gatam abhimukhaṃ saṃnivṛttaṃ tathaiva |
cakṣuḥ khedāt sajalagurubhiḥ pakṣmabhiś chādayantīṃ
sābhre 'hnīva sthalakamalinīṃ na prabuddhāṃ na suptām || *Meghadūta* 89

From time to time she pushes away the braid,
Hard and rough, from the apples of her cheeks
That she plaited discarding her chignon
On the first day of our separation,
That I, when grief-rid, shall free at curse-end,
Pushes with a hand whose nails are untrimmed –
I fear your friend is filled with fierce sorrow
At night when entertainments diminish –
By day such sorrow would not torment her
Because she would be busy with her chores
Behold therefore that good woman by night
In order to delight her with my news
In a window near the floor, where sleepless she lies.
Anxious, cast sidelong on estrangement's bed
Like the moon's last digit bestride the east,
Craving sleep, though tears prevent its onset,
Because in nought but dreams can she unite with me.
With a sigh that burns the petal of her lip
She blows away the hair that surely hangs
Over her cheeks roughened by water-baths,
Passing the nights that once passed in a flash
With me in the love-play of our fancy
With scalding teardrops on estrangement's bed.
As a hibiscus on a cloudy day
Closes not nor opens fully she stays
Neither wide awake nor fast asleep
Concealing in her grief with lashes full of tears
Her eyes that out of tender habit glance
At the moonlight, nectar-cool, when through
The lattice it enters, but soon turn away.

Tears and sleepless eyes are the predominant images here. There is stillness in the grief presented in these verses and the only movement belongs to the *yakṣiṇī*'s eyes: literally her eye 'goes to (*gatam abhimukham*) the rays of the moon' but 'just as quickly turns away' (*saṃnivṛttaṃ tathaiva*). Personified, and indeed representing the *yakṣiṇī's* heart's desire, her glance runs in glee toward the welcome moonlight, her dear friend in nights of lovemaking with the *yakṣa*, but turn back, by which is meant that the eyes close, because the moon reminds her of her separation from him. She inhabits a frontier land between sleep and wakefulness, a state compared to a hibiscus (*sthalakamalinī*), its petals, partially unfurled on a cloudy day. The anatomy of melancholy, though of sombre nature, is paradoxically always exquisite in the *Meghadūta*: it is never dreary but ripe with colour (blues and greens being predominant), delicacy, life and beauty.

In verse 90 he asserts why his conjectures about his wife's ailing state are not random imaginings but accurate renderings[18] the veracity of which will soon be apparent to the cloud. The reason for the statement of his wife's malady of melancholy is his knowledge of her true love:

jāne sakhyās tava mayi manaḥ saṃbhṛtasneham asmād
itthaṃbhūtāṃ prathamavirahe tām ahaṃ tarkayāmi |
vācālaṃ māṃ na khalu subhagaṃmanyabhāvaḥ karoti
pratyakṣaṃ te nikhilam acirād bhrātar uktaṃ mayā yat || 90
sā saṃnyastābharaṇam abalā pelavaṃ dhārayantī
śayyotsaṅge nihitam asakṛd duḥkhaduḥkhena gātram |
tvām apy asraṃ navajalamayaṃ mocayiṣyaty avaśyaṃ
prāyaḥ sarvo bhavati karuṇāvṛttir ārdrāntarātmā || 91
ruddhāpāṅgaprasaram alakair añjanasnehaśūnyaṃ
pratyādeśād api ca madhuno vismṛtabhrūvilāsam |
tvayyāsanne nayanam uparispandi śaṅke mṛgākṣyā
mīnakxsobhākulakuvalayaśrītulām eṣyatīti || *Meghadūta* 92

Since I know your friend is in love with me
I imagine she'll be this way the first time
We are apart. Assuredly it's not
Because I think myself a lucky man
That makes me say any old thing to you.
All that I have said to you O brother
Very soon you will see to be the truth.
That weakened woman will make even you
Shed a fresh tear droplet I'm certain,
Her dainty body shorn of all her jewels
Cast more than once in anguish on her bed –
They who have moist quintessences often
Are disposed to compassion in their acts.
Imagine I my doe-eyed lady's eye
Bereft of oily kohl, its sidelong stares
Hidden by her hair; its play of eyebrows
Forgotten through her rejection of wine,
When you come near is like a lily blue
Resplendent, made to tremble by the fish
Leaping, while its upper eyelid trembles.

Here again the overlap between water and tears is illuminated, especially through the eyes of the *yakṣiṇī* being blue. The meticulousness of the portrayal is in keeping with the travelogue style of the previous part of the poem, in which every verse had provided a variegated insight into a feature of what the cloud encounters on its journey. In this sense the *yakṣiṇī* is one of the many sights the cloud is told he will see in his itinerary. On the other hand, grief is not represented here as just another aspect of the poem's particular 'list of sights' style, but it also contains an allusion to related depictions of it in earlier literature, in which almost forensic interest is shown in the development of despair. The stages of grief Sundarī inhabits in the *Saundarananda* are worth reiterating now, as they provide a parallel frame of reference for the vision of the *yakṣiṇī*:

> Hearing this news of her husband she immediately leaped up, shaking; she clutched at her arms and screamed piercingly, like a she-elephant struck in the heart with a poisoned arrow. Her eyes reddened and smeared with tears, and her thin limbs wracked with burning pain, she fell down with her strings of pearls broken and in disarray, like the branch of a mango-tree breaking due to its burden of fruit.
>
> She moaned loudly, like a *chakravaka* bird when a hawk has wounded the tip of her mate's wing, as if to compete with the pigeons gathered on the palace roof, their throats tremulous with cooing. The couch she lay on though decked in soft-coloured rugs, though decorated with cat's-eye gems and diamonds, though with feet of gold and extremely valuable, gave her no comfort in her restlessness. Beholding her husband's ornaments and clothes and his items of amusement such as his *vina* she entered a state of darkness, howling loudly and collapsing as though sinking into the mire.
>
> For as her diaphragm heaved with her hard breathing like cave's interior rent by a fiery thunderbolt, and her innermost heart burned with the fire of grief, Sundari at that moment seemed to have lost her mind. She wept, grew exhausted, yelled, fell weary, wandered about, stood still, lamented, broode; she raged, scattered her garlands, tore at her face and pulled at her clothes.
>
> The violent sobbing of this girl of the beautiful teeth greatly distressed her ladies in waiting when they heard it. (*Saundarananda* 6.24–5 and 6.30–5 in Covill 2007, pp. 121, 123–5)

Sundarī's anguish is portrayed as an unstoppable and frightening loss of control – and this is in contrast to the slow dolour of the *yakṣiṇī*, who carries the hope of the *yakṣa*'s return unlike the hopeless Sundarī whose husband has left never to return. On the other hand the overall images certainly resonate. The *yakṣa* describing his wife as a bereft *cakravāka* bird matches also – as it does with the description of Sītā previously mentioned – with *Saundarananda* 6.30. Sundarī is described as a *cakravāka* bird lamenting the wounding of her husband. But where the similarity with Sītā is simply in the state of alteration, with Sundarī the *yakṣiṇī* shares the violent, ignominious, physicality of despair. Sītā's dejection is described in almost sedate terms in contrast to that of the *yakṣiṇī*. Lovesickness for the *yakṣiṇī* is a powerful, physical malady – a true depression – not a temporary aberration of the soul. Thus too in the case of Sundarī. Like the *yakṣiṇī* in *Meghadūta* 91, 'she of beautiful teeth' (*Saundarananda* 6.35a *cārudantīm* = *Meghadūta* 79a, *śikharadaśanā*) collapses on her couch unable to sleep, in intense grief, dishevelled, unable to do anything except sob. She tries to play a *vīṇā* belonging to her husband (*Saundarananda* 6.32). In *Meghadūta* 83 the *yakṣiṇī* too tries fruitlessly to sing while playing her *vīṇā*, except in this case, the song is one that is a creation of her husband's. Verse 81, in which the *yakṣiṇī* is imagined cupping her face and crying recalls Sundarī in *Saundarananda* 6.10 'with her face in her hands, suffering because she couldn't see her husband, and burning with desire and anger' (Covill 2007, p. 117).

A further analogy to the physical process of despair, in which all thought and action become incapacitated, is provided by Damayantī's lovesickness in the *Mahābhārata*. After hearing the goose's message that Nala is in love with her, Damayantī falls dangerously ill (*Mahābhārata* III.51.1–4): Instead of feeling happy, love sickened her body and mind. She was not healthy. She was intent in anxious thinking. She was wretched, her face colourless and thin. Her gaze was fixed upwards. She was intent on brooding and at no time did she find comfort in the delights of bed and couch. She could not sleep by night or day. She continuously cried out, 'Alack! Alack!' Through such indications, her friends understood that she was ill.

In this way the vision of bereaved women in all three works echo and are in unison with each other. While the image of Sītā is most certainly a common wellspring for the figure of the separated lover, the other depictions, particularly the Buddhist portrayal in the *Saundarananda*, construct dejection as real psychological trauma, physically and mentally crippling. The Buddhist writer is interested in the subtleties of anguish such as the powerful frenzy of a mourner losing control, the inability to find comfort in repose or the painful memories brought up by objects associated with the departed lover. As such, the *Meghadūta*'s *yakṣiṇī* is more in the tradition of the Buddhist Sundarī. What is of significance in these portrayals of grief which post-date the *Rāmāyaṇa*'s Sītā is the changed state of psychology – these experiences are not temporary disturbances of emotions, but something the *Mahābhārata* calls in its description of Damayantī *asvastha*, unhealthy. Loss has turned the women, as well as the *yakṣa* in the *Meghadūta* and Purūravas in the *Vikramorvaśīya*, into persons other than themselves. They inhabit an otherness, akin to a living death, like the lotus pond killed by frost.

In seeking to represent experience and the experiencing subject starkly severed from his true healthy nature, these descriptions construct for us a phenomenology of grief.

Conclusion

In the previous chapters we have seen the persistent presence of a tragic middle in the majority of Kālidāsa's compositions. This middle aligns with the idea of rupture in medias res in theories of narrative development. In *alaṃkāraśāstra*, the nature of rupture in the narrative, called *vimarśa* or *avamarśa*, was understood in a number of different ways, according to the *Abhinavabhāratī*.

Some, possibly the logicians, understood its nature to be doubt, and some an impediment to the final goal that renewed optimism and, at least according to Śaṅkuka, offset and nourished into being the final *rasa*. Some found it to be death or, it seems according to Udbhaṭa, to be registered in thoughts of failure, and some in thoughts about a disaster. In all these interpretations, it seems that this core rupture was not considered final but purposeful for the effort depicted in the narrative.

Examples in *alaṃkāraśāstra* show that the *vimarśa* need not be strictly tragic – it is the moment within both happy and sad stories when the final fruit of the narrative is temporarily thwarted. On the other hand, Kālidāsa treats the *vimarśa* as a fully tragic moment involving loss, sometimes even inventing an episode to supplement his sources with such a *vimarśa* where tragedy is absent, or investing more interest in potentially tragic incidents than that shown in the source.

As I have understood them in this book, these episodes of *vimarśa* are, first, reflective studies of how the phenomenon of grief is experienced by a subject and the kinds of core philosophical questions it provokes in all humans (as such, some of these episodes can stand independently); second, they are inevitable, indeed existentially germane, for all beings in Kālidāsa's narrative universe; and third, in many cases, they form a second birth as it were in the narrative, presenting tragic rupture as an optimistic, maturing, even transformative 'test' for characters, in order for the remaining story to continue anew. As such these *vimarśa* sections coincide closely with the way *vimarśa* was understood within aesthetics, as the turning point for renewal. They even seem to metaphorically represent an idea of time as death followed by birth in potentially infinite repetition. This idea closely harmonizes with conceptions in Indian ascetic traditions, particularly within Buddhist traditions, concerning *saṃsāra* (transmigration) and objective transience that were, in all probability, far more widely known in Kālidāsa's time than the views in *alaṃkāraśāstra*.

What, then, are the core characteristics of the emotional experiences portrayed in the Kālidāsean *vimarśa*? First: the confrontation with the absence of the beloved other, the second self, or to use Kālidāsa's own words, the 'shadow-self' (*chāyātmā*). In the case of Aja and Rati, the other is transformed from a vital, living body into a horrific corpse or is burnt to ashes. In the case of Śakuntalā, the other is transformed into a starkly altered person, with no sense of an older shared time. In the cases of Purūravas and the *yakṣa*, the other is physically absented as a punishment. In each instance a sense of shock, disbelief and panic overcomes the subject.

This confrontation leads to a severe disturbance in the character's perception of time: the subject continues to dwell in a period that was shared with and made familiar by the loved one; but now appears a new time, emptied of the warm, beloved living body and the interpersonal events connected with it. He or she lives in two separate times at once, as it were, the shared time, the time that is really 'real', but that has past, and the present, which is continually interpenetrated and rendered unreal by the former.

While past time was dynamic and in flow, present time, permeated by absence, is slow, and in fact seems to stop completely, or return to the same point in an endless eddy. The subject feels lost and disoriented (Purūravas).

The loved one continues to live in the present time – his or her ghost is resurrected in items of familiarity. But the constant conflict with present time leads to a feeling of uncanniness in the subject, to a feeling of some kind of terrifying unreality in which everything is unfamiliar, horrific and cold. The subject grapples with a new, altered self in his or her new, ongoing life: feelings of alienation, mistrust or even abjuration of one's habitual self, and a sense that his or her experience is exclusive and unshared, lead to a severe contraction and impoverishment of the self so that he or she becomes wholly other (Duṣyanta on his realization). The wish of suicide may prevail when there is an inability to welcome the altered self, or there may be a severe detachment, a kind of death in life (Aja), when suicide is not an option.[1]

The phenomenology of grief is also filled with questions about tragic causality and the true nature of things. 'Who did this?' 'Why did this happen?' 'What did

I do?' What could I have done to prevent this? Most importantly perhaps, the bereaved asks: 'What is true and what is false?' or 'What is reality, what illusion?' In the *Śakuntalā* and in the *vimarśa* in the *Vikramorvaśīya*, the latter question forms the structuring theme to the dramatic process depicted, and in showing the dawning of true awareness, allusions are made to false knowledge and its rectification in terms of Mīmāṃsā epistemology and to intuitive memory-based knowledge (*pratyabhijñā*) in Nyāya.

Questions of causality are sometimes accompanied by anger toward the mysterious 'cause' – the uncanny 'unknown' with which the griever is confronted – and by a feeling of being controlled by this 'unknown', of losing one's own power and choice in the process. For Kālidāsa, the experience is similar, to a small degree, to schizophrenic disembodiment. Often the images whereby the 'unknown' is constructed are of something circular or of a thick impenetrable black mass (*tamas*) fogging the mind – of the person being manipulated and entered into. However, the articulation of feeling helpless and disembodied, accompanied by anger at all the unknown culprits responsible for taking away one's power (or, as for the *yakṣa*, the vivid image of a future time together), restores lost sense of self to the subject. In fact the *vimarśa* in Kālidāsa comprises a tension between the selfhood lost and selfhood gained, powerlessness overturned by the assertion of power, uncanniness by healing.

Notes

Preamble: A Note on the Indian Medieval

1 Stein 2010, p. 105.
2 Ibid., p. 106.
3 Kulke and Rothermund 1998, pp. 103–51.
4 Ibid., p. 103.

Introduction, Part I: The tragic middle

1 *Nāṭyaśāstra* 18.93cd–96; cf. *Abhinavabhāratī* 18.94–96; *Sāhityadarpaṇa* 6.250–1.
2 'Perhaps the most outstanding feature in the dramatic literature is the entire absence of tragedy or violent action of any kind. Although … the hero and heroine pass through a time of suffering, the play invariably ends with the optimism of a fairy tale' (Holme 1902, p. xi).
3 'The atmosphere of the Sanskrit drama is of the fairy story taken to an ultimate pitch of sophistication. … There is the same blend of gentleness, grace and fantasy with a calm maturity and wisdom. Tragedy in the Greek sense does not occur, and unhappy endings of any kind are as foreign to the conventions of Sanskrit drama as they are, for instance, to the novels of Jane Austen' (Coulson 1981, p. 19).
4 See, for example, Tatar 1999, pp. ix–xviii.
5 Gerow 1984, p. 48.
6 '[Greek] tragedy resides in a conflict, the seemingly ineluctable opposition of the man's good and the good of those who constitute his universe.… The classical tragedy is always in some form self-induced in terms of a "tragic flaw" (*hamartia*).… Tragedy seems to presume the possibility that in some ultimate sense, all is not well with the world, that man, because of what he truly is, may perish in the interest of others' (Gerow 1984, p. 48).
7

> Character is constant … The idea that a certain kind of hero is essential to the play reflects the Indian view that character and action are not adventitiously related. In an important sense, nothing 'happens' to the hero, for he is suited to the action that constitutes the play. … Since the true protagonist is inseparable from the nature and quality of his action, and must therefore be successful, the

exploration of failure is, in the Indian view, a self-defeating task. In other words the 'tragic' perspective is an inappropriate way of viewing Sanskrit drama … tragedy seems antithetical to the basic Indian notion that the ultimate good of the individual is integrally bound to the good of all. (ibid., 46–8)

Similary Bhat, in his study of Indian tragedy, concludes after an overview of an 'absence of tragedy' in Sanskrit: 'It appears, therefore, that the Sanskrit poets were either incapable of conceiving the tragic drama, or preferred to avoid it deliberately' (Bhat 1974, p. 95).

8 *The Varieties of Religious Experience*, p. 381.

9 Goodall 1996, pp. 154–5.

10 Ibid., p. 159.

11 Ibid., p. 161.

12 Ibid., p. 127.

13 Ibid., pp. 65–6.

14 Ibid., p. 90.

15 Ibid., p. 157.

16 One would expect *māgamaḥ* instead of *mā … agamaḥ*. On the other hand examples of the prohibitive with *mā* followed by the augmented form of the aorist appear in Vedic and also in epic Sanskrit: *mā … udagāḥ* (Taittirīya Āraṇyaka 1.14.1); *mā vālīpathaṃ anvagāḥ* (Rāmāyaṇa 4.29.48d in Brockington, *Epic Threads*, p. 22). For other examples in the epic sources, see Oberlies 2003, p. 184. I am grateful to Dr Elizabeth Tucker for these examples.

17 Goldman's translation of the *Bālakāṇḍa* followed herein is: 'Since, Nisháda, you killed one of this pair of *krauñchas*, distracted at the height of passion, you shall not live for very long.' It does not exactly translate *śāśvatīḥ samāḥ* (for all time), while the imperative value of *mā*, which it seems Goldman translates not as a prohibition but simply as *na*, remains unclear in Goldman's 'shall'.

18 In the words of Sheldon Pollock 'In this story we find the first acknowledgement not only that the specific power of the literature lies in the expression of emotion – the phonemic correspondence *śoka/śloka* maps an ontological one – but also that the expression of the poet's own emotion constitutes this power' (Pollock 2016, p. 5).

19 For a summary see Vaudeville 1963, pp. 327–8.

20 Vaudeville 1963, p. 327.

21 According to this argument (Vaudeville 1963) the tale up to the arrival of Brahmā forms the content of an ur-legend telling of the rise of poetry in general, especially folk poetry, and is linked to a clan of bards, the Kuśīlavas. The curse, the first verse of *śloka*, was originally uttered not by Vālmīki but by the female *krauñca* bird: 'One may surmise that the verse is a quotation from an older ballad, in which a cruel Niṣāda was cursed by a female Krauñcī bird, symbolising a sorrowful wife

separated from her Lord' (ibid., p. 332). It is also pointed out that the word *krauñca*, deriving from the root *kruñc* (to cry), can imply a class of waterbirds (including the *sārasa* crane) having a sorrowful cry who are mentioned in numerous places in Vedic literature (ibid., pp. 330–1), and that there was a popular belief that 'the cry of those water-birds is caused by sorrow or mourning, *śoka*, so that the *śloka* sung by *krauñca* birds is really born of *śoka* and expresses pathos, *karuṇam*' (ibid., p. 331). The original story of the rise of poetry can thus be imagined to centre on a pair of *krauñca* birds, anthropomorphized to suggest a wife and a noble (which is retained as an evocation in the *krauñcī*'s human-like *karuṇāṃ giram*, 'mournful invocation' in *Vālmīki Rāmāyaṇa* 1.2.11). 'In telling how *śloka* was once born of *śoka*, the Kuśīlavas meant to uphold their own traditional belief on the source of Vālmīki's inspiration: the Krauñca-vadha episode points to popular songs on the popular theme of the sorrow of a faithful wife in separation – a type of song whose heroine was commonly a Krauñcī bird – as one of the main sources of the *rāmāyaṇam kāvyam*' (ibid., p. 335). Vaudeville also suggests, in a perceptive reading, that the *krauñcī* bird symbolically evokes Sītā, the heroine of the *Rāmāyaṇa*. The importance given to her thereby would harmonize with non-Vālmīkian traditions of the Rāmāyaṇa such as the Jain Rāmāyaṇa in which Sītā is the primary character (pp. 334–5).

22 Noticed by Vaudeville 1963, pp. 331–2, n. 15.

23 *tām abhyagacchad ruditānusārī kaviḥ kuśedhmāharaṇāya yātaḥ | niṣādaviddhāṇḍajadarśanotthaḥ ślokatvam āpadyata yasya śokaḥ || Raghuvaṃśa M 14.70.* To her [Sītā] came the poet [Vālmīki], while following her wails, when he had gone to pluck *kuśa* grass as fuel, he whose grief, arisen from the vision of the bird pierced by the hunter, had become poetry.

24 *atha sa brahmarṣir ekadā mādhyāndinasavanāya nadīṃ tamasām anuprapannaḥ | tatra yugmacāriṇoḥ krauñcayor ekaṃ vyādhena vadhyamānaṃ dadarśa | ākasmikapratyavabhāsāṃ devīṃ vācam ānuṣṭubhena chandasā pariṇatām abhyudairayat |mā niṣāda pratiṣṭhāṃ tvam agamaḥ śāśvatīḥ samāḥ | yat krauñcamithunād ekam avadhīḥ kāmamohitam ||*

> *[…] tena hi punaḥ samayena taṃ bhagavantam āvirbhūtaśabdaprakāśam ṛṣim upasaṃgamya bhagavān bhūtabhāvanaḥ padmayonir avocat ṛṣe prabuddho'si vāgātmani brahmaṇi | tad bruhi rāmacaritam | avyāhatajyotir ārṣaṃ te cakṣuḥ pratibhātu | ādyaḥ kavir asi ity uktvāntarhitaḥ | atha sa bhagavān prācetasaḥ prathamaṃ manuṣyeṣu śabdabrahmaṇas tādṛśaṃ vivartam itihāsaṃ rāmāyaṇaṃ praṇināya |* (*Uttararāmacarita*, II.5, pp. 29–30).

Once, that sage arrived at the Tamasā River to have the midday ritual bath. There he beheld one amongst two krauñcas, roaming as a couple, being slain by a hunter. When the Goddess Speech suddenly appeared to him, he gave her expression, transformed as the metre Anuṣṭubh (śloka): 'Never, for all time, O Hunter, may you attain stability, since you slew one among the pair of krauñcas while they were entranced in lovemaking!' At that time, the Lord who is born from a lotus [Brahmā], the creator of beings came to that revered sage in whom the light of the sacred word had arisen and said 'O Sage, you are knowledgeable about the ultimate Truth Brahman whose nature is the sacred word. Thus, declare the deeds of Rāma. May your seer's eye, in which the light [of imagination] is unimpeded, flash forth. You shall be the first poet.' Saying thus, he disappeared. Then the lord, descendant of Pracetas, conveyed the history [called] Rāmāyaṇa, which, among men, is the first such transformation of Brahman in the form of sacred Sound.

25 *mā* + *ālabdhāḥ*; the latter is the aorist *ātmanepada*, 2 p sg of *ā-labh* = to reach.

26 *sa gatvā tamasātīraṃ tīrthe snātvā kṛtārcanaḥ* |
cacāra śiṣyasahitaḥ puṇyāsu vanabhumiṣu || *1.15*
tasyāgre krauñcamithunād ekaṃ manmathamohitam |
sa dadarśa niṣādena nihataṃ niśiteṣuṇā || *1.16*
tataḥ ślokacchalāt tasya śokānalasamīritaḥ |
dayayā hṛdayālīno nirgataḥ karuṇo rasaḥ || *1.17*
aho niṣkaruṇenedaṃ niṣādena viṣādakṛt |
kṛtaṃ kukṛtaśīlena karma marmavidāraṇam || *1.18*
mā niṣāda pratiṣṭhāṃ tvam ālabdhāḥ śāśvatīḥ samāḥ |
yat krauñcamithunād avadhīḥ kāmamohitam || *1.19*
ity uktvā karuṇāsindhuḥ samīpasthaṃ punaḥ punaḥ |
ślokaṃ paṭhan muhuḥ śokād iti śiṣyam abhāṣata || *1.20*
tatas tatra nadītīre sthitaḥ śiṣyayuto muniḥ |
dadarśa tatra ślokasaṃtoṣāt svayaṃ brahmāṇam āgatam || *1.21*
muninābhyarcitas tatra pādyapūjāsanādibhiḥ |
so'vadat puṇyapīyūṣaṃ dantakāntyā kirann iva || *1.22*
aho sārasvataḥ ko'pi taruṇaḥ karuṇāvataḥ |
avatīrya tava mune prasaraḥ sarasaḥ svayam || *1.23*
rāmasya caritaṃ cāru kāvyabandho vidhīyatām |
astu caiva sudhādhautā kṛtakṛtyā sarasvatī || *1.24*
lokeṣv anekakalpāntasthāyi karṇāmṛtaṃ satām |
kuru rāmāyaṇaṃ puṇyaṃ yaśo nijam ivojjvalam || *1.25*
ity uktvāntarhite kṣipraṃ prajāsṛji munīśvaraḥ |
kartuṃ pracakrame rāmacaritaṃ jñānalocanaḥ || 1.26 Rāmāyaṇamañjarī

He [Vālmīki] having gone to the bank of the Tamasā, having bathed in the sacred waters and worshipped, wandered with his students on the auspicious grounds of the forest. He witnessed before him one amongst a pair of *krauñca*s slain by a hunter with a pointed arrow while it was entranced in passion.

Then, the tragic *rasa*, abiding in his heart effused out of his compassion in the guise of a verse, impelled by the fire of his grief. 'Alack a heartless hunter, whose practice is to conduct cruelties, did this deed, a cause of anguish that tears at my mortal part! Never, for all time, O Hunter, may you gain stability, since you slew one amongst the pair of *krauñca*s while it was entranced in lovemaking.'

Saying this, that ocean of compassion taught his student standing nearby by reciting the verse over and over again, which had momentarily arisen in that way out of grief. Then the sage while on that riverbank with his student saw Brahmā himself arrive there in his satisfaction with the verse. Honoured by the sage at that place with offerings of water for washing the feet and worshipped with auspicious cries, he spoke, scattering with the lustre of his teeth, it seemed, auspicious nectar. 'Ah, Sage, what an indescribable, fresh, offspring of the goddess Sarasvatī that having descended in you, when you were filled with compassion, [became] a *rasa*-laden torrent of its own accord. Let an epic poem set down the delightful deeds of Rāma! And in this way may Sarasvatī, bathed in nectar, be one whose duties are acquitted! Compose the auspicious *Rāmāyaṇa*, that shall abide till the end of many *kalpa*s among men, the nectar for the hearing of the virtuous, as brilliant as your own fame.' When, having spoken thus, the creator of subjects [Brahmā] had swiftly disappeared, the lord of sages, eye of knowledge, began to compose the deeds of Rāma.

27 *Dhvanyāloka* 1.5 and *Dhvanyālokalocana* 1.5; Ingalls, Masson, Patwardhan 1990, pp. 113–15).

28 Pollock 2016, p. 5.

29 Ingalls, Masson and Patwardhan 1990, p. 115; see also pp. 113–14; for Sanskrit text see *Dhvanyālokalocana* 1.5, pp. 84–6. For a response to this view by Jaina scholars, see Restifo 2019.

30 G. K. Bhat too bases his exposition of the tragic in Sanskrit literature on Western tragedy: 'Tragedy is a Western concept. It will have to be viewed, I assume, according to the direction provided by Western thinkers from Aristotle downwards, and by the criteria implicitly present in the tragedies written by Western dramatists. Very little has been written on the subject of tragedy in Sanskrit drama by Indian scholars; and the one or two articles that have been published seem to be written with the ostensible purpose of proving the existence of tragic drama in Sanskrit. It appears to me that these attempts are either misguided as to the proper criteria for a formal tragedy, or else, they are an apology for a possible shortcoming in Sanskrit literature' (Bhat 1974, preface, p. v).

31 Thus Aristotle in the *Poetics*: 'Tragedy is a representation of an action of a superior kind – grand, and complete in itself – presented in embellished language, in distinct forms in different parts, performed by actors rather than told by a narrator, effecting through pity and fear, the purification of such emotions' (Kenny 2013, p. 23).

32 Lewes quoted by A. S. Byatt, introduction to *The Mill on the Floss*, p. xxxvii.
33 A. S. Byatt, introduction to *The Mill on the Floss*, p. xxxvii.
34 Eliot quoted by A. S. Byatt, introduction to *The Mill on the Floss*, p. xxvi.
35 'But if hostile to light irony, religion is equally hostile to heavy grumbling and complaint. The world appears tragic enough in some religions, but the tragedy is realized as purging, and a way of deliverance is held to exist. We shall see enough of the religious melancholy in a future lecture; but melancholy according to our ordinary use of language, forfeits all title to be called religious when, in Marcus Aurelius's racy words, the sufferer simply lies kicking and screaming after the fashion of a sacrificed pig. The mood of a Schopenhauer or a Nietzsche, – and in a less degree one may sometimes say the same of our own sad Carlyle, – though often an ennobling sadness, is almost as often only peevishness running away with the bit between its teeth. The sallies of the two German authors remind one, half the time, of the sick shriekings of two dying rats. They lack the purgatorial note which religious sadness gives forth' (*The Varieties of Religious Experience*, p. 38).
36 Tolstoy quoted in *The Varieties of Religious Experience*, p. 156.
37 Frye 2010, p. 7.
38 In the same vein Bhat 1974, p. 2: 'One of the characteristic themes of tragic representation in the ancient days is the conflict … resulting in the hero's death and resurrection; this symbolises the death and rejuvenation in nature.'
39 Frye 2010, pp. 7–8. I am grateful to Pirachula Chulanon for first pointing out this article to me and its importance for my work.
40 See Chapter 4 in this book for an analysis.
41 *Nāṭyaśāstra* 6.39–45 in Pollock 2016, pp. 52–3.
42 *Nāṭyaśāstra* 6.39–45 in Pollock 2016, p. 52.
43 *Nāṭyaśāstra* 6.45 in Pollock 2016, p. 53, section 304.

Introduction, Part II: Doubt, obstacle, deliberation, death, disaster: The trial in Indian aesthetics

1 I am grateful for Dr Andrew Ollett's careful reading of and detailed comments on this section and for his suggestions of various resources on plot development in Sanskrit. Prof. Diwakar Acharya, with whom I read the *Abhinavabhāratī*, clarified many of the philosophical issues discussed in that work. I am indebted to both of them for their time and patience.
2 Warder 1972, I, pp. 54–76; Byrski 1974; Tubb 1979, pp. 119–86; Gerow 1979–80 and Kane 1983. Kane's (1983) is by far the most exhaustive and in-depth study of the subject, while Byrski's (1974) is the most original and the most perceptive

regarding the *vimarśa*. The arguments about the *pañcakatraya* here are largely a summary of their findings.

3 Date according to Pollock 2016, p. 47.

4 On the other hand, a theory of art appears to have long been known prior to its systematization in the *Nāṭyaśāstra* in the fourth century CE and was propounded by other teachers, of both drama and erotics it seems, whose names alone are later recalled though their works were lost (such as Suvarṇābha, Kucumāra, Nandikeśvara) (De 1988, p. 2, with reference to the *Kāvyamīmāṃsā* and the *Kāmasūtra*). De (1988, pp. 1–17) discusses some important antecedents to poetical concepts of word and meaning in the grammatical tradition. On this basis one can concur with the historian of Indian aesthetics Pollock in his view that: 'Some organized body of knowledge of the sort presented here [in the *Nāṭyaśāstra*] had therefore long been in existence' (Pollock 2016, p. 47).

5 Cf. Haas 1912, pp. 8–32.

6 The full verse is as follows:

> *taṃ taha soūṇa puṇo bhaṇiyaṃ ubbiṃbabālahariṇācchi* |
> *jai evaṃ tā suvvau susaṃdhibaṃdhaṃ kahāvatthuṃ* ||

7 Tubb 1979, p. 19.

8 *Nāṭyaśāstra* 19.2–5. See also *Abhinavabhāratī* 19.3–4; and Kane 1983, p. 9.

9 *Abhinavabhāratī* 19.3; *Avaloka* 1.11ab; *Sāhityadarpaṇa* 6.67ab; Kane 1983, p. 10.

10 Kane 1983, p. 14.

11 *autsukyamātrabandhas tu yadbījasya nibadhyate / mahataḥ phalayogasya sa phalārambha iṣyate // Nāṭyaśāstra* 19.9; cf. *Abhinavabhāratī* 19.9; *Daśarūpa* 1.20ab; *Avaloka* 1.20ab; *Sāhityadarpaṇa* 6.71cd; Byrski 1974, p. 104; Kane 1983, pp. 14–16.

12 *apaśyataḥ phalaprāptiṃ vyāpāro yaḥ phalaṃ prati / paraṃ cautsukyagamanaṃ sa prayatnaḥ prakīrtitaḥ // Nāṭyaśāstra* 19.10; cf. *Abhinavabhāratī* 19.10; *Daśarūpa* 1.20cd; *Avaloka* 1.20cd; *Sāhityadarpaṇa* 6.72ab; Byrski 1974, p. 104; Kane 1983, pp. 17–19.

13 *īṣatprāptir yadā kācit phalasya parikalpate / bhāvamātreṇa tu prāhur vidhijñāḥ prāptisambhavam // Nāṭyaśāstra* 19.11; cf. *Abhinavabhāratī* 19.11; *Daśarūpa* 1.21 ab; Haas 1912, p. 10; *Avaloka* 1.21 ab; *Sāhityadarpaṇa* 6.72cd; Byrski 1974, p. 104; Kane 1983, pp. 19–20 (including consideration of the *Sāhityadarpaṇa*).

14 Kane 1983, p. 20, translates, apparently without taking into account the *Avaloka*: *upāyāpāyaśaṅkābhyām prāptyāśā prāptisambhavaḥ (Daśarūpa* 1.21ab): 'The possibility of obtaining the fruit is a hope for its attainment accompanied by doubts as to what will prove helpful or hurtful.'

15 *niyatāṃ tu phalaprāptiṃ yadā bhāvena paśyati / niyatāṃ tāṃ phalaprāptiṃ saguṇāṃ paricakṣate //Nāṭyaśāstra* 19.12; *Abhinavabhāratī* 19.12; *Daśarūpa* 1.21cd;

Avaloka 1.21cd; *Sāhityadarpaṇa* 6.73ab; Byrski 1974, p. 136 (interpreting as restriction of the attainment); Kane 1983, p. 21.

16 *abhipretaṃ samagraṃ ca pratirūpaṃ kriyāphalam / itivṛtte bhaved yasmin phalayogaḥ prakīrtitaḥ // Nāṭyaśāstra* 19.13; *Abhinavabhāratī* 19.13; *Daśarūpa* 1.22cd; *Avaloka* 1.22cd; *Sāhityadarpaṇa* 6.73cd; Byrski 1974, p. 112; Kane 1983, p. 22.

17 Abhinavagupta summarizes the stages succinctly: 'And the means, when resorted to by one undertaking action, undergoes five stages as follows: the means in its essential nature, the means when somewhat swollen beyond its essential nature, the means when potentially able to effect the fruit, the means when placed in doubt by the onslaught of obstacles and the means when certain to lead to the fruit of the annulment of hindrances on the cessation of opposition. Thus those who are capable of enduring suffering, who dread disappointment, and who think before they act, employ a cause [of attaining their goal] having this extent', *Dhvanyālokalocana* 3.14.75–88 in Tubb 1979, pp. 139–40.

18 'The course of the mythological action-sacrifice has the following invariable succession of events or elements: (A) desire (B) effort as well as continuation denoted in the sacrifice by *śrama*, *tapas*, *śraddhā*, *yajña* and *āhuti*; (C) obstruction marked by an attack of the Asura Rākṣasas; (D) its overcoming and completion of the sacrifice. ... The import and aim of the action-sacrifice is a mystical reconstruction of the body of the Lord of Creatures and through it the fulfilment of all desires. ... Since *Yajña* claims to be the pattern for all happening in the Universe, then the elements of it outlined above will naturally remain a true expression of the Universe as well. On the other hand, since *Nāṭya* claims to be the representation of the true state of the Three Worlds and as such claims to deserve the name of sacrifice itself (*ijyā*, NŚ.V.108), then these elements of the sacrifice have to be represented by *Nāṭya*' (Byrski, 1974, p. 100). In a similar vein, Byrski 1974, p. 137: 'Since *Yajña* must reach a positive conclusion, it cannot therefore be overrun by the adverse forces of the Asuras, for then the disintegrated body of the Lord of Creatures will not be reconstructed and the whole order of the Universe will be perilously disturbed. *Nāṭya* is supposed to reflect the nature of the world to such an extent that it is itself called a sacrifice ... so that it cannot disregard this pattern and consequently be an untrue representation of the Three Worlds.'

19 McCrea 2009, pp. 62, 65, 70, 89–97.

20 *Abhinavabhāratī* 19.20; Kane 1983, p. 25.

21 *Abhinavabhāratī* 19.22.

22 *svalpamātraṃ samutsṛṣṭaṃ bahudhā yad visarpati / phalāvasānaṃ yac caiva bījaṃ tat parikīrtitam || Nāṭyaśāstra* 19.22; *Abhinavabhāratī* 19.22; *Daśarūpa* 1.17ab; *Avaloka* 1.17ab; *Sāhityadarpaṇa* 6.65cd–6.66ab; Byrski 1974, pp. 118–19 (he develops the plant analogy in p. 119); Kane 1983, p. 26.

23 The *Daśarūpaka* has *avāntarārtha* instead of *prayojana*, which is translated by Haas as 'secondary matter'.

24 *prayojanānāṃ vicchede yad avicchedakāraṇam / yāvatsamāptir bandhasya sa binduḥ parikīrtitaḥ // Nāṭyaśāstra* 19.23; cf. *Abhinavabhāratī* 19.23; *Daśarūpa* 1.17cd; *Avaloka* 1. 17 cd; *Sāhityadarpaṇa* 6.66cd; Byrski 1974, p. 121; Kane 1983, pp. 26–7.

25 *yad vṛttaṃ tu parārthaṃ syāt pradhānasyopakārakam pradhānavac ca kalpyeta sā patāketi kīrtitā // Nāṭyaśāstra* 19.24; cf. *Abhinavabhāratī* 19.24; *Daśarūpa* 1.18 (dealt with tersely); *Avaloka* 1.18; *Sāhityadarpaṇa* 6.67cd (correlating the *prāsaṅgikam itivṛttam* with the *patākā*); Byrski 1974, p. 123; Kane 1983, p. 29, Rangacharya 1996, p. 158). Rāmacandra and Guṇacandra, Jaina literary critics, see Śūdraka's *Mṛcchakaṭikā* to be dominated by the development of the *patākā* (Warder 1972, III, p. 34).

26 *phalaṃ prakalpyate yasyāḥ parārthāyaiva kevalam / anubandhavihīnatvāt prakarīti vinirdiśet // Nāṭyaśāstra* 19.25; cf. *Abhinavabhāratī* 19.25; *Daśarūpa* 1.18 (dealt with tersely); *Avaloka* 1.18; Byrski 1974, p. 123; Kane 1983, p. 33.

27 *yad ādhikārikaṃ vastu samyak prājñaiḥ prayujyate / tadartho yaḥ samārambhas tat kāryaṃ parikīrtitam // Nāṭyaśāstra* 19.26; cf. *Abhinavabhāratī* 19.26; *Daśarūpa* 1.18 (dealt with tersely); *Avaloka* 1.18; Byrski 1974, p. 131; Kane 1983, p. 33; Warder 1972, I, p. 54.

28 *Daśarūpa* 1.16cd; Haas 1912, p. 8.

29 *Sāhityadarpaṇa* 6.69cd–6.70ab, Kane 1983, pp. 34–8.

30 *Sāhityadarpaṇa* 6.69cd–6.70ab.

31 *Daśarūpa* 1.13cd; *Avaloka* 1.13cd.

32 In similar vein Byrski 1974, who feels that the '*bīja* appears to be the most universal, and, therefore, the most important of the five *arthaprakṛtis*' (Byrski 1974, p. 119).

33 Cf. Byrski 1974, p. 118.

34 Warder describes the *sandhis* as 'conjunctions between the actions, and activating emotions, of different characters in the story as arranged by the playwright. The opening will thus be when the actions of two (or more) characters cross in such a way as to produce the seed' (Warder 1972, I, p. 58).

35 *Daśarūpa* 1.23cd; *Avaloka* 1.23cd; Haas 1912, p. 12.

36 *yatra bījasamutpattirnānārtharasasambhavā / kāvye śarīrānugatā tanmukhaṃ parikīrtitam // Nāṭyaśāstra* 19.39; cf. *Abhinavabhāratī* 19.39; *Daśarūpa* 1.24cd–1.25ab; *Avaloka* 1.24cd–1.25ab; *Sāhityadarpaṇa* 6.76; Haas 1912, p. 12; Byrski 1974, p. 134; Kane 1983, p. 45.

37 *bījasyodghāṭanaṃ yatra dṛṣṭanaṣṭam iva kvacit / mukhanyastasya sarvatra tad vai pratimukhaṃ smṛtam // Nāṭyaśāstra* 19.40; cf. *Abhinavabhāratī* 19.40; *Daśarūpa* 1.30, *Avaloka* 1.30; *Sāhityadarpaṇa* 6.77; Haas 1912, p. 15; Byrski 1974, p. 134; Kane 1983, p. 45.

38 *udbhedas tasya bījasya prāptir aprāptir eva vā / punaścānveṣaṇaṃ yatra sa garbha iti saṃjñitaḥ // Nāṭyaśāstra* 19.41; cf. *Abhinavabhāratī* 19.41; *Daśarūpa* 1.36; *Avaloka* 1.36; *Sāhityadarpaṇa* 6.78; Haas 1912, p. 20; Byrski 1974, p. 134; Kane 1983, p. 47; Rangacharya 1996, p. 159.

39 *garbhanirbhinnabījārtho vilobhanakṛto 'thavā / krodhavyasanajo vāpi sa vimarśa iti smṛtaḥ // Nāṭyaśāstra* 19.42; cf. *Abhinavabhāratī* 19.42; *Daśarūpa* 1.43; *Avaloka* 1.43; *Sāhityadarpaṇa* 6.79; Haas 1912, p. 24; Byrski 1974, p. 134; Kane 1983, p. 47; Warder 1972, I, p. 59; Rangacharya 1996, p. 159.

40 *Sāhityadarpaṇa* VI.79cd–6.80ab.

41 *samānayanam arthānāṃ mukhādyānāṃ sabījinām / nānābhāvottarāṇāṃ yad bhaven nirvahaṇaṃ tu tat // Nāṭyaśāstra* 19.43; cf. *Abhinavabhāratī* 19.43; *Daśarūpa* 1.48 cd–1.49ab; *Avaloka* 1.48cd–1.49ab; *Sāhityadarpaṇa* 6.90; Haas 1912, p. 28; Byrski 1974, p. 134; Kane 1983, p. 50.

42 The *ḍima* and the *samavakāra* do not show the phase of Trial. The *vyāyoga* and the *ihāmṛga* do not have either the Embryo or the Trial. The *bhāṇa*, the *prahasana* and the *vīthi* only have the Source and the End (*Nāṭyaśāstra* 19.45–7).

43 Kane 1983 p. 51.

44 *Abhinavabhāratī* 19.18; Kane 1983, p. 51.

45 Warder 1972, p. 59.

46 Kane 1983, pp. 52–3. For Rāmacandra and Guṇacandra on aesthetic experience, see Restifo 2019.

47 Kane 1983, pp. 52–3.

48 'The positive progression of the play's action as conveyed by the avasthās may in effect be thwarted or temporarily suspended by various aspects of the middle three sandhis. the two groups work together: the sandhis are the vehicle for the expression of the stages of action in the drama, and in opposition to each other: the sandhis also do not permit the avasthās to become overly linear. The tension and balance between these two groups is perhaps the most important factor in the formation of a successful plot based on dramaturgical theory (Kane 1983, p. 52).

49 'It should be clear from what the *Nāṭyaśāstra* says that the conjunctions do not necessarily match the stages of the action. These latter apply to any action and presumably to any kind of play, including those in which there are only two conjunctions. The stages are regarded as inevitable, even in real life. The conjunctions are not inevitable, but some or all of them should be used by the playwright in his art, depending on the scale, especially the length, of his presentation. The conjunctions are all related to the seed of the objective and its development, or in other words to the plot as devised by the playwright out of his original story material. They are largely concerned with impediments to this development, with the dramatic conflict. The stages on the other hand are distinguished in a straightforward manner in relation to the fruit and the means to attain it. We may conclude that a

straightforward narration (without a "plot") is to be transformed into a work of art by the introduction of the conjunctions' (Warder 1972, I, p. 60).

50 'The already quoted definition of the *niyatāpti* stage of action does not indicate whether the word *niyata* should be translated as 'suppressed' or as 'sure', 'certain'. In our view the following arguments speak for the first alternative … the hitherto accepted interpretation brought to its logical conclusion practically excludes the last *avasthā* (*phalāgama*), which according to NŚ [the *Nāṭyaśāstra*] has to be present along with the first one in the form of the first and the last *sandhi*s in absolutely all plays. Besides, the old interpretation inadmissibly dilutes the conflict so that there is hardly any place left for it in a play. From the very beginning a hero will steadily approach his aim without any really serious setback. After the Possibility of Attainment (*prāptisambhava*) comes immediately the Certainty of Success (*niyatāpti*) which is followed by the Attainment of Fruit (*phalāgama*). Despair (*duḥkha*) which according to the definition of *Nāṭya* has to be present in it, is totally absent from such a theoretical play. Yet as if yielding to this obvious requirement, supported also by dramatic practice, Abhinavagupta, Dhanika, Viśvanātha and others mention in the course of their discussion the existence of the element of disruption at the *niyatāpti* stage. Nevertheless, for them the true *niyatāpti* stage seems to follow the overcoming of difficulties. This unnatural shift of stress is, of course, forced upon them by their wrong interpretation of the word *niyata*. Once this word is taken in its negative meaning of "suppressed", "curbed" or "restrained", then a conflict in a play carrying with itself an element of despair gains a legitimate and prominent place in a drama. Such an interpretation is also justified from the point of view of an emotional reaction. The joy of a final victory is immensely augmented when contrasted with the very-near-to defeat situation which precedes it.'

51 I am grateful to Prof. Diwakar Acharya for clarifying this passage.

52 For Abhinavagupta's use of the *Nāṭyaśāstra*, see Tubb 1985.

53 A possibility is that they could have read *so 'vamarśa*, apparently seeing the initial *a* of *avamarśa* elided through *sandhi* which they assumed from seeing an *avagraha* – the *avagraha* and the short *i* are similar in writing.

54 Kane 1983, pp. 48–9, translates *sandehātmako vimarśa…katham na sandehaḥ* thus: 'The reconsideration consists of doubt. But an objector says that the notion that the possibility [of obtaining the fruit] occurs first, and then any doubt is not proper, because the followers of Nyāya say that the reasoning comes in between doubt and certainty. Moreover, the reconsideration is pervaded by the Niyataphalaprāpti avasthā, and how can certainty and doubt exist [at that time]? The following is the reply to the objection. Even after reasoning [that the fruit could be obtained], doubt may exist if the pervasiveness [of the certainty] has been removed by some other cause, and why should that not be the case

here? Even though a fruit may be possible due to the strength of a cause, when it is contradicted by a strong [cause], and when strong causes [for a different conclusion] exist, then how can there fail to be doubt, because the productive and obstructive [causes] have equal force.

55 For Nyāya definitions of *vimarśa* as logical doubt, see Chapter III; see also *Nyāyasūtra* 1.1.23.

56 The phrase used is *sutarām uddhūrakandharībhavati*: 'strenuously stretches its neck.'

57 Cf. Kane 1983, p. 59: translates *yata eva … ucyate* as: 'Whether the setback is due to the efforts of an adversary or due to one's own endeavours [directed toward another goal], one who is ready for human effort partakes of action even though previously opposed, because of the development of the desire to succeed. The attainment of the fruit is said to be certain because of this intention [of the hero].'

58 *tadalobhe*] ed., p. 28, *tadalābhe* correction.

59 *āvṛtt-*] ed., p. 28, *āvṛtta-*, em. D. Acharya.

60 *-nirbhinno*] ed. p. 28, *-nirbhinnam*, em. D. Acharya.

61 It is unclear whether this camp understood *vimarśa* to be either doubt or obstacle.

62 The syntax of *punar apy asya saraṇir eva* and its correlation to *sā ca …* is odd.

63 cf. *asakṛduccāritasyaikasya śabdasya śaktyā anekārthapratipādakatvaṃ tantram iti śābdikā vadanti* | [quotation unattributed] *vivakṣitārthajñāpakaṃ tantram it vedāntinaḥ* | [quotation unattributed], *Nyāyakośa* p. 318. I am grateful to Prof. Diwakar Acharya for kindly pointing out this reference.

64 See for instance his reanalysis of Vāmana's interpretation of the *Nāṭyaśāstra* on the *guṇas* of literature in Tubb 1985.

1 Kālidāsa and his inheritance of grief

1 The date of Kālidāsa is far from certain. For various arguments and theories, see Mirashi andNavlekar 1969, pp. 1–35. I have here followed their conclusion, based on the Aihole inscription of Pulakeśin II forming the lower limit and an inscription from Mandasor of *c.*473–4 CE, verse 10 (in which the poet Vatsabhaṭṭi emulates the *Meghadūta*), forming the upper limit (ibid., p. 29). Cf. Lienhard 1984, p. 115, who similarly locates Kālidāsa in *c.*400 CE, in the court of Candragupta II (375–413 CE), also known as 'Vikramāditya' of Ujjayinī.

2 On the basis of his work, Bhat 1974 undertook a study of tragedy (in the Greek formal sense) in Sanskrit.

3 Devadhar 1962, pp. 489–508 (Sanskrit text); Gerow 1985b, pp. 57–70; Gerow 1985a, pp. 405–12.

4 S. Lévi and B. Winternitz cited in Devadhar 1962, p. iii; K. Rama Pisharoti cited in Devadhar 1962, p. ix; Devadhar 1962, pp. i–x; M. M. Kuppuswami Sastri in Venkatachalam 1986, p. 16; P. V. Kane in Venkatchalam 1986, p. 16. A strong pro-Bhāsa camp also exists. For a summary of the 'vivacious controversy', see Venkatachalam 1986, pp. 9–17.

5 *Dhvanyālokalocana* p. 335.

6 For example: Jhala 1943; Sabnis 1966; Sarma 1968; Mirashi and Navlekar 1969; Yadav 1974; Warder 1972, III, pp. 122–54; Lienhard 1981, pp. 114–21; and n. 173; Miller 1984. For more, see A. Wezler's preface to the *Meghadūta*, p. xi.

7 These tend to be general comments on the beauty of pathos, for example: Mirashi and Navlekar 1969, pp. 126–7 (*Rativilāpa*) and ibid., pp. 174–77 (*Ajavilāpa*); and Jhala 1943, p. 171 (on the repudiation of Śakuntalā by Duṣyanta).

8 'His [Kālidāsa's] *kāvyas* may be said to exemplify a trend in the art … the lyrical one, which carries to an extreme the possibilities suggested by the independence of the stanzas in an epic, together with an assumed implication of the theory that it is the emotions which constitute the essential content of a work of art. We have traced above [in the analysis of Pāli literature] the role of lyric poetry in the development of the *kāvya* medium and seen how its techniques pervaded epic poetry, drama and prose composition. We are also familiar with the originally dramatic theory of the presentation of emotions, producing the aesthetic experience. The trend which Kāldāsa represents would reduce all *kāvya* to lyric poetry, eliminating the narrative element necessary to the epic form, and would concentrate on depicting emotion whilst neglecting the action which constitutes the matter of drama and the real basis of emotional experiences' (Warder 1972, III p. 124).

9 See Chapter 3.

10 Moreover, the word *prayoga*, literally 'use'/'employment', is frequently used for performance in the *Nāṭyaśāstra* (while, deriving from the same basal formation *pra-yuj*, the word *prayoktṛ* meaning an executor/agent is used to refer to an actor/performer), and there is a certain, definite ring of Bharata in that word in the *Kumārasambhava.* For the use of prayoktṛ and similar words in the Nāṭyaśāstra to denote actors and poets, see Byrski 1974, p. 128.

11 It is not certain that this Bharata was the same as the author of the *Nāṭyaśāstra.*

12 On more on Rāma's vulnerability, see Sattar 2011, and on this lament, ibid., p. 89.

13 'The Birth Story of Vessantara,' in Appleton and Shaw 2015, Vol. 2, pp. 507–640. For Maddī, see ibid., pp. 607–17. I am sincerely grateful to Dr Sarah Shaw for first telling me about Maddī, for sharing so generously her research and for engaging in stimulating conversations about the tragic middle in Indian and other literature. I learnt much from her, especially concerning how one can make wider literary connections.

14 Carvings of Vessantara's giving away of his children are to be found in Bharhut, Sanchi, Amaravati, Goli, Ajaṇṭā, Gandhāra and in Miran in Chinese Turkestan: Cone and Gombrich 1977, p. xxxv, pp. xliv–xlvii; see also Appleton and Shaw 2015, Vol. 2, p. 507.

15 Cone and Gombrich 1977, pp. 109–10.

16 Appleton and Shaw 2015, Vol. 2, pp. 602–6.

17 'The story is completely simple and unified in its construction, with an internal logic that can lead to one, and only one, deeply shocking and near tragic crisis, but also to one, and only one, happy resolution. The utterly absurd and wonderful premise of its plot is this: that each Bodhisatta, in order to find complete awakening, must in a life shortly before the final one give absolutely everything they have away. This includes his wealth, possessions, inheritance of the kingdom, for this Bodhisatta the seven-hundredfold gift of alms to renunciates (a very important gift), carriage, and indeed his wife and children. The Bodhisatta in this story does all of these things; Gombrich has provided analysis of the function and meaning of the gifts in his introduction (PGPV xii–xvii). If the Bodhisatta were a tragic hero in a Shakespearean or ancient Greek drama, this impassioned giving away of what is most precious to him would constitute an act of terrible *hubris*, an action against the gods, produced from some fatal flaw (*hamartia*) that can lead only to *nemesis*, the terrible and often agonizingly appropriate destruction of the hero and his family. It very nearly does this: he really is like a tragic hero in his immense conviction, utterly undiverted focus, and complete commitment to his mission. And, after being banished to the forest and giving away his children, who suffer terribly at the hands of the brahmin, he does seem to be facing an end like a great tragic hero, alone and weeping over his wife who seems near death, like Othello over Desdemona or King Lear over his daughter Cordelia, with all worldly happiness and good fortune thrown away. But this is not a tragedy, nor even a comedy, though its outcome fulfils many classical expectations of both genres. For it is the very generosity of the Bodhisatta's initial vow, made aeons before, that ensures he is protected in his great acts of giving. The world systems themselves quake even when he first thinks of his acts of generosity. It quakes again when he makes his gifts, and again at the end. The gods, and even the *yakkha*s who speed the exiled family's journey from their own kingdom, know his aspiration and do not allow the family to come to harm. *Deva*s prevent Maddī from being harmed but also ensure she does not intervene to prevent his gift. King Sakka, protecting the Bodhisatta from the possibility of being alone and unprotected, comes to ask for her, and then at what is the turning point of the story, gives her back and offers him eight wishes, ensuring their future happiness. Gods also come to the children's aid when they are in captivity, tucking them up in divine garments and bedding when their cruel captor has gone to sleep. By the end of the story, in, as Gombrich points

out, exactly the reverse order that the gifts had been given and the banishment had taken place, the family return triumphantly, gifts successively returned, accompanied by the king and queen and their magnificent entourage back to their own city (PGPV xiii–xvi). The end does not only offer a simple palindrome, or chiasmus, unraveling events back to their beginning; it is a creative return. When they are welcomed home, the Bodhisatta is made king, and festivals are celebrated, with now universal acceptance of his code and way of life. So the Bodhisatta, with his great deed undertaken, immediately continues his acts of giving, now within the protected sphere of his kingdom and aided by King Sakka and his own people' (Appleton and Shaw 2015, Vol. 2, pp. 508–9).

18 Cone and Gombrich 1977, p. xxxvi.

19 Haribhaṭṭa reveres the high standard of Āryaśūra's compositions in the very beginning of the *Jātakāmālā* (verse 2) in Hahn 2007, p. 3 (Sanskrit), p. 4 (English translation).

20 Meiland 2009, p. xix.

21 'The story of Vessantara is included with exactly a hundred verses. This version presupposes the VJ verses and much of the material in the Pali prose … [showing] that Āryaśūra has borrowed directly from the Pali or something close to it' (Cone and Gombrich 1977, p. xxxvi).

22 The synonyms for 'unwanted', *aniṣṭa* and *anīpsita*, seem to refer here specifically to omens.

23 *Api* with the optative strengthens the latter.

24 *atha madrī vipriyopanipātaśaṃsibhir aniṣṭair upajanitavaimanasyā mūlaphalāny ādāyā kṣiprataram āgantukāmāpi vyāḍamṛgoparudhyamānamārgā ciratarenāśramapadam upajagāma | ucitāyāṃ ca pratyudgamanabhūmāv ākrīḍāsthāne ca tanayāv apaśyantī bhṛśataram arativaśam agāt | anīpsitāśaṅkitajātasaṃbhramā tataḥ sutānveṣaṇacañcalekṣaṇā | prasaktam āhvānam asaṃparigrahaṃ tayor viditvā vyalapac chucāturā || [9.]78.*

samājavad yat pratibhāti me purā sutapralāpapratināditaṃ vanam | adarśanād adya tayos tad eva me prayāti kāntāram ivāśaraṇyatām || 79 kiṃ nu khalu tau kumārau krīḍāprasaṅgaśramajātanidrau suptau nu naṣṭau gahane vane vā | cirān madabhyāgamād atuṣṭau syātāṃ kvacid bālatayā nilīnau || 80 ruvanti kasmāc ca na pakṣiṇo 'apy amī samākulās tadvadhasākṣiṇo yadi | taraṅgabhaṅgair avinītakopayā hṛtau nu kiṃ nimnagayātivegayā || 81 apīdānīṃ me vitathā mithyāvikalpā bhaveyuḥ | api rājaputrāya saputrāya svasti syāt | apy aniṣṭanivedināṃ nimittānāṃ maccharīra eva vipāko bhavet | kiṃ nu khalv idam animittāpavṛttapraharṣam aratitamisrayāvacchādyamānaṃ vidravatīva hṛdayaṃ | visrasyanta iva me gātrāṇi | vyākulā iva digvibhāgāḥ | bhramatīva cedaṃ paridhvastalakṣmīkaṃ vanam iti | athānupraviśyāśramapadam ekānte nikṣipya mūlaphalaṃ yathopacārapuraḥsaraṃ bhartāram abhigamya kva dārakāv iti prapaccha | atha bodhisattva jānānaḥ snehadurbalatāṃ mātṛhṛdayasya durnivedyatvāc ca viprayasya naināṃ kiṃcid vaktuṃ śaśāka |

janasya hi priyārhasya vipriyākhyānavahninā | upetya manasas tāpaḥ saghṛṇena suduṣkaraḥ || 82 atha madrī vyaktam akuśalaṃ me putrayoḥ | yad ayam evaṃ tuṣṇīṃbhūtaḥ śokadainyānyvṛttyaivety avadhārya samantataḥ kṣiptacitteva vilokyāśramapadaṃ tanayāv apaśyantī sabāṣpagadgadaṃ punar uvāca | dārakau ca na paśyāmi tvaṃ ca māṃ nābhibhāṣase | hatā khalv ahaṃ kṛpaṇā vipriyaṃ hi na kathyate || 83 ity uktvā śokāgninā pargatahṛdayā chinnamūleva latā nipapāta | Viśvantarajātaka in the *Jātakamālā*, pp. 64–5.

25 *athavā suramālyarūpabhāg aśanir nirmita eṣa karmaṇā | yad anena taru na pātitaḥ kṣapitā tadviṭapāśrayā latā || Raghuvaṃśa* V 8.47.

26 *dhṛtir astamitā ratiś cyutā virataṃ geyaṃ ṛtur nirutsavam | gatam ābharaṇaprayojanaṃ pariesūnyam śayanīyam adya me | Raghuvaṃśa* A 8.91.

27 See Introduction, Part 1.

28 *svaśarīraśarīriṇāv api smṛtasaṃyogaviparyayau yadi | virahaḥ kim ivānutāpayed vada bāhyair viṣayair vipaścitam ||* 8.87.

29 I have translated *antara* as 'particular' following Mallīnātha, who explains: *ātmadaśāntareṣu svadaśāviśeṣu | antaraśabdo viśeṣavācī |*

30 The word *cuṇṭhī* is attested in for example the *Rājataraṅgiṇī* 13 of Jonarāja (Slaje 2014, p. 56). Reference provided by H. Isaacson.

31 *Oṣadhipatibhṛt* can mean both the supporter of the 'Moon' and 'the best of medicinal herbs'; *kāṃdiśīka* is defined by Amara in the *Amarakośa* as *bhayadrutaḥ* ('having fled in or from terror'): I am grateful to Prof. H. Isaacson for providing me with the *Amarakośa* reference.

32 I am grateful to Dr Csaba Dezso for clarifying Vallabhadeva's interpretation and for sharing with me the notes to this passage taken by the editors of the *Raghupañcikā*.

2 The map of melancholy: Lamentation and the philosophical pause

1 Peacock 1903, p. 7.

2 The text of the *Kumārasambhava* usually followed is the one with Vallabhadeva's commentary. The verse numbers in this tally with *Kumārasambhava* M. The text of the *Raghuvaṃśa* usually followed is *Raghuvaṃśa* A (with Aruṇagirinātha's commentary). I also refer to *Raghuvaṃśa* V (with Vallabhadeva's commentary) and *Raghuvaṃśa* M (with Mallīnātha's commentary). For details, please see the Bibliography.

3 Warder 1972, III, p. 129.

4 In this vein, Warder 1972, III, p. 129: 'It does not observe the requirements for an epic usually given by the theorists, that it should have a single hero and unity of action, the story being developed with the five conjunctions.'

5 Dezső 2014, p. 159.

6 This is also the view held by the commentator Aruṇagirinātha (Tubb 1979, p. 26).

7 This is the view of Nārāyaṇapaṇḍita (Tubb 1979, pp. 165–6).

8 Aruṇagirinātha believes that Rati's lament enhances our perception of the hero, 'for it is well-known that when this (grief) resides in the party of the opponent [Kāma is the opponent in the *Kumārasambhava* according to him] it contributes to the excellence of the hero' (Tubb 1979, p. 165).

9 A similar concept called *ākṣipti* is presented in poetics (*Nāṭyaśāstra* 19.86cd, *Abhinavabhāratī* 19.86cd) as part of the constitutive limbs of either the *garbha* or the *vimarśa* and though also understood as a shocking revelation of concealed matter that brings back the seed of the story to the forefront, it is not tragic in nature, as anagnorisis is: this is made clear by the extant examples.

10 *Alteritas* (Latin 'difference') is used by Alain de Lille in *Liber du planctu naturae*, 0435C and Bernard of Cluny in *De contemptu mundi* II.363–4 and II.705–8: I am grateful to Dr A. Ruppel for very kindly sending me these Latin references in a personal communication.

11 See Chapter 3 for internal patterning in the *Śakuntalā*.

12 *viṣame samajā guruḥ same sabharālo 'tha gurur viyoginī.*

13 I experimented by setting the *viyoginī* verses from these two poems to *tīn tāla* and they lend themselves well to this pattern. The *rāga* was Miyā ki Malhār.

14 From *Raghuvaṃśa* A:

sa kadācid avekṣitaprajaḥ saha devyā vijahāra suprajaḥ |
nagaropavane śacīsakho marutāṃ pālayiteva nandane || 8.32
atha rodhasi dakṣiṇodadheḥ śritagokarṇaniketam īśvaram |
upavīṇayituṃ yayau raver udayāvṛttipathena nāradaḥ || 8.33
kusumair grathitām apārthivaiḥ srajam ātodyaśironiveśitām |
aharat kila tasya vegavān adhivāsaspṛhayaiva mārutaḥ || 8.34
bhramaraiḥ kusumānusāribhiḥ parikīrṇā parivādinī muneḥ |
dadṛśe pavanāvalepajaṃ sṛjatī bāṣpam ivāñjanāvilam || 8.35
abhibhūya vibhūtim ārtavīṃ madhugandhātiśayena vīrudhām |
nṛpater amarasrag āpa sā dayitorustanakoṭisusthitim || 8.36
kṣaṇamātrasakhīṃ sujātayoḥ stanayos tām avalokya vihvalā |
nimimīla narottamapriyā hṛtacandrā tamaseva kaumudī || 8.37
vapuṣā karaṇojjhitena sā nipatantī patim apy apātayat |
nanu tailaniṣekabindunā saha dīpārcir upaiti medinīm || 8.38
ubhayor api pārśvavartināṃ tumulenārtaraveṇa vejitāḥ |
vihagāḥ kamalākarālayāḥ samaduḥkhāḥ iva tatra cukraśuḥ || 8.39

15 I was inspired to coin a phrase from Māgha: *anutsūtrapadanyāsā sadvṛttiḥ sannibandhanā | śabdavidyeva no bhāti rājanītir apaspaśā* || *Śiśupālavadha* 2.112.
16 Also examined in Chapter 3 under *Vidhi, śāpa, karma, Īśvara.*
17 I Vallabhadeva glosses *paralokanavapravāsinaḥ … tava* as *yamalokagāmino'pi tava.*
18 In the words of the commentator Vallbhadeva: 'While there lives Kāma, the god of pleasure, the sense organs bring pleasure … the meaning is that you [Kāma] are the lord of pleasure' (*sati hi kāme viṣayāḥ sukhakāriṇaḥ … tvaṃ [kāmaḥ] sukhasyeśvara ity arthaḥ*) *Kumārasambhava* V, pp. 97–8). Similarly Mallīnātha: 'The meaning is that in the absence of the giver of pleasure, from where [can we find] pleasure? (*sukhapradābhāve kutaḥ sukham iti bhāvaḥ*, *Kumārasambhava* M, p. 89).
19 *gativibhrama* can mean both restlessness of your walk and the blunders of fate. I am grateful to Professor James Benson for suggesting the second meaning. Vallbhadeva glosses *anumṛteva* as *paścān mṛteva* (it seems to have died after you). Aruṇagirinātha similarly interprets and reads an additional *tvām* in his version that clarifies the object of *anumṛtā* (*tvām … anumṛteva*), explaining 'because of the fact that *anu* is a preposition, *tvām* is in the accusative case' (*anoḥ karmapravacanīyatvāt tvām iti dvitīyā*).
20 Goodall 2009.

3 On losing and finding love: Conflict, obstacle and drama

1 All citations from the *Śakuntalā* unless otherwise indicated are from the Devanāgarī version of the play with Rāghavabhaṭṭa's commentary.
2 My point of view is in contrast to Gerow's: 'An interpretation based primarily on the play's content tends to … undervalue the moments of incipient violence, cruelty and pathos … for these appear quite clearly secondary, functions of chance or error, and ultimately are erased in the final reintegration' (Gerow, E., 1979, p. 564).
3 Vasudeva 2006, pp. 23–5.
4 Johnson 2001, pp. xii–xiv.
5 Gerow 1979, pp. 565–6.
6 Gerow 1979, p. 566 thinks otherwise: 'The fourth and the sixth acts are also ethically parallel, and show the principal characters being shorn of that which till then had been their very "nature": in the fourth Śakuntalā leaves the hermitage … and experience "*viraha*" for the first time … in the sixth, the King experiences *viraha* for the girl he now knows he has abandoned'.
7 Sītā though is an emblem of ploughed earth/agriculture while Śakuntalā represents wild/undomesticated earth: whereas the former moves from palace to wilderness, the latter moves from forest to palace.
8 See Chapter 2.

9 Rāghavabhaṭṭa, *Śakuntalā* Act IV: *atha caturtho 'ṅkādipañcamamadhye 'yathoktaṃ karoti' ity anena garbhasaṃdhir uktaḥ | tallakṣaṇam ādibharate 'udbhedas tasya bījasya prāptir aprāptir eva ca | punaś cānveṣaṇaṃ yatra sa garbhaḥ prakīrtitaḥ || iti | pūrvasaṃdhi upakṣiptāptiḥ | durvāsasaḥ śāpād apraptiḥ | punas tasya prasādenābhijñānadarśanena punaḥ prāptir iti | atra prāptyāśāpatākānurodhād aṅgāni kalpayet* | For a detailed discussion following Rāghavavabhaṭṭa, see Gerow 1979, pp. 565–7.

10 Gerow 1979, p. 570.

11 Ibid.

12 Ibid.

13 Ibid., p. 567.

14 Ibid., p. 571.

15 *Tarkabhāṣā, Pramāṇa, Śabda pṛ* 19 in the *Nyāyakośa*, p. 543. I am grateful to Prof. Diwakar Acharya, All Souls, Oxford, for first providing me with the *Nyāyakośa* references and reading these passages on *pratyabhijñā* with me. In the same vein:

atra taddeśakālavṛttitvarūpatattāsaṃskārāt sa evāyaṃ ghaṭaḥ iti pratyabhijñā jāyate iti bodhyam | (*Nīlakaṇṭhī*, 1 *pṛ* 14, *Nyāyakośa*, p. 543).

tadanugṛhītas tadanusaṃdhānaviṣayaḥ pratyayas tadbhāvaviṣayaḥ pratyabhijñānam (*Nyāyavārtikam*, *Nyāyakośa*, p. 543).

16 *Padārthacandrikā Saptapadārthaṭīkā*, *Nyāyakośa*, p. 543.

17 *Dīdhitiḥ, bādha*. *Nyāyakośa*, p. 543.

18 *Vācaspatyam*, *Nyāyakośa*, p. 543.

19 *Lakṣaṇāvaliḥ Nyāyasiddhāntadīpaḥ pṛ* 59, *Nyāyakośa*, p. 543.

20 *Tarkabhāṣā, Hetvātmā Pṛ*. 50, *Nyāyakośa*, p. 543.

21 *Sarvadarśanasaṃgraha pṛ. 193 pratybhi.* in *Nyāyakośa*, p. 543.

22 There are some puns here: *-parigṛhītam* can mean both known and married; *rūpam* can mean both form/shape/thing and beauty.

23 After hearing the heavenly voice confirming that the boy was his son Duṣyanta:

tac chrutvā pauravo rājā vyāhṛtaṃ tridivaukasām |
purohitam amātyāṃś ca saṃprahṛṣṭo 'bravīd idam ||
śṛṇvantv etad bhavanto 'sya devadūtasya bhāṣitam |
ahaṃ cāpy evam evainaṃ jānāmi svayam ātmajam ||
yady ahaṃ vacanād eva gṛhṇiyām evam ātmajam ||

bhaved hi śaṅkyo lokasya naiva śuddhā bhaved ayam || *Mahābhārata* I.69.34-36. See Johnson 2001, pp. 109–37 for a translation of the entire episode.

24 M. Gangopadhyaya 1982, p. 424 (I have applied *sandhi* in the transliteration).

25 *sulabhāvakāḥ* literally means 'one whose access is easily gained'.

26 *kathaṃ jñāyate, yadā hi śuktikāyām api rajataṃ manyamāno rajatasaṃnikṛṣṭo me cakṣur iti manyate* | *bādhakaṃ hi yatra jñānam utpadyate naitad evaṃ*

mithyājñānam iti tad anyasaṃprayoge viparītaṃ tatsaṃprayoga iti | prāg bādhakajñānotpatteḥ katham avagamyate yadā na tatkāle saṃyagjñānasya mithyājñānasya ca kaścid viśeṣaḥ | yadā kṣudādibhir upahataṃ mano bhavatīndriyaṃ vā timirādibhiḥ saukṣmyādibhir vā bāhyo viṣayas tato mithyājñānam anupahateṣu saṃyagjñānam | indriyamanorthasaṃnikarṣo hi jñānasya hetuḥ…tadantargato doṣo mithyājñānasya hetuḥ | duṣṭeṣu hi jñānaṃ mithyā bhavati | katham avagamyate | doṣāpagame saṃpratipattidarśanāt | kathaṃ duṣṭāduṣṭāvagama iti cet prayatnenānvicchanto na ced doṣaṃ upalabhemahi pramāṇābhāvād aduṣṭam iti manyemahi | tasmād yasya ca duṣṭaṃ karaṇaṃ yatra ca mithyeti pratyayaḥ sa eva asamīcīnaḥ pratyayo nānya iti | (*Śabarabhāṣya* 1.1.4a). I am grateful to Prof. Diwakar Acharya, All Souls, Oxford, for reading *Śabarabhāṣya*'s section on *pramāṇa* with me over the summer of 2019.

27 *śailānām avarohatīva śikharād unmajjatāṃ medinī*

> *parṇābhyantaralīnatāṃ vijahati skandhodayāt pādapāḥ |*
> *saṃtānais tanubhāvanaṣṭasalilā vyaktiṃ bhajanty āpagāḥ |*
> *kenāpy utkṣipateva paśya bhuvanaṃ matpārśvam ānīyate ||* *Śakuntalā* VII.8

28 *upoḍhaśabdā na rathāṅganemayaḥ pravartamānaṃ na ca dṛśyate rajaḥ | abhūtalasparśatayā 'niruddhatas tavāvatīrṇo'pi ratho na lakṣyate ||* *Śakuntalā* VII.10

29 For a translation, see Johnson 2001, pp. 109–37.

30 Chalmers 1969, pp. 28–9.

31 Ibid.

32 In this vein, Cowell, the earliest English translator of the *Vikramorvaśīya*, says of Purūravas's madness:

> He is mad but his madness is not that of 'Orestes' or 'Lear,' for we are in the world of the soft contemplative Hindú; and wherever we turn in Indian poetry, we find the gentler feelings of the heart, not the fiercer. The reader must bear this in mind as he follows Pururavas through the forest, and forget for the while Orestes' frenzied call for his bow, or Lear's desolation in the storm. (Cowell 1851, p. v)

33 *Ṛgveda* 10.95; *Śatapathabrāhmaṇa* (*Yajurveda*) 11.5.1; *Harivaṃśa* 1.26 in Warder 1972, III, p. 137.

34 Barnard 2014, Letter of 22 November 1817, pp. 79–80.

35 Barnard 2014, p. 263.

4 The altered heart: Anguish, entreaty and lyric

1 The text used most frequently here is that interpreted by Vallabhadeva, and verse numbers correspond to those given in that text. When referring to the text

commented upon by Dakṣiṇāvartanātha (*c.*1200) I identify it as *Meghadūta* D, by Pūrṇasarasvatī (*c.*end of the fourteenth century CE), as *Meghadūta* P, by Mallīnātha (*c.*fifteenth century CE), as *Meghadūta* M.

2 It spawned many imitation poems such as the *Pavanadūta* and a section of the *Mālatīmādhava* (IX, pp. 25–6). Translations of it appear in Tibetan and Sinhalese; while in the eighth century, the *Pārśvābhyudaya*, a Jaina version incorporating the *Meghadūta*'s verses through *samasyāpūraṇa*, was composed by Jinasena (Lienhard 1981, p. 118). Around fifty commentaries in Sanskrit exist (ibid.).

3 For Bhāmaha's date, see Bronner 2012, pp. 67–112.

4 *ayuktimad yathā dūtā jalabhṛnmārutendavaḥ* |

tathā bhramahārītacakravākaśukādayaḥ ||
avāco 'vyaktavācaś ca dūradeśavicāriṇaḥ |
kathaṃ dūtyaṃ prapadyerann iti yuktyā na yujyate || *Kāvyālaṅkāra* 1.42–3.

5 *yadi cotkaṇṭhayā yattad unmatta iva bhāṣate* | *tathā bhavatu bhūmnedaṃ sumedhobhiḥ prayujyate* | | *Kāvyālaṅkāra* 1.44.

6 *Yakṣas* may have been called *guhyakas* because they were felt to have guarded treasures in caves. Vallabhadeva also glosses *guhyaka* with 'auspicious being' (*puṇyajana*). Mallīnātha notes a quote differentiating *yakṣas* from *guhyakas* but remarks that Kālidāsa did not accept this distinction: *vidyādharāpsaroyakṣarakṣogan dharvakinnarāḥ* | *piśāco guhyakaḥ siddho bhūto'mī devayonayaḥ ity abhidhānaśāstre yakṣaguhyakayaor bhedaḥ pradarśitaḥ tathāpy avāntarabhedāpakṣayā sa mantavyaḥ* | *kavīnāṃ tu na tādṛśabhedeṣv āsthā* | *Meghadūta* M, p. 12.

7 See also arguments made by Lienhard 1984, pp. 113–14, 117.

8 Olivelle 1997, p. xii.

9 Lienhard 1984, p. 114.

10 Similarly Jhala 1943, p. 57, opines: 'Indeed, the *Meghadūta*, as Kālidāsa has conceived it, is one deep sigh of a love-stricken heart doomed to separation – its beats being heard from stanza to stanza. Descriptions of scenes of Nature … are now suffused with the longing of the lover's heart and become invested with a deeper meaning. The tenderness and pathos of the description of the heroine become doubly justified as they spring from the wistful anguish of her lover's heart. What poignant anguish the Yakṣa must have suffered as he conjured up the figure of his beloved.'

11 For a discussion see Sarkar 2017, pp. 102–3.

12 Vallabhadeva's gloss to *bhava … rasabhyāntaraḥ*: *'apaḥ piver ity arthaḥ*, 'the sense is 'drink water!'

13 Müller 1879, pp. 55–7.

14 '*O bird, that fliest*,' *etc.* – This story the Master told at Jetavana, about a man who pined for his former wife. The circumstances which called it forth are explained

in the Puppharatta Birth-tale, and the tale of the past in the Indriya Birth-tale. So the man was impaled alive. As he hung there, he looked up and saw a crow flying through the air; and, nought recking of the bitter pain, he hailed the crow, to send a message to his dear wife, repeating these verses following:

'O bird, that fliest in the sky!
O winged bird, that fliest high!
Tell my wife, with thighs so fair:
Long will seem the time to her.
'She knows not sword and spear are set:
Full wroth and angry she will fret.
That is my torment and my fear,
And not that I am hanging here.
'My lotus-mail I have put by,
And jewels in my pillow lie,
And soft Benares cloth beside.
With wealth let her be satisfied.'
With these lamentations, he died.

When the Master had ended this discourse, he declared the Truths and identified the Birth (now at the conclusion of the Truths, the lovesick brother attained the fruition of the First Path): 'The wife then was the wife now; but the spirit who saw this, was I myself' (Rouse 1895, pp. 302–3).

15 Dakṣiṇāvarta introduces the Meghadūta with: *iha khalu kaviḥ sītāṃ prati hanumatā hāritaṃ sandeśaṃ hṛdayena samudvahan tatsthānīyanāyakādyutpādyena sandeśaṃ karoti* and identifies verse 97 as the source for this interpretation in: *rāmakathābhilāṣe liṅgam ity ākhyāte pavanatanayaṃ maithilīvonmukhī sā ity vakṣyamāṇam vacanam* (*Meghadūt*a D, p. 1). Mallīnātha writes: *sītāṃ prati rāmasya hanumatsaṃdeśaṃ manasi nidhāya meghasandeśaṃ kaviḥ kṛtavān ity āhuḥ* | (*Meghadūta* M, p. 2).

16 *Kanaka* can also mean *datura*. *Datura* ointment or oil is used to cleanse the skin in ayurveda.

17 *Vā* as 'like' is interprereted following Vallabhadeva's comment *vāśabda ivārthe*.

18 Thus also interpreted by Vallabhadeva who introduces the verse with: *katham evaṃvidhāṃ tām asvasthām avaiṣīty āha*.

Conclusion

1 Modern phenomenology understands the basic experience of grief as 'a conflict of consciousness between a presentifying and a "de-presentifying" intention: Bereaved

individuals experience a fundamental ambiguity between presence and absence, between the present and the past, indeed between two worlds they live in – an ambiguity which may also manifest itself in being painfully torn between acknowledgment and denial of the loss. In this disturbing ambiguity, grief resembles an otherwise quite different emotional state, namely the feeling of uncanniness: The anxious person in an uncanny environment experiences a menacing presence of something which yet remains invisible in the background. Like grief, it is an experience of a presence in absence' (Fuchs 2017, p. 44).

Bibliography

Primary sources

Abhinavabhāratī, Abhinavagupta: see *Nāṭyaśāstra*.

Ajavilāpa: See Raghuvaṃśa A and Raghuvaṃśa V under *Raghuvaṃśa*.

Caupannamahāpurasacariam, Śīlāṅka. ed. A. M. Bhojak, Prakrit Text Society: Varanasi, 1961.

Avaloka, Dhanika. See *Daśarūpaka*. For an English translation, see Maharaj (1969).

Daśarūpaka, Dhanaṃjaya, *The Daśarūpaka of Dhanaṃjaya with the commentary Avaloka by Dhanika and the sub-commentary Laghuṭikā by Bhaṭṭanṛsiṃha*, ed. T. Venkatacharya, Adyar Library and Research Centre, Vasanta Press: Adyar, 1969. For English translations, see Haas (1912) and Maharaj (1969).

De Profundis, Oscar Wilde, *De Profundis and Other Writings*, ed. C. Tóibín, Penguin Classics: Penguin Random House, UK, 2013.

Dīnākrandanastotra, Loṣṭaka, ed. Paṇḍita Durgāprasāda, Paṇḍita Kāśīnāthaśarman and Paṇḍita Vāsudevaśarman, Kāvyamālā Series No. 6, Nirnaya Sagar Press: Bombay, 1960, pp. 21–30. For text with Hindi commentary, see Sharma (2004).

Dhvanyāloka, Ānandavardhana, *The Dhvanyāloka with Locana of Abhinavagupta and Bālapriyā of Rāmaśāraka*, ed. P. Pattābhirāma Śāstrī, Kashi Sanskrit Series 135, Chowkhamba Sanskrit Series Office: Benares, 1940.

Dhvanyālokalocana, Abhinavagupta: See *Dhvanyāloka*.

Jātakamālā Āryaśūra, *The Jātaka-mālā; or, Bodhisattvāvadāna-mālā, by Ārya-Çūra*, ed. H. Kern, Harvard Oriental Series: Cambridge, MA, 1891.

Jātakamālā, Haribhaṭṭa, *Haribhaṭṭa in Nepal: Ten Legends from his Jātakamālā and the Anonymous Śākyasiṃhajātaka*, ed. M. Hahn, The International Institute of Buddhist Studies: Tokyo, 2007.

Kaṭṭhahārijātaka, see Chalmers (1969).

Kāvyādarśa, Daṇḍin, ed. V. P. Rangacharya Raddi Shastri, Bhandarkar Oriental Research Institute: Poona, 1938.

Kāvyālaṅkāra, Bhāmaha, *Kāvyālaṅkāra of Bhāmaha, edited with English translation and notes*, ed. and trans. P. V. Naganatha Sastry, Motilal Banarsidass: Delhi, 1970.

Kumārasambhava, Kālidāsa:

(i) *Kumārasambhava*: commented on by Vallabhadeva, *Vallabhadeva's Kommentar (Śāradā version) zum Kumārasambhava des Kālidāsa*, ed. M. S. Narayana Murti and K. L. Janert, Franz Steiner Verlag: Wiesbaden, 1980. Also cited as *Kumārasambhava* V.

(ii) Kumārasambhava M: commented on by Mallīnātha, *Kālidāsa's Kumarasambhava with the Commentaries of Mallinath, Charitravardhana and Sitarama*, Nag: Delhi, 1989 (1898).

Līlāvaī, Koūhala, *Līlāvaī of Koūhala*, ed. A. N. Upadhye, Singhi Jain Sastra Sikshapitha, Singhi Jain Series no. 31, Bharatiya Vidya Bhavan: Mumbai, 1949.

Mahābhārata, *The Mahabharata. For the first time critically edited by Vishnu S. Sukthankar with the cooperation of Shrimant Balasaheb Pant Pratinidhi [et al.]; and illustrated from ancient models by Shrimant Balasaheb Pant Pratinidhi*, ed. V. S. Sukthankar, B. Pant Pratinidhi, S. K. Belvalkar et al., Vol. I (*Ādiparvan*), Vol. III, Part 1 (The *Āraṇyakaparvan*), Bhandarkar Oriental Research Institute: Poona, 1933–42.

Mālavikāgnimitra, Kālidāsa, *Malavikagnimitra: A Sanskrit play by Kālidāsa*, ed. and trans. C. H. Tawney and R. P. Dwivedi, Indological Book House: Varanasi, 1964.

Meghadūta, Kālidāsa:

(i) *Meghadūta*, Kālidāsa, *Kālidāsa's Meghadūta edited from manuscripts with the commentary of Vallabhadeva*, ed. E. Hultzsch, Foreword: A Wezler, Munshiram Manoharlal Publishers: Delhi, 1998 (first edition 1911). Also cited as *Meghadūta* V.

(ii) *Meghadūta* D, with the commentary of Dakṣiṇāvarta, ed. T. Gaṇapati Śāstrī, *Sarvamatasangraha*, Trivandrum Sanskrit Series No. LXII, Superintendent Government Press: Trivandrum 1918, pp. 1–70.

(iii) *Meghadūta* P, with the commentary of Pūrṇasarasvatī, *Meghasandesa of Kalidasa with the Commentary 'Vidyullata' by Purnasarasvati*, ed. R. V. Krishamachariar, Sri Vani Vilas Press: Srirangam, 1909.

(iv) Meghadūta M, with the commentary of Mallīnātha, *Kālidāsa's Meghadūta or the Cloud-Messenger (as Embodied in the Pārśvābhyudaya) with the Commentary of Mallīnātha*, ed. K. Bapu Pathak, Aryabhushan Press: Poona, 1916.

Mūdrārākṣasa, Viśākhadatta, *Mūdrārākṣasa of Viśākhadatta with the Commentary of Dhuṇḍirāja*, ed. M. R. Kale, Motilal Banarsidass: Delhi, 1965.

Nāṭyaśāstra, Bharata, *Nāṭyaśāstra with the Commentary of Abhinavagupta*, ed. M. Ramakrishna Kavi, in four volumes, Vol. III (Chapters 19–27), Gaekwad Oriental Series No. 124, Oriental Institute: Baroda, 1954.

Nyāyakośa or Dictionary of Technical Terms of Indian Philosophy, ed. B. Jhalakīkara and V. S. Abhyankar, The Bhandarkar Oriental Research Institute: Poona, 1978 (1928).

Nyāyasūtra, Gautama, see Gangopadhyaya (1982).

Poetics, Aristotle, see Kenny (2013).

Raghuvaṃśa, Kālidāsa:

(i) Raghuvaṃśa A: commented on by Aruṇagirinātha, *Raghuvamsa by Mahakavi Kalidasa with Prakasika commentary of Sri Arunagirinatha and Padarthadeepika commentary of Sri Narayana Panditha*, ed. P. K. Achyuta Poduval and D. D. Pisharodi, Sanskrit College Committee: Tripunithura, year unknown.

(ii) *Raghuvaṃśa* V: commented on by Vallabhadeva, draft of unpublished critical edition of Canto 8, edited by C. Dezső, H. Isaacson, D. Goodall, C. Kiss et al., to be published as *Raghupañcikā*, Vol. II, Groningen Oriental Series, Brill: Leiden. The draft of the text was kindly put at my disposal by Dr C. Dezső and Dr C. Kiss.

(iii) Raghuvaṃśa M: commented on by Mallīnātha: *The Raghuvaṃśa of Kālidāsa, with commentary Sanjīvanī of Mallīnātha, extracts from Vallabhadeva, Hemādri, Dinkara Misra, Charitravardhan, Sumativijaya*, with an introduction by H. D. Velankar, ed. Narayan Ram Acharya, Nirnaya Sagar Press: Bombay, 1948.

Ratīvilāpa: see *Kumārasambhava*

Rāmāyaṇa I (*Bālakāṇḍa*), trans. Robert P. Goldman, New York University Press and the JJC Foundation: New York, 2005.

Rāmāyaṇa II (*Ayodhyākāṇḍa*), ed. and trans. Sheldon Pollock, containing Sanskrit original, New York University Press and the JJC Foundation: New York, 2005.

Rāmāyaṇa III (Araṇyakāṇḍa), *Vālmīki Rāmāyaṇa* Critical Edition, Volume III, The Araṇyakāṇḍa, ed. P. C. Divanji, Oriental Institute: Baroda, 1971..

Rāmāyaṇa V (*Sundarakāṇḍa*), ed. and trans. Robert P. Goldman and Sally J. Sutherland Goldman, containing Sanskrit original, New York University Press and the JJC Foundation: New York, 2006.

Rāmāyaṇa VI (*Yuddhakāṇḍa*), *Vālmīki Rāmāyaṇa Critical Edition, Volume VI, The Yuddhakāṇḍa*, ed. P. L. Vaidya, Oriental Institute: Baroda, 1971.

Rāmāyaṇamañjarī, Kṣemendra, ed. Pandit Bhavadatta Śāstrī and Kāśīnāth Pāṇḍurang Parab, Nirṇaya Sāgara Press: Bombay, 1903.

Sāhityadarpaṇa, Viśvanātha, *Sāhityadarpaṇa with the commentary Lakṣmī*, ed. K. M. Shastri, Chaukhamba Sanskrit Series Office: Benares, 1955.

Saundarananda, Aśvaghoṣa, see Covill (2007).

Śabarabhāṣya to *Jaiminīmīmāṣāsūtra*, electronic text by S. Vasudeva of Erich Frauwallner *Materialien zur ältesten Erkentnislehreder Karmamimimsi*, Sitzungsberichte / Österreichische Akademie der Wissenschaften, Vienna, 1968, pp. 10–61, Göttingen Register of Electronic Texts of Indian Languages (GRETIL), accessed from http://gretil.sub.uni-goettingen.de/gretil/1_sanskr/6_sastra/3_phil/mimamsa/sabbha1u.htm.

Śakuntalā, Kālidāsa:

(i) *Śakuntalā*, Devanāgarī version with Rāghavabhaṭṭa's commentary *Abhijñānaçakuntalā with the commentary styled Arthadyotanika of Raghavabhaṭṭa*, ed. M. R. Kale, Bombay 1961 (1898).

(ii) *Śakuntalā* (B) Bengali version, *Kâlidâsa's Çakuntalâ, the Bengâlî Recension with Critical Notes*, ed. R. Pischel, Schwers Carl Friedrichs: Kiel & Trübner, London, 1877.

(iii) *Śakuntalā* (K) Kashmiri version, see Vasudeva (2006).

Śaṅkarabhāṣya to the *Chāndogyopaniṣad*, Śaṅkara, *The Chandogya Upanishad of the Samaveda with the Commentary of Sankaracharya and the Gloss of Ananda Giri*, ed. Jibananda Vidyasagara, Sucharoo Press: Calcutta, 1873.

The Mill on the Floss, George Eliot, ed. A. S. Byatt, Penguin Classics: London, 2003.

The Varieties of Religious Experience, William James, ed. M. E. Marty, Penguin Classics: London, 1985.

Troilus and Criseyde, Chaucer, see Benson (2008).

Uttararāmacarita, Bhavabhūti, *Uttararamacharita of Mahākavi Bhavabhūti with Ramā Sansrkit-Hindi Commentary*, ed. R. Tripathi, Chaukhamba Surbharati Prakashan: Varanasi, 2005. For an English translation (with parallel Sanskrit text), see Pollock (2007).

Vakroktijīvita, Kuntaka, *The Vakroktijīvita of Kuntaka*, ed. K. Krishnamoorthy, Karnatak University: Dharward, 1977.

Vibudhānanda, Śīlāṅka, see *Caupannamahāpurasacariam*.

Vikramorvaśīya, Kālidāsa, *The Vikramorvaśīya of Kālidāsa with the commentary of Ranganātha*, ed. K. P. Parab and M. R. Telang, Nirnayasagara Press: Bombay, 1888. For an English translation, see Cowell (1851).

Secondary sources

Appleton, N. and S. Shaw 2015 (trans.), *The Ten Great Birth Stories of the Buddha: The Mahānipāta of the Jātakatthavaṇṇanā*, vols 1 and 2, Silkworm Books: Thailand.

Barnard, J. 2014, John Keats, *Selected Letters*, Penguin Classics: UK.

Benson, D. 2008 (ed.), *The Riverside Chaucer*, Oxford University Press: Oxford.

Bhat, G. K. 1974, *Tragedy and Sanskrit Drama*, Popular Prakashan: Bombay.

Bronner, Y. 2012, 'A Question of Priority: Revisiting the Debate on the Relative Chronology of Daṇḍin and Bhāmaha', *Journal of Indian Philosophy* 40 (1), pp. 67–118.

Byrski, M. C. 1974, *Concept of Ancient Indian Theatre*, Munshiram Manoharlal: Delhi.

Chalmers, R. 1969, *Kaṭṭhahārijātaka* (Jātaka No. 7), in *The Jātaka Or Stories of the Buddha's Former Births*, Vol. I, Pali Text Society, UK. (First Published by The Cambridge University Press in 1895.) Also available online http://obo.genaud.net/dhamma-vinaya/pts/kd/jat/jat.1/jat.1.007.chlm.pts.htm.

Cone, M., and R. Gombrich, 1977, *The Perfect Generosity of Prince Vessantara*, Oxford Clarendon Press: Oxford.

Covill, L. 2007, *Handsome Nanda by Aśvaghoṣa* (Sanskrit text with parallel English translation), Clay Sanskrit Library, New York University Press and the JJC Foundation: New York.

Coulson, M. 1981 (trans.), *Three Sanskrit Plays: Śakuntalā by Kālidāsa, Rākṣasa's Ring by Viśākhadatta, Mālatī and Mādhava by Bhavabhūti*, Penguin Classics: London.

Cowell, E. B. 1851 (trans.), *Vikramorvaśī: An Indian Drama*, Stephen Austin: Hertford.

De, S. K. 1957, *The Meghadūta of Kālidāsa*, Sahitya Academy, Delhi.

De, S. K. 1988, *History of Sanskrit Poetics*, Firma K.L.M.: Calcutta.

Devadhar, C. R. 1962, *Bhāsanāṭakacakram: Plays Ascribed to Bhāsa*, Oriental Book Agency: Poona, India.

Dezső, C. 2014, 'We do not fully understand the learned poet's intention in not composing a twentieth canto: Addiction as a structuring them in the *Raghuvaṃśa*', *South Asian Studies*, 30(2), 159–72, published online https://www.tandfonline.com/doi/full/10.1080/02666030.2014.962335.

Frye, N. 2010, 'The Argument of Comedy', in *Northrop Frye's Writings on Shakespeare and the Renaissance*, Volume 28, ed. T. Y. Grande and G. Sherbert, University of Toronto Press: Canada, pp. 1–13.

Fuchs, T. 2017, 'Presence in Absence: The Ambiguous Phenomenology of Grief', *Phenomonology and the Cognitive Sciences* 17 (2018), 43–63.

Gangopadhyaya, M. 1982 (ed. and trans.), *Nyāya: Gautama's Nyāyasūtra with Vātsyāyana's Commentary*, Indian Studies: Calcutta.

Gerow, E. 1979, 'Plot Structure and the Development of *Rasa* in the Śakuntalā, Pt. I', *Journal of the American Oriental Society* 99 (4), 559–72 (564).

Gerow, E. 1971, *A Glossary of Indian Figures of Speech*, Mouton: The Hague.

Gerow, E. 1980, 'Plot Structure and the Development of *Rasa* in the Śakuntalā, Pt. II', *Journal of the American Oriental Society*, 100 (3), 267–82.

Gerow, E. 1984, 'Sanskrit Dramatic Theory and Kālidāsa's Plays', in *Theatre of Memory: The Plays of Kālidāsa*, Columbia University Press: New York, ed. B. Stoler Miller, pp. 42–62.

Gerow, E. 1985a, 'Bhāsa's Ūrubhaṅga and Indian Poetics', *Journal of the American Oriental Society*, 105(3), 405–12.

Gerow, E. 1985b (trans.), 'Ūrubhaṅga: the Breaking of the Thighs', *Journal of South Asian Literature*, Vol. 20, No. 1, *Part 1: Essays on the Mahābhārata*, Asian Studies Centre: Michigan State University, pp. 57–70.

Goodall, D. 1996 (ed. and trans.), *Hindu Scriptures*, based on an anthology by R. C. Zaehner, University of California: Berkeley.

Goodall, D. 2009, 'Retracer la transmission des textes littéraires à l'aide des textes "théoriques" de *l'Alaṅkāraśāstra* ancien: quelques exemples tirés du *Raghuvaṃśa*', in *Écrire et transmettre en Inde classique*, ed. Colas and Gerschheimer, Ecole francaise d'Extreme Orient: Paris, pp. 63–77.

Haas, G. C. O. 1912 (trans.) *The Daśarūpa a Treatise on Hindu Dramaturgy by Dhanaṃjaya*, Columbia University Press: New York.

Hahn, M. 2007, *Haribhaṭṭa in Nepal: Ten Legends from His Jātakamālā and the Anonymous Śākyasiṃhajātaka*, The International Institute for Buddhist Studies: Tokyo.

Holme, T. 1902 (ed.) *Sakuntala; or, The Fatal Ring [tr. by Sir W. Jones]. To which is added Meghaduta [tr. by H. H. Wilson] the Bhagavad-gita, or Sacred Song [tr. by C. Wilkins]*, Walter Scott: Paternoster Square, London, E.C.

Ingalls, D., J. Moussaieff Masson and M. V. Patwardhan 1990 (trans.), *The Dhvanyāloka of Ānandavardhana with the Locana of Abhinavagupta*, Harvard University Press: Cambridge, MA.

Jhala, G. C. 1943, *Kālidāsa: A Study*, Padma Publications: Bombay.

Johnson, W. 2001 (trans.), *Kālidāsa: The Recognition of Śakuntalā*, Oxford University Press: Oxford.

Kane, M. L. 1983, *The theory of plot structure in Sanskrit drama and its application to the Uttararāmacarita*, PhD Thesis, University of Harvard, Department of Sanskrit and Indian Studies.

Kenny, A. 2013 (trans.), *Aristotle: Poetics*, Oxford University Press: Oxford.

Kulke, H., and D. Rothermund. 1998, *History of India*, Routledge: London.

Lienhard, S. 1984, *A History of Classical Poetry* (A History of Indian Literature, ed. J. Gonda, Vol. III Fasc I), Otto Harrassowitz: Wiesbaden.

Mahaharj, J. C. 1969 (ed. and trans.), *The Daśa-rūpaka of Dhanañjaya with the Daśarūpāvaloka Commentary by Dhanika*, Chowkhamba Sanskrit Series Office: Varanasi.

McCrea, L. 2009, *The Teleology of Poetics in Medieval Kashmir*, Harvard Oriental Series 71, Harvard University Press: Cambridge, MA.

Meiland, J. 2009, *Garland of the Buddha's Past Lives by Āryaśūra*, Vol. I, New York University Press and the JJC Foundation: New York.

Miller, B. Stoler1984 (ed.), *Theatre of Memory: The Plays of Kālidāsa*, Columbia University Press: New York.

Mirashi, V. V., and N. R. Navlekar 1969, *Kālidāsa: Date, Life and Works*, Popular Prakashan: Bombay.

Müller, M. 1879 (trans.), *The Upanishads*, Part 1, Clarendon Press: Oxford.

Oberlies, T. 2003, *Grammar of Epic Sanskrit*, De Gruyter: Berlin.

Olivelle, P. 1997, *The Pañcatantra: The Book of India's Folk Wisdom*, Oxford University Press: Oxford.

Peacock, W. 1903, *Selected English Essays*, OUP/Humphrey Milford: London.

Pollock, S. 2007, *Rāma's Last Act by Bhavabhūti*, New York University Press and the JJC Foundation: New York.

Pollock, S. 2016, *A Rasa Reader*, Columbia University Press: New York.

Rangacharya, A. 1996, *The Nāṭyaśāstra: English Translation with Critical Notes*, Munshiram Manoharlal: Delhi.

Restifo, A. 2019, 'Demystifying Kashmiri Rasa Ideology: Rāmacandra–Guṇacandra's Theory of Aesthetics in Their Nāṭyadarpaṇa', *Journal of Indian Philosophy* 47, 1–29. https://doi.org/10.1007/s10781-018-9374-2.

Rouse, W. H. D. 1895, *The Jātaka, or Stories of the Buddha's Former Births*, Vol. II, Cambridge University Press: Cambridge.

Sabnis, S. S. 1966, *Kālidāsa: His Style and His Times*, N. M. Tripathi: Bombay.

Sarma, D. 1968, *An Interpretative Study of Kālidāsa*, Chowkhambha Sanskrit Series Office: Varanasi.

Sarkar B. 2017, 'Licence and faithfulness: Taking liberties with Kathā in classical Sanskrit poetry and aesthetics', *Journal of Indological Studies*, Nos 26–27 (2014–15), University of Kyoto: Japan, pp. 102–3.

Sattar, A. 2011, *Lost Loves: Exploring Rāma's Anguish*, Penguin Books: Delhi.

Sharma, K. N. 2004, *Kaśmīrī Stotraparamparā evaṃ Dīnākrandana stotra*, Eastern Book Linkers: Delhi.

Slaje, W. 2014, *Kingship in Kaśmīr (AD 1148–1459) From the Pen of Jonarāja, Court Paṇḍit to Sulṭān Zayn al-'Ābidīn*, Universitätsverlag Halle-Wittenberg: Halle an der Saale.

Stein B. 2010, *A History of India*, Wiley-Blackwell: Chichester.

Tatar, M. 1999, *The Classic Fairy Tales: Texts, Criticism*, W. W. Norton: New York.

Tubb, G. 1979, *The Kumārasambhava in the Light of Indian Theories of the Mahākāvya*, PhD thesis, Harvard University: Cambridge, MA.

Tubb, G. 1985, 'Abhinavagupta on phonetic structure', *Journal of the American Oriental Society*, 105(3), Indological Studies Dedicated to Daniel H. H. Ingalls (July–September 1985), American Oriental Society, pp. 567–78.

Vasudeva S. 2006 (ed. and trans.), *The Recognition of Shakúntala* (Sanskrit text of the Kashmiri version with parallel English translation), New York University Press and the JJC Foundation: New York.

Vaudeville, Ch. 1963, 'The *Krauñca-Vadha* episode in the Vālmīki Rāmāyaṇa' in *Journal of the American Oriental Society*, 83(3)(August–September 1963), 327–35.

Venkatachalam, V. 1986, *Bhāsa*, Sahitya Akademi: New Delhi.

Warder, A. K. 1972, *Indian Kāvya Literature* (Vols I–VIII), Motilal Banarsidass: Delhi.

Yadav, B. R. 1974, *A Critical Study of the Sources of Kalidasa*, Bhavana Prakasha: Delhi, Aligarh.

Index

Abhijñānaśakuntalā 21–2, 32, 52, 53
  see also Śakuntalā
abhijnās ('knowledge symbols') 102
Abhinavabhāratī 10, 25, 26, 31, 32, 36–8, 165, 174 n.1
Abhinavagupta 9, 10, 25–7, 35–48
abodhapūrvaṃ smaraṇam ('unconscious recollection') 116
adbhutanirdeśa (indication of something absurd) 96–7
ādhikārikam itivṛttam see narrative structure
ādikavi 6
ādikāvya 6
ādiśloka 9
aesthetics *see* Indian aesthetics
Agnimitra (King) 61
ahiṇṇāṇam/abhijnānam 110
Aja 24, 67, 77, 83, 85, 87, 89, 90, 166
Ajavilāpa (Aja) and *Rativilāpa* (Rati) 67, 83, 85, 90, 93–107, 142
  adbhutanirdeśa (indication of something absurd) 96–7
  asamāptaparikarma (a verse about an unfinished decoration) 102–3
  dehivākya (a statement about embodied beings) 98–9
  maraṇecchā (a death-wish) 106–7
  mohabhaṅga, the (the swoon broken) 94–5
  rahaḥsmaraṇa and *kāmacihnāni* (a recollection of intimacy and the signs of the beloved) 99–102
  utsūtratānirdeśa (an indication of an anomaly) 97–8
  vācyanirdeśa (an indication of censure) 103–4
  vidhyāropa (attribution to Fate) 104–5
  vilāpavarṇana, The (description of the lament) 95–6
ākṣipti ('disclosure') 113
Alakā 21, 102, 135, 148–50, 154
alaṃkāra conventions 59
alaṃkāraśāstra 165
alteritas 4, 63, 66, 91, 108, 129, 131, 141
Ānandavardhana *see Dhvanyāloka*
anaṅga ('bodiless') 92
antaḥsāram (with internal essence) 145, 146
antarbāṣpa (tearful) 145
antastoyam (watery) 149
anekadharmopapatti ('apprehension of the unique characteristic') 121
aṅgulīyaka, nāmamudrā 109
anupalabdhyavyavasthā ('irregularity of non-apprehension') 121
anyathāvṛtti cetah 57, 82
Appleton, N. 64, 181 n.13, 182–3 n.17
'Argument of Comedy, The' 16–18
Aristotle 91
Aristotelian anagnorisis 90
Aruṇagirinātha 107–8, 129–30
Āryaśūra 62–7, 70, 127, 151, 152
  see also Jātakamālā, *Mādrīvilāpa*, and *Viśvantarajātaka*
Aśvaghoṣa 10–11, 13, 18, 20, 58, 68–72
Atithi 87
Aurelius, Marcus 107
Avaloka see Dhanika
avamarśa/vimarśa 13–14, 21, 25, 59, 69, 83, 121, 165
avamṛṣṭi ('pondering') 27
avasthās (stages of action), 26–30, 32, 34–43, 45–9, 102
  see also narrative structure
'awareness/identity' 128
Ayodhyākāṇḍa (*Rāmāyaṇa*) 74–6, 81
ayuktimat ('unreasonableness') 139
Āyus 23

Bacon, Francis 87
bādhakajnāna (falsifying knowledge) 124
Bālakāṇḍa 6–8, 79
Barnard, J. 188 n.34

bāṣpagadgadaḥ ('stuttering in tears') 67
Benson, J. 186 n.19
Bhāmaha 26, 139–41
Bharata and Kālidāsa 19, 22, 25, 26, 38, 39, 42, 47, 49, 55, 56, 59–62, 81, 136
Bhāsa 56
Bhat, G. K. 11, 89, 170, 173 n.30, 174 n.38, 180 n.2
Bhavabhūti 8–9, 18, 58
bīja 27, 31, 32, 36, 37, 39, 45, 50, 76, 88
see also narrative structure
bindu (Drop) 31, 36, 56
see also narrative structure
Brahmadatta (king of Benaras) 127
Bṛhadāraṇyakopaniṣad II (iv) and IV (iii) 5
Bronner, Y. 189 n.3
Buddha in the *Saundarananda* 68–71
Buddha, life story of 3
Buddhism 79
Buddhist literary prototype 64
Byatt, A. S. 11
Byrski, M. C. 27, 29, 32, 34, 38, 174 n.2, 176 n.18, 178 n.38, 181 n.10

cakragati (the motion of a wheel) 86
cakranemi (chariot wheel) 86
cakravāka bird 156
Cākyārs of Kerala 56
calamity (vipad) 78
candrakāntāḥ (moonstones) 150–1
cātaka birds 126
chalita (song) 61
Chalmers, R. 188 n.30
Chāndogyopaniṣad VIII (iii–iv, vii, ix and xii) 5
chāyātmā ('shadow-self') 166
Citrabhānu 27
Cone M. 63, 182 n.14, 183 n.18
Consolation of Philosophy 120
Coulson, M. 2, 11, 55, 169 n.3
Covill, L. 69, 70, 161, 162
Cowell, E. B. 188 n.32
Criseyde tale 82
curse (*śāpa*) 6, 8–10, 19, 22–4, 34, 42, 52, 55, 60, 61, 75–86, 104, 110–15, 117, 118, 120–3, 125, 132, 133, 136, 143, 159, 170–1

Dakṣiṇāvarta 146, 190 n.15
Daṇḍin 26, 144
Dante's *Inferno* 80–1
Daśaratha 18, 24, 74, 76, 82, 87, 90
Daśarūpaka/Daśarūpa 26, 177 n.23
see also Dhanaṃjaya
date-palm and the Jambū trees 154
dehivākya (a statement about embodied beings) 98–9
see also Ajavilāpa (Aja) and *Rativilāpa* (Rati)
De Profundis 1, 3, 109
De, S. K. 141
Devadhar, C. R. 181 n.4, 188 n.3
Dezso, C. 88, 184 n.32, 185 n.5
Dhanaṃjaya *see Daśarūpaka/Daśarūpa*
Dhanika 26, 29, 32–4, 37, 39, 45
dharma (religious piety) 88, 113
Dhvanyāloka 9, 10, 36, 57
Dhvanyālokalocana 36
Dilīpa 87
Dīnākrandanastotra 56, 79–80, 143
doṣa (epistemological fault) 115, 125
doṣas (literary defects) 125, 139
duḥkhātmaka ('characterized by suffering) 25
dukkha (suffering) 5
Duṣyanta 16

Eliot, G. 11–14, 86, 139
emotional cleansing (catharsis) 11
epische breite (epic breadth) 11, 12

Fatal Ring, The 2
fate (*vidhi*) 13, 21, 37, 42, 45, 53, 55, 57, 70, 74–86, 90, 93, 97–9, 104–5, 108, 131, 132, 137, 186 n.19
'Form of the Good' (Platonic) 18
Frye, Northrop 13, 16–18, 171 n.37
Fuchs, T., 191 n.1

Gambhīrā River 147, 148
gāndharva marriage 109
Gangopadhyaya, M. 121, 187 n.24
garbha (embryo) *see* narrative structure
Gerow, E. 2, 11, 111, 113, 114
A Glossary of Indian Figures of Speech (1971) 2
Godāvarī River 62

Goethe 11–12
Goldman, Robert P. 7
Gombrich, R. 63, 182 n.14, 183 n.18
Goodall, D. 104, 170 n.9

Haas, G. C. O. 175 n.13, 178 n.38
Hahn, M. 183 n.19
Hamlet or *King Lear* 1
Haribhaṭṭa 64
Harṣa of Kannauj x
Holme, T., 2, 11, 169 n.2
House of Fame, The 145
Hunter, O. 7

idyll 109
Indian aesthetics 4, 10, 19–20, 25–7, 39, 51, 56, 60, 115, 175 n.4
Indumati 16, 18, 24, 51, 52, 57, 67, 77, 81–4, 89, 90, 92, 95, 99–101, 104, 105
Indumatī and Aja's marriage 57
Ingalls, D. 173 n.27, 173 n.29
īśvarecchā (will of God) 85

Jainism 79
James, William 3, 14–16, 107
Jānuśruti Pautrāyaṇa (King) 151
Jātakamālā 64, 66, 151
Jhala, G. C. 181 n.6, 189 n.10
Johnson, W. 111, 186 n.4, 187 n.23
Jones, William 2, 126–7

kāmacihnāni (of the signs of the beloved) *see Ajavilāpa* (Aja) and *Rativilāpa* (Rati)
Kāma (god of love) 88, 89
Kāmavilāpajātaka 142, 151
Kane, M. L. 27, 36, 37, 174 n.2, 175 n.11, 175 n.14, 176 n.16, 177 n.25, 178 n.48
Kaṇva 112
karmavipāka 84
karuṇarasa 2, 4, 9, 19, 56
kārya 31, 32, 36, 87–9
  see also narrative structure
Kaṭṭhahārijātaka 127
Kāvyādarśa see Daṇḍin
kāvya 1–3, 8, 15, 16
Kāvyālaṅkāra see Bhāmaha

Keats, John 135
kelikāvya 144–5
Kenny, A. 173 n.31
Kirātārjunīya 143–4
Kouhala 27
Krauñca 6–11, 16, 18, 57, 75, 76, 170–1 n.21, 171–2 n.24
kṛtānta ('agent of ends') 74
Kṣemendra 8–9
  see also Rāmāyaṇamañjarī
Kubera 21, 52, 81, 143, 146, 151
Kulke, H. 169 n.3
Kumārasambhava 16, 18, 21, 23, 32, 52, 53, 56, 59, 60, 71, 85, 87–9, 112, 136, 138

Lakṣmīsvayaṃvara (*Lakṣmī's Choice of Husband*) 60
Lewes, George Henry 12
Lienhard, S. 180 n.1, 181 n.6, 189 n.2
Līlāvaī see Kouhala
Lineage of the Raghus, The see Raghuvaṃśa
Loṣṭaka *see Dīnākrandanastotra*
love messages and 'insentient' messengers 151–4

Maddīvilāpa (Pāli) 63–4
Madrīvilāpa (Sanskrit, Āryaśūra) 64–7, 138
Mahābhārata 57, 58, 108, 119, 125, 127, 140, 143, 151, 162–3
mahākāvya /sargabandha 18, 20–1, 26–7, 48, 53, 56–8, 68, 75, 87, 144
Mālavikāgnimitra 61–2
Mallīnātha 144
maraṇecchā (a death-wish) *see Ajavilāpa* (Aja) and *Rativilāpa* (Rati)
McCrea, L. 176 n.19
Medieval/Indian medieval x–xi, 169 n.1–4
Meghadūta 5, 16, 18, 20, 21, 52, 53, 56, 57, 86, 128, 139, 140, 142–5, 154–63
Meiland, J. 183 n.20
Miller, B. 181 n.6
Mill on the Floss, The 11–12, 86, 139
Mīmāṃsā (theory of language) 30, 49, 117, 123, 124, 167
Mirashi, V. V. 180 n.1, 181 n.6
mithyājnāna (false perception) 125, 133

mohabhaṅga, the (the swoon broken) 90–1, 94–5
see also Ajavilāpa (Aja) and *Rativilāpa* (Rati)
moha (fault of error) 122–3
mṛdu vastu (gentle object) 92
mṛgatṛṣṇikā (mirage) 134
Mūdrārākṣasa 48
Müller, M. 189 n.13

Nala and Damayantī 151, 162–3
nandavilāpa ('Nanda's lament') 69–70
nandabhāryāvilāpa ('The Lament of Nanda's Wife') 68–9
narrative structure
avasthā (stages of action)
niyatā phalaprāpti (the Certain attainment of Fruit) 28, 38
prayatna (Effort) 28, 29, 36
prāptisambhava (the Possibility of Success) 29
prārambha (Initiation) 28–9, 31, 36
ādhikārikam itivṛttam 27–8, 31
prakṛtis/arthaprakṛtis (narrative means)
bindu (the Drop) 31, 36, 56
bīja (the Seed) 27, 32–7, 39, 41–2, 45, 46
kārya (the Purpose) 31, 32
patākā (the Flag) 32
prakarī (the Interlude) 32, 131
prāsaṅgikam itivṛttam 27–8, 32
sandhi (Junctures)
garbha (the Embryo) 33, 35, 37, 48–50, 113
mukha (the Source) 33, 35–7, 48, 49
nirvahaṇam (the End) 35, 44, 48–50
pratimukha (the Reflection) 33, 35–7, 48, 49
vimarśa/avamarśa (the Trial) 13–14, 21, 25–7, 34–53, 59, 83, 90, 113, 114, 121, 122, 130, 144, 165–7
'natural evil' 13, 14, 19
Nāṭyaśāstra 25–8, 31–3, 35, 36, 38, 39, 59
'neglect of action' 57
nirvahaṇam see narrative structure
nirveda 2
Nirvindhyā River 133, 147
niyatā phalaprāpti 39, 41
see also narrative structure

non-Naiyāyikas 45
Nyāya 40, 44, 45, 47, 116, 120, 121, 167, 179
Nyāyasūtra 25, 26, 120

Oberlies, T. 7, 170 n.16
Olivelle, P. 189 n.8

paḍiboho ('re-recognition') 117
see also *pratyabhijñā*
Pāli 57, 62
pañcakatraya see narrative structure
Pañcatantra 141
patākā see narrative structure
Peacock, W. 184 n.1
phala (narrative fruit) 18, 27, 28, 87
see also narrative structure
phalaprāpti ('the acquisition of the narrative fruit') 13, 27–9, 37–41, 49, 61
see also narrative structure
phalayoga (the addition of fruit') 28, 29
see also narrative structure
Poetics 91
Pollock, S. 58, 59, 76, 170 n.18, 173 n.28, 175 n.3
prakaraṇa 35
prakṛtis/arthaprakṛtis 26–8, 31–2, 35–7, 41, 48–9, 73, 77, 78, 83, 117, 134, 148, 154
see also narrative structure
prāptisambhavam 29
see also narrative structure
prārambha 28, 31, 36
see also narrative structure
prāsaṅgikam itivṛttam see narrative structure
pratimukha 33, 35–7, 48, 49
see also narrative structure
pratyabhijnā 116, 117, 120, 133, 134, 136, 167
prayatna (Effort) 28, 29, 36, 40
see also narrative structure
Pūrṇasarasvatī 156
Purūravas 60, 131–138, 154, 166
Puruṣasūkta 18
puruṣārthas 88
puruṣavyasanas concept 88

Rāghavabhaṭṭa 59, 113, 114, 186 n.1, 187 n.9
Raghu 18, 23, 24, 87, 90

Raghuvaṃśa 8–9, 16, 21, 23–4, 32, 52, 53, 57, 87–9, 112, 136, 138
'Rama's Last Act' 58
 see also *Uttararāmacarita*
rahaḥsmaraṇa (recollection of lovemaking) 99–102
 see also Ajavilāpa (Aja) and *Rativilāpa* (Rati)
rasa 4, 10, 19, 33, 44, 47, 60–2, 114, 148, 165, 177
Rāmāyaṇa 6, 8, 18, 56, 57, 62, 72–4, 140, 154
 curse in 75–6
 fate in 74–5
 see also Ayodhyākāṇḍa; *Yuddhakāṇḍa*
Rāmāyaṇamanjarī 8–9
Rāmāyaṇa's kraunca bird 57
Rangacharya, A. 177 n.25, 178 n.38
rasābhyantaraḥ ('one whose interior is filled with liquid') 145, 147, 148
Rati bereavement 89
Rativilāpa 90
Ratnāvalī 29, 33, 34, 45
recognition 116
Restifo, A. 173 n.29, 178 n.46
retribution (*karma*)
 curse 77–86, 104
 fate 13, 77–86, 104
 retribution 13, 77, 84, 104
Revā River 146
Rothermund, D. 169 n.3
Rouse, W. H. D. 190 n.14
Ṛtusaṃhāra 53

Śabarabhāṣya 188
śabdabrahman 9
śabdapramāṇa 118
Sabnis, S. S. 181 n.6
Sāgarikā 29, 33, 34, 41, 42
Sāhityadarpaṇa 26, 34
Śakas xi
Śakuntalā 16, 21, 56, 58, 59, 78, 109
 see also *Abhijñānaśakuntalā*
samānadharmopapatti ('apprehension of common characteristics') 121
saṃcāribhāvas 19
saṃgamamaṇi ('jewel of union') 132
sammoha (error) 122, 135
saṃsāra (transmigration) 166
sandeha (doubt) 20, 114, 121
sandeśakāvya/dūtakāvya (messenger poetry) 140–1
sandigdhabuddhi ('one of conflicted knowledge') 118–19
sandhi (junctures) 33–5, 48–52, 55, 59
 see also narrative structure
śāpa 6
Sarkar, B. 189 n. 11
Sarma, D. 181 n. 6
Sastri, T. Ganapati 56
Sattar, A. 181 n.12
Saundarananda 56, 68–72, 161, 162
'the second birth' 14–16, 18–19
self-awareness 126, 127
Shaw, S. 64, 181 n.13, 182–3 n.17
'Sick Soul, The' 14
Slaje, W. 184 n. 30
śloka 6–8
śokaḥ ślokatvam āgataḥ 9–10
ślokatvam āpadyata yasya śokaḥ ('he whose grief had become poetry') 9
śṛṅgārarasa 19
Stein, B. 169 n. 1
subhāṣitas 151
Sundarakāṇḍa 156
Sundarī in the *Saundarananda* 68–72, 156
'supernatural good' 15–16

Tamasā River 171
tamas (heavy substance) 91, 122, 167
Tatar, M. 169 n. 4
Teachings on Drama 26
 see also Nāṭyaśāstra'
Tolstoy, L. 13, 14
tragic middle 55, 57, 59, 66, 67, 71, 72
 and vilāpa 88–9
 see also Vikramorvaśīya; *Meghadūta*; narrative structure
'tragicomedies' 6
'transitory emotions' 19
 see also *saṃcāribhāvas*
Troilus and Criseyde 120, 186 n.19
Troilus tale 82
Tubb, G. 27, 36, 59, 174 n.2, 176 n.17, 180 n.64

Udayana 29, 33, 34
Udbhaṭa 43
Ujjayinī (city) 147, 152, 180 n.1

upacitarasāḥ (they in whom fluid/emotion is abundant) 145
upalabdhyavavasthā ('irregularity of apprehension') 121
Upaniṣadic Brahmanism 79
Ūrubhaṅga 2, 56
Urvaśī 23, 60
utsṛṣṭikāṅka/aṅka 2
utsūtratānirdeśa (an indication of an anomaly) 97–8
see also Ajavilāpa (Aja) and Rativilāpa (Rati)
Uttararāmacarita 8–9, 56, 58

vācyanirdeśa (an indication of censure) 103–4
see also Ajavilāpa (Aja) and Rativilāpa (Rati)
Vakroktijīvita 143
Vallabhadeva 84, 100, 141
Vālmīki 6
Varieties of Religious Experience, The (1902) 14–15
Vāsavadattā 29, 33, 34, 41, 42
vastunirdeśa 143
Vasudeva, S. 110, 111, 186 n.3
Vaudeville, Ch. 8, 170 n.19–21
Venkatachalam, V. 181 n.4
Vessantarajātaka 62, 127
Vessantara (King) 63
Vibudhānanda 2, 56
vidhyāropa (attribution to fate) 104–5, 137
see also Ajavilāpa (Aja) and Rativilāpa (Rati)
Vikramorvaśīya 22, 52, 53, 56, 60, 109, 117, 131, 141, 167
vilāpa/lament 13, 53, 56–7, 66–7, 80, 85, 88–9, 93, 98, 99, 107, 136–7, 142, 144
vilāpavarṇana, The (description of the lament) 95–6
see also Ajavilāpa (Aja) and Rativilāpa (Rati)
vimarśa see avamarśa/vimarśa; narrative structure
vipratipatti ('contradictory assertions about the same object') 121
Viśākhadatta 48
see also Mudrārākṣasa
Viśvanātha 26, 27, 31–2, 36, 39, 144
Viśvantarajātaka 62–7
see also Āryaśūra

Walder, Coulson 55
Warder, A. K. 26, 36, 56, 57, 59, 141, 174 n.2, 177 n.25, 177 n.27, 177 n.34, 178–9 n.49, 178 n.39, 181 n.6
Western tragedy 11, 17–20
Wezler, A. 142, 144
Wilde, Oscar 1, 3, 109
"Willow Song" 108
Woodhouse, Richard 135

Yadav, B. R. 181 n.6
yakṣa 16, 135, 139–40, 145–6
yācnā 142
yogavibhāga 46
Yuddhakāṇḍa (*Rāmāyaṇa*) 151

www.ingramcontent.com/pod-product-compliance
Lightning Source LLC
Chambersburg PA
CBHW072235290426
44111CB00012B/2102
* 9 7 8 0 7 5 5 6 3 9 2 4 3 *